SYNERGIC INQUIRY

SYNERGIC INQUIRY

A Collaborative Action Methodology

Editors

Yongming Tang
California Institute of Integral Studies

Charles Joiner

SAGE Publications
Thousand Oaks ▪ London ▪ New Delhi

For information:

Sage Publications, Inc.
2455 Teller Road
Thousand Oaks, California 91320
E-mail: order@sagepub.com

Sage Publications Ltd.
1 Oliver's Yard
55 City Road
London EC1Y 1SP
United Kingdom

Sage Publications India Pvt. Ltd.
B-42, Panchsheel Enclave
Post Box 4109
New Delhi 110 017 India

Printed in the United States of America on acid-free paper

Library of Congress Cataloging-in-Publication Data

Synergic inquiry : a collaborative action methodology / editors, Yongming Tang, Charles Joiner.
    p. cm.
Includes bibliographical references and index.
ISBN 0-7619-1208-8 (cloth) — ISBN 0-7619-1209-6 (pbk.)
   1. Group relations training. 2. Problem solving. 3. Conflict management.
4. Interpersonal relations. 5. Intergroup relations. 6. Difference (Psychology)
7. Consciousness. I. Tang, Yongming. II. Joiner, Charles W. III. Title.
HM1086.S86 2006
303.6'9—dc22

                                                2006002938

06   07   08   09   10   9   8   7   6   5   4   3   2   1

Acquiring Editor:	Lisa Cuevas Shaw
Editorial Assistant:	Margo Beth Crouppen
Production Editor:	Sanford Robinson
Copy Editor:	Cheryl Duksta
Typesetter:	C&M Digitals (P) Ltd.
Indexer:	Julie Sherman Grayson
Cover Designer:	Michelle Kenny

Contents

Foreword

S *ynergic Inquiry* is an invaluable addition to the range of approaches to the emancipation of human consciousness embraced within the participatory worldview (Reason & Bradbury, 2001). I am grateful to Sage for taking the risk of publishing the work of a Chinese social artist whose genius is expressed more clearly as art than as social science. The vision of *Synergic Inquiry* is not easily captured in the language of the contemporary northern United States mind-set, especially when English is the visionary's second language.

Synergic Inquiry grew quite directly out of Yongming Tang's life experiences. He was a spiritually sensitive man raised under the materialist ideology of the People's Republic of China. He was a student socialized to formal learning in the hierarchical and didactic educational system of China who found himself a graduate student in the radically democratic classrooms of Antioch College in 1988–1990. He was a Chinese faculty member in a European-U.S. graduate school dominated by a pervasive White consciousness. He engaged in deep self-exploration to survive emotionally and spiritually. He engaged in careful study of U.S. culture, especially so he could understand the hidden web of privilege that race confers on European-U.S. people. He explored the intellectual paradigms that dominate the U.S. academic establishment. Through it all, he grew to appreciate the wisdom in both the East and West, in both traditional and modern approaches to life. With a group of friends, he began to find ways to transcend differences and achieve a transformed state of knowing.

Yongming searched through his experience for insights that might help him describe these moments of emancipation. He reexamined his study of biology while a student in China; his doctoral study in systems dynamics in the United States; his study of the Eastern philosophies of Taoism, Confucianism, and Buddhism that, ironically, he encountered first in California; and his later study of Western philosophy and developmental psychology. He recognized a common developmental process in these many sources, a process that had enabled him to begin to transcend destructive polarities in his own experience and, he believed, had promise for transforming the experience of groups and organizations.

With what was still an inchoate conceptual model, Yongming had the chutzpah to take a group of northern U.S. consultants to apply the nascent model with executives in a major enterprise in China. Out of that successful experience, and with the collaboration of several U.S. citizens led by Charles Joiner, Yongming first developed a coherent conceptual model. In short order, he experimented with organizations in India, Mexico, and the United States and developed a set of rich practices to help individuals, groups, and organizations to open and expand consciousness through confronting and engaging points of deep difference. The process was made rich by the sequence of steps in his approach. He engaged the domains of experience that are preverbal and kinesthetic as well as those that are archetypal and mythic before drawing on intellectual categories: He accessed the imaginal before drawing on existing constructs. From my experience, this seems to be one key to permitting the emergence of synergies that can transcend differences.

During the 1990s, I had the privilege of working with Yongming as a colleague in a university and in a consulting practice, and I grew to love him like a brother. What stands out to me from my experience with Yongming and with synergic inquiry are some lessons and a question that might inform your exploration:

• First, the transformation of consciousness is the journey of a lifetime, not the product of a workshop. Synergic inquiry offers a window into that ongoing process and in so doing stirs inspiration and hope and provides tools to facilitate progress. I experience synergic inquiry as a complement to my own spiritual discipline and my practice as an educator, and I commend it to you from my own experience.

• Second, as a student of organizational change and transformation, I know that leaders for change must be able to create synergy. Immersion in synergic inquiry can help leaders develop a mind-set that will enable them to invite synergy to emerge in groups and organizations.

• Third, in his focus on the nonverbal and imaginal domains, the practice of synergic inquiry as described by Yongming draws on streams of experience regarding learning and change that, unfortunately, remain on the margin of practice in most institutions. For what it's worth, as an adult educator, I am helped to more fully understand Yongming's exploration of the nonverbal and the imaginal by looking to John Heron's work (1996) and that of Lyle Yorks and Elizabeth Kasl (2002).

• Fourth, as pointed out in the text that lies ahead, synergic inquiry does not magically dispel power differences between individuals or groups. Differences in power and privilege may be among the most corrosive in our culture. In confronting such differences, the indispensable seems to be trust: Without trust, such a confrontation seems too risky. For all the potential risk, this seems an arena where synergic inquiry might be helpful.

• Fifth, the process of synergy invited by synergic inquiry suggests an advanced state of consciousness, akin to what Robert Kegan (1994) describes as Order 5 Consciousness, what Ken Wilber (2001) might call integral consciousness, what Bill Torbert (2004) calls the Alchemist. Such models raise a question in my mind: To what extent do we only have access to these advanced states of consciousness by moving through all preceding stages in linear sequence (do we have to go through Stage 4 to get to Stage 5?), and to what extent are the advanced stages latent in all of us all of the time? Experimenting with synergic inquiry may help us penetrate this mystery.

In a deep sense, Yongming's work transforms the old saying "you can be right or you can be in relationship" from representing a polarity between self-righteous judgment on one hand and commitment to preserve the relationship at any cost on the other to an understanding of the creative alchemy that can emerge only from the dance of difference between two engaged consciousnesses. e. e. cummings (1994) puts it as follows:

one's not half two. It's two are halves of one:
All lose, whole find

As cummings might have it, the work of synergic inquiry is more art than science, an emergence from Being more than a plan for Doing.

Given the immense need to transcend polarities and find new and creative ways to engage the seemingly intractable problems humans have created in the 21st century, people desperately need to cultivate the mind-set and capacity envisioned by synergic inquiry. I hope that, with appreciation of the book's genesis, you will experiment boldly with the practice and add to the growing body of experience that helps inform us all.

—Dean Elias, EdD
Saint Mary's College of California
Moraga, CA

References

cummings, e. e. (1994). *Complete poems 1904–1962*. New York: Liveright Publishing.

Heron, J. (1996). *Co-operative inquiry: Research into the human condition*. Thousand Oaks, CA: Sage.

Kegan, R. (1994). *In over our heads: The mental demands of modern life*. Cambridge, MA: Harvard University Press.

Reason, P., & Bradbury, H. (2001). *Handbook of action research: Participative inquiry and practice*. Thousand Oaks, CA: Sage.

Torbert, W. (2004). *Action inquiry: The secret of timely and transforming leadership*. San Francisco: Berrett-Koehler.

Wilber, K. (2001). *A theory of everything: An integral vision for business, politics, science and spirituality*. Boston: Shambhala.

Yorks, L., & Kasl, E. (2002). Toward a theory and practice for whole-person learning: Reconceptualizing experience and the role of affect. *Adult Education Quarterly, 52*(3), 176-192.

Preface

While this book was being reviewed by academic experts organized by Sage Publications, both of us embarked on new journeys for our lives. Yongming took off to use the synergic inquiry methodology to facilitate a process that would help a U.S.-based company create a culturally synergic operation in China. Soon after that, he launched a synergic educational project, which started in Beijing and is now quickly spreading to other parts of China. This project involves using the synergy process to educate students (elementary, high school, and college), workers, managers, and governmental personnel about language, culture, and personal development. Charlie, in contrast, moved from California to South Carolina to pioneer a new community, whereby he could experiment with ways to harmonize humans and nature. In this process, he and his communal friends intentionally bring different cultural wisdoms into synergy to benefit the development of the community. Meanwhile, he worked on his dissertation research project, which focused on the spiritual dimension of synergic inquiry. This timely immersion of the synergic inquiry method in his native culture has been a valuable resource and inspiration to both of us. So, while the book was being printed, our journeys of synergy continued.

With regards to this book, we have many people to thank. First, we are grateful to each other: This book is a synergic product between both of us. Our differing cultural backgrounds, experiences, and styles of thinking and writing have been sources of cocreation and synergy. We are also deeply indebted to many others, especially those who have co-led synergy projects with either one of us. It was through those meaningful collective experiences that we were able to articulate the foundation and various dimensions of the methodology. Yongming is especially grateful to his mentor, friend, colleague, and partner Dean Elias, whose intellect, wisdom, and styles influenced the growth of Yongming as a person, including his intellectual development. Particularly, Yongming gratefully acknowledges Dean's contribution to the structure of the last chapter and his detailed feedback to previous drafts of the book, which helped us improve the book's presentation. Sometimes Yongming jokes that his U.S. self is Dean, and there is some truth to that statement.

We are also thankful to Joanne Gozawa, who had the courage to join the first synergy project in China, which led to the birth of synergic inquiry. Joanne's belief in synergy was indeed inspirational to us, and the numerous projects Yongming co-led with her helped add dimensions to the book that otherwise would not have been possible. Joanne also gracefully made her comments about the book, which helped improve the drafts. We are equally thankful to other key project leaders, who in various ways helped contribute to the book. We'd like to name just a few: Lien Cao, Colette Winco, Taj Johns, Susan Cannon, Dean Michelson, Carole Barlas, Professor Yi-fu Yin (a distinguished professor in China), Dr. David Golf, Dr. Cynthia McReynolds, and Dr. Elizabeth Campbell. Along the same line, we also want to thank those project leaders and key participants whose project reports were educational to us.

Both of us are deeply indebted to the other writers in the book, whose names are properly recognized in their respective chapters. We felt that their experiences helped illuminate different parts of the methodology, and their stories are powerful for readers to read.

Last, both of us want to express our wholehearted gratitude to our faithful editor Sandra Stacey, who made a large contribution to the previous drafts of the book. Her unique capability to grasp the differences between the East and the West; her editorial expertise, which helped clarify issues that are normally difficult to understand; and her exquisite language skills, which helped articulate what we were trying to say made significant differences for us. And our sincere, heartfelt gratitude belongs to Joyce Cassells, who with short notice helped to update our references and made appropriate suggestions for modifying the book.

1

Introduction

No problem can be solved by the same consciousness that created it.

—Albert Einstein

Scientists are further beginning to recognize that—like the artificial conflict between spirit and nature, between woman and man, and between different races, religions, and ethnic groups fostered by the dominator mentality—the way we view conflict itself needs to be reexamined.

—Riane Eisler (1987)

This book introduces a new, collaborative action methodology called synergic inquiry (SI) for both investigating and effecting transformative change among individuals and collectives. This methodology is a formalization of the very means by which it was created. It was formalized into methodology so that it could be shared with others and explored more widely.

In this opening chapter, we begin by presenting a perspective on current issues and their root causes, which provides a rationale for understanding the intent of SI. Then, we situate SI in the context of research to discuss the distinctive contributions that SI makes as a methodology. We also describe the structure of the book to help orient readers. Finally, we end with a brief account of the history of SI.

Worldly Violence, Primary Causes, and the Root Problem

Our world is full of violence. This violence begins within each of us. We have multiple forces within us that are colliding with each other, causing us pain, agony, and misery. Further, external complexities in our personal as well as professional lives also affect the intricate internal dynamics between these multiple forces. These external demands and struggles can easily overwhelm us, causing a sense of crisis of personal identity and growth (Kegan, 1994).

The violence we experience in our inner world manifests itself in our outer world. At the relationship level, we have yet to learn how to relate to each other without violence. Our internal reactions to significant external changes tend to disrupt our relationships. In our relationships with our lovers and friends, we tend either to lose our own sense of self, to dominate the other, or to compromise our senses of self and others. These dynamics leave us confused and afraid of each other (Johnston, 1991). Our dealings in groups suffer in similar ways. We rarely know how to work well together and do not truly know how to collaborate. Team efforts are often undermined by competition or domination between members of the team, and group decisions tend to be compromises rather than creative solutions that use the strengths and insights of all involved (Katzenback & Smith, 1993; Lipnack & Stamps, 1993; Mouton & Blake, 1984; Reddy, 1988). These violent symptoms continue outward to the organizational level, where we cultivate organizational cultures that crush individual differences and exploit individual egos for organizational success (Kanter, 1983; Senge, 1990). Or organizations exist without a sense of a cohesive whole because they are so full of conflicts and confrontations (Lawrence & Lorsch, 1967).

At the levels of community and society, we find these same kinds of problems repeated in racism, sexism, and other forms of exploitation, exclusion, and intolerance that are widespread throughout the world (Eisler, 1987). People of one race or belief exclude, beat, and even kill people of other races and those who are different. Those who are on the receiving end of this tend to do the same to others, as shown in the horrible struggles between the United States and Muslim extremists, between Whites and Blacks and other minorities in the United States, between Israelis and Palestinians in the Middle East, and between Palestinians and Indians in the Near East, between the Chinese and the Tibetans in the Far East, and so forth. These "isms" between different groups also tend to cause a superficial feeling of unity among members within each constituency, which does not respect human differences. Instances of violence are also extended beyond global boundaries in subtle and yet profound ways. We seem to suffer from egocentrism (in which we believe that we are the only right group) or ethnocentrism (in which we believe our group is better than others' groups) (Adler, 1997), and these incompatible beliefs lead to historic imperialism of one culture over others, as happened with the European domination over Africans, Asians, and other people in other parts of the world (Ani, 1994).

The violence does not stop at the human realm. It expands itself to the ecological realm. The human domination over nature is leading to the kinds of severe breakdown that scientists call entropy, and the living system of earth's biosphere seems to be taking a road toward deterioration and inexorable death (Harman, 1994). Warnings from those who study these problems have even taken the form of a statement from a group consisting of 1,680 scientists from 70 countries around the globe, including 104 Nobel laureates, saying that humanity is on a course of self-destruction (Union of Concerned Scientists, 1992).

What are the sources for these divergent forms of violence within each of us, for all of us, and the whole ecology of us? After pondering this for many years, what came to us is that each of us, all of us, and the whole ecology of us suffer from one paramount incapacity: our inability to engage differences in ways that are harmonious, creative, and transformative. Differences in each of the realms are often turned into polarities, and these in turn polarize our relationships with each other and the ecological world in which we live. It is those polarizations that catalyze varied forms of violence in our individual lives, social and organizational lives, and ecological lives.

The futurist, Charles M. Johnston (1991), developed a marvelous framework that helps illuminate the underlying causes for these problematic symptoms. In his framework, he identifies three major human errors—separation fallacy, unity fallacy, and compromise fallacy—in our business of dealing with differences and polarities. Separation fallacy simply means that differences are polarized to the extent that one is fully differentiated from others. In addition, separation fallacy associates a positive value to one end of the pole. "Our modern defining of such things as objective and subjective, human kind and nature, masculine and feminine as distinct has made not just a statement about difference, but as well about where 'real' truth ultimately lies" (Johnston, 1991, p. 35). When this happens, "mind remains separate from body, matter from energy, moral from immoral. East is East and West is West and never the twain shall meet" (Johnston, 1991, p. 35).

In contrast, unity fallacy refers to the human tendency to be incapable of or unwilling to differentiate the self from others. In the name of searching for oneness, unity, or sameness, differences between self and other and part and whole are either unseen or framed as unimportant. If the separation fallacy is the pendulum swinging to the left, unity fallacy is the pendulum swinging to the right.

The compromise fallacy is the idea that the pendulum must be somewhere in the middle. In the world of self meeting others, boundaries are colliding to the extent that everyone loses some by gaining some. This idea does not lead to the extremity that either the unity fallacy or the separation fallacy does, nor does it work with differences and polarities to the extent that uniqueness is being leveraged. It confuses "integration with some additive middle ground. Rather than revealing the rich spectrum of colors that lies beyond black and white, they lead us to conclude that reality simply shows varying shades of gray" (Johnston, 1991, p. 38).

It is our belief that these fallacies are the primary causes of all forms of violence in our social and ecological realms. In addition, we also believe that most people individually suffer from one or more forms of these fallacies. These fallacies also exist in our social collectives. They constitute a matrix of dynamic interactions that affect us both internally as well as externally.

A common theme penetrating these fallacies is an either-or mentality that leads to a power-over dynamic. It is either I win or you win, or we both win a bit by losing some. The perspective is further confirmed by the work of Riane Eisler (1987)—the futurist and activist—on gender relations. In her internationally acclaimed book, *The Chalice and the Blade,* she posits that underlying the great surface diversity of human culture there exists the dominator model, which is about "the ranking of one half of humanity over the other" (p. xvii). In our history, people took on this dominator model, which caused social and ecological perils. As quoted in the opening of the chapter, scientists are further beginning to recognize that—like the artificial conflict between spirit and nature, between woman and man, and between different races, religions, and ethnic groups fostered by the dominator mentality—the way we view conflict itself needs to be reexamined.

Yet it is also our belief that there is something deeper and more fundamental and alarming than these important causes for our violence in our social and ecological lives. This has to do with a root problem that seems to reach at the core of our challenges: That is, we seem to suffer from a fundamental pathology in the way we mythize or spiritualize the world. We share Raimon Panikkar's (1979) belief that our most basic crisis is one of myth. Basically, we seem to suffer from the pathological belief that reality is fundamentally stable, ultimately definable, and fully knowable. There is one truth, and we will try to get it right. Then, when we find out that we have different beliefs and perspectives, violence against each other occurs.

For us, the discussion just recounted leads to a critical realization. We do not believe that these varied forms of violence arise of themselves, nor do we believe they come from inherent human evil or the perversity of the physical world. Our experience with SI substantiates the statement by Albert Einstein used at the beginning of this chapter. From our point of view, we cannot solve our problems as long as we stay locked within the pathological belief within which these violent problems were created. The underlying root cause for our ever-increasing problems is the pathology that exists in our own individual and collective consciousnesses.

The pathology at our mythical level, manifested as the dominator model in the form of the three major fallacies, imposes heavily on our ability to learn from, accept feedback from, and respond effectively to the challenges and opportunities that we now face. As a species, humans could well be diagnosed as learning challenged. That is to say, we do not even know how to learn to transform the deep-rooted pathology that causes the kinds of problems and crises we now face.

Indeed, our time calls for a new, refreshing perspective to approach the crises we face, one that reexplains the world (Thompson, 1991). Such a new approach has to be able to transform the pathology in our consciousnesses and expand capacities so that we can think anew and relate to each other differently in social and ecological contexts to make a difference for everyone. As the poet and activist Audre Lorde so powerfully expresses, "It is not our differences that divide us. It is our inability to recognize, accept, and celebrate those differences."

The SI methodology grew out of the need and the desire to do just this, to learn how to transform and expand individual and collective consciousness by drawing on our individual and cultural diversity as sources of wisdom rather than of friction. It was developed and refined to help us reframe and reassess the richness within our diversity and learn to solve problems collaboratively, creatively, efficiently, and effectively by moving us beyond barriers of culture, training, knowledge, status, and belief. We present this methodology in hopes that it can be used to help you collectively enhance your capacities to work with the problems of varied proportions that cut across national and cultural boundaries to affect all of our lives.

Synergic Inquiry and Purposes of SI

SI was created in response to the problems that resulted from our inability to engage in differences that challenge all parts of our lives—our work and educational lives; our personal and professional relationships; our leadership, business, and community lives; and our diversity issues and cross-cultural interactions. Many new approaches have been developed to deal with these problems. But it seems that solutions have always come from the same two places—out of the mindsets that created the problems or out of their polar opposites. As a result, the solutions often end up not being effective or causing more problems than they solve.

SI is inspired to be a qualitatively different approach. Coming out of the notion of synergy—identified by us as a grand pattern underlying the evolution of the universe—it is a methodology that attempts to enhance human creativity and harmony through the way it addresses problems and crises. It is developed to break open the three major human fallacies by expanding human consciousnesses and capacities.

SI is a collaborative, action-oriented methodology that cultivates our capacities for problem solving, conflict resolution, learning, and growth through transforming and expanding human consciousnesses. SI does this by means of the unique way in which it focuses on and uses differences. Within SI, differences are not regarded as sources of friction and conflict; they are used for the wisdom inherent in them and the learning they can promote. The methodology allows people with differences—be they differences in personality, learning style, status, or culture—to come into the same process with equality and fairness. Developed to creatively use differences to help us make a difference for ourselves and the world, SI creates a container to hold all who engage in it and invites their participation.

Over the years, SI has been applied to contexts as varied as individual development, relationship enhancement, conflict resolution, team development, organizational development and transformation, community development, and racial, ethnic, and gender differences. There have been cross-cultural applications in China, Mexico, India, and the United States.

With our intention to uphold our vision and desire for helping make a fundamental shift for our societies, SI works within the four levels of our individual and collective lives—the mental, the social, the political, and the spiritual:

1. *Mental: Fostering synergic capacity for resilience, adaptability, and change.* SI is designed to help develop and actualize human potential. It does this by facilitating expansion of participants' consciousness and capacities for transformative change. It intends to have participants learn to embody a process through which they can continually expand themselves on their own future journeys.

2. *Social: Solving problems for social systems of various levels and complexities.* On the social level, SI enables participants to identify and use differences creatively. In the process, inclusivity, motivation, and performance are increased. Thus, SI fosters creativity for solving social and organizational problems.

3. *Political: Transforming power relationships in ways that enable humans to flourish.* SI is designed to transform adversity into synergy so that all can benefit. In this way, it addresses fundamental causes for social alienation, injustice, oppression, and domination and enhances equity, justice, and harmony.

4. *Spiritual: Aligning self with the evolutionary pattern of the universe.* Crystallized from our understanding about how the universe evolves, SI is a process that expands the normal egoistic self to seek out the spiritual connection of oneself to the larger whole. We believe that the power of SI lies in this ultimate spiritual intention.

Features of SI

There are several features of SI that distinguish it from traditional research methodologies. These include its orientation toward action and collaboration, its ability to transform consciousness; and its view of research as a living quest, a balance between theory and practice, and an intention that is ultimately spiritual.

Following the emphasis in Plato and Aristotle on pure knowledge and pure truth, traditional research focuses on generating knowledge for the sake of knowledge itself (Harman, 1996; Heron, 1996; Reason, 1994, 1996). Research in general, and science in particular, have been kept as privileged disciplines in which researchers and scholars develop objective knowledge about the world (Reason, 1988, 1994, 1996). The knowledge generated by this kind of research is usually not accessible to the general public. Even when the general public does have access to it, the forms and contents of this research do not make much sense to the general populace.

In contrast, SI fosters research as a way of life, empowering humans of all cultures to learn, grow, and expand. Research is no longer a privileged discipline controlled by traditional academies. It treats research as a living quest for learning, growth, collective problem solving, and even spiritual development. It generates subjective knowledge and collective human processes that are catalytic for transformative changes. The knowledge SI develops from human action will be poignant and directly applicable for participants. Because any knowledge with use must have both consequences and efficacy, this method is designed to help participants take learnings and new awareness into their own actions and behaviors and use them productively.

Traditional research also separates the researcher from the researched. Whereas the researcher has power over design strategy, data analysis, and report writing, the researched does not have much say, either in terms of the research process or in terms of its outcomes (Heron, 1996; Reason, 1988, 1994, 1996). In sharp contrast, SI is highly collaborative. It breaks down barriers and power differentials between researcher and researched. Everybody participates in the whole process of research, and everyone is empowered to integrate new knowledge into actions at both the individual and collective levels. Each participant is both researcher and researched, or both object and subject; research is *for, by,* and *with* people. In this way SI joins in the powerful sentiment expressed by Peter Reason (1988, 1994) and John Heron (1996), and it belongs to participative schools of inquiry, such as cooperative inquiry, action inquiry, and participatory action research.

SI was developed to help at various human system levels because we firmly believe that the fundamental pathology also exists in every social system level, and every system suffers from one or more forms of fallacies. Therefore, for us the only fundamental solution to all social and ecological predicaments is to expand consciousness at all possible human system levels.

SI transforms consciousness by building in reflective practices that help in examining the underlying premises of one's own presuppositions, assumptions, values, and beliefs. In contrast, most traditional research approaches are not transformative. They tend to focus on generating knowledge for objective and external purposes, without active processes that reflect on one's own consciousness.

SI also maintains a careful balance between theory and practice. Most traditional research generates knowledge or theories and has little to no interest in guiding practices. The result is that most traditional research is difficult to apply to the issues and problems people actually face, and most practitioners lack an adequate theoretical foundation and their research outcomes are not designed to reflect back onto the methodological framework itself. Inspired by theorist Kurt Lewin's position that "there is nothing so practical as a good theory," SI inherently maintains balance between theory and practice in two different ways. First, SI has a solid theoretical foundation. It has a theoretical framework underlying its methodological processes and steps: its solidity within, identified by us as universal domains through what Gregory Bateson (1979) called a pattern that connects, as well as its definition and description of consciousness and its dimensions. Further, a product of continuing theorizing and practicing, the outcomes of SI research are used to reflect on and improve the theoretical and the methodological.

SI also maintains a balance between theory and practice through the ways in which new insight or awareness learned about the self or others becomes living theory for living action. Participants apply their new awareness within the inquiry itself and use the new awareness to develop new skills and capacities for action. Although this localized kind of theory does not have the generalizability of a grand or metatheory, it is certainly a good use of theory for the participants themselves.

Finally, and most ambitiously, SI has what some would call a spiritual intention, that of facilitating the evolution of human consciousness. The mental, social, and political purposes just outlined are all informed by this spiritual core. Underlying SI is the principle that we recognize that, in its essence, the universe itself evolves. The universe unfolds its mystery in ways that tend to go beyond any human action and imagination. This principle is used to guide both human practice of SI and the development of the methodology itself to facilitate the evolution of human consciousness to access more of this mysterious universe.

The spiritual dimension of science and research is beginning to be noted by research methodologists. A champion of this front, Peter Reason (1993), argues that science is sacred and has a spiritual character. Building on this theme propounded by Reason, the position is forcefully elaborated by Lincoln (1995):

> The spiritual, or sacred, side of science emerges from a profound concern for human dignity, justice, and interpersonal respect. The sacredness in the enterprise of science issues from the collaborative and egalitarian aspects of the relationships created in the research-to-action continuum. Researchers who conceive of science in this way make space for the life ways of others and create relationships that are based not on unequal power, but on mutual respect, granting of dignity, and deep appreciation of the human condition. (p. 284)

We would like to extend this position further. It is our belief that the very attention that informs science and research, and thus human action, is spiritual. This is what links both science and human action to the mythical dimension of reality (Panikkar, 1979; Vachon, 1995) or the sacredness of reality (Reason, 1993). Taking to heart the quotation by Albert Einstein used earlier, we use SI in an attempt to help people to continually grow beyond the limitations of their own consciousnesses. In other words, SI was designed to help facilitate the evolution of consciousness by enabling us, as participants, to consciously integrate ever-larger evolutionary patterns into ourselves.

Structure of This Book

The purpose of this book is to introduce this new methodology so that it may be used more widely to address both the questions and the problems that people face. The book is divided into two basic parts: methodology and theory and SI practices. Part I, "The SI Methodology and Its Theoretical Foundation" (Chapters 2–4), explicates SI in terms of its methodological framework, theoretical foundation, and relationship to other research paradigms and methodologies. Detailed descriptions of the processes and phases, with tools and exercises for guiding practice, are also given. Part II, "SI

Practices" (Chapters 5–16), provides guidance for potential SI practitioners and case studies. In our concluding chapter (Chapter 16), we reflect on these cases and explore implications for future research.

In Part I, Chapter 2, "Overview of Synergic Inquiry," the basic premises on which SI is based are described, and an overview of the methodology is presented. For those who wish to seriously consider analyzing or using SI as a research or change methodology, Chapters 3 and 4 are especially important. Chapter 3 discusses the theoretical foundation on which SI is developed. It presents the argument for a universal principle—the synergy principle—drawing from various sources of cultural wisdoms, social sciences, and natural sciences. Chapter 4 places this methodology in the context of other research paradigms and change methodologies. These provide a wider context from which to understand the uniqueness of SI in the larger context of research paradigms and methodologies for change and transformation.

Part II, Chapter 5 describes how to get started, and some of the major issues that arise from using SI are addressed. Chapters 6–15 are a collection of case studies. These give a more concrete picture of the scope of SI and its applications. They range from the level of the individual and personal relationships through the group level to that of organizations. Intersecting these levels are such issues as personal development, team development, organizational development, conflict resolution, racism, sexism, and cross-cultural synergy.

The case studies include one by an individual demonstrating how she uses SI to embody change in the nature of her being and the foundations of her behavior. Another presents a husband and wife who synergize with each other to uncover the sources of friction and address a longstanding logistic problem. A third shows how family members use synergy to uncover layers of selves and to move beyond the conventional explanations of intergenerational conflict to simultaneously strengthen family ties and encourage the independence of a child approaching adulthood.

At the level of the group, cases demonstrate the use of SI to forestall conflict and allow forward movement with vision and plans, to solve a previously intractable collective problem, and to address issues between Blacks and Whites in a way that enables the Black subgroup to come to grips with previously invisible differences among themselves and the White subgroup to delve more deeply than usual into the cultural foundations of their beliefs and behavior. Other studies include a case in which a group was formed specifically to use SI as a workshop addressing gender issues between men and women and one in which a teacher in a high school with a diverse student body uses SI as a new pedagogy.

At the organizational level, one chapter demonstrates the application of SI to management practices in a business in China in which synergy created between U.S. and Chinese approaches to business helps improve the organization's performance. In the process, important differences in approach to organizational and cultural expectations of employees become visible. Another organizational case study shows SI being used to help a U.S. organization deal with its start-ups in Mexico: The heavy impact of the unrecognized cultural and historical issues behind these problems is brought to the surface in such a way that revitalization for the whole organization emerges out of this SI intervention.

In our concluding chapter, we reflect on these SI cases from our own perspectives and interpretations. The central themes as well as the interesting particularities of these cases are discussed. The implications of SI work for future of research are also explored.

A Brief History of SI

Synergic inquiry was initiated and led by Yongming Tang with many people contributing to its development. It was born out of Yongming's painful struggles to make sense of experiences in graduate school in the United States, without rejecting the Chinese culture in which he had been raised and educated. He wanted to find a means by which he could live productively, if not always harmoniously, in both Chinese and U.S. worlds.

Yongming eventually did find a way to use these experiences to expand his understanding and thinking. Seeing the range of benefits this approach brought him as an individual, he wondered if it would be possible to bring these same kinds of benefits to an organization. Dissertation research on transferring management models from European and U.S. cultures to China led him to strive for ways that might allow Chinese organizations to experiment with Western ideas differently. Would it be possible for Chinese organizations to synergize these ideas with their own existing beliefs, practices, and culture, rather than merely trying to adopt the foreign as "new and better" and ending up with negative outcomes?

In the process of exploring synergy in relation to organizations, Yongming came across Nancy Adler's (1997) cultural synergy process for problem solving in multicultural organizations. In this work, she outlines a process involving two phases: differentiation of different cultural perspectives and then their subsequent integration. This process provided the initial framework for what is now called synergic inquiry.

Because we did not yet know how to differentiate and how to integrate as groups, the first project is best described as a chaotic experience. It took place in China and, after a brief introductory session in the United States, began with lectures and a tour of Beijing to introduce a Chinese perspective to the U.S. team. This was followed by a 30-hour train ride to a remote community in northern China, where the business was located. Once there, our hosts did not know how to receive us, and we, as a group, did not know how to relate to them.

Everyone was overwhelmed by the cultural differences, and there was no formal process to help with integration and learning. The U.S. team did manage to organize itself, conduct interviews, and observe the lives and work of their Chinese counterparts. More important were efforts to make sure that both the Chinese and the U.S. teams had as many as possible of the kinds of experiences Yongming had found so beneficial for himself. The Americans readily immersed themselves in the differences they found in China. They played and toured together. They visited people's homes, conducted interviews, and argued and discussed endlessly. In the end, a talk was organized so that some of the executives and managers could listen to the Americans report on how Western management approaches might effectively be used to improve their situation. Then the project ended.

Everything was so extremely hectic that Yongming had doubts that any real benefits at all could come out of such a project. Despite the wealth of exciting ideas that were developed, he wondered whether the Chinese would actually be able to use them. Or would these too be treated the way that ideas from the West were usually treated in China? Remaining in China after the project, he was told that those who had intensely interacted with the team from the United States felt that they had learned a lot.

Some of these learnings had to do with their cultural stereotypes: Their views about Americans had changed. Others talked about how they had been personally transformed by their experiences with the U.S. team and about how these transformations would now enable them to try using the new ideas in practice.

Back in the United States, there was a team retreat for reflection and closure. Because the whole project had been so "messy" by the standards of Yongming's training as a consultant, he was prepared for some very stiff criticism from participants. To his surprise the team members talked about how much this brief experience affected their lives. Participants felt that the experience had been extraordinarily transformative, and the amount of gratitude they expressed was overwhelming. These responses energized Yongming so much that he began to formalize the activities of this project into what became the core of the SI methodology.

Into this Yongming fed all that he had learned as a Chinese man immersed in the U.S. culture, drawing on his personal experiences with culture shock and his scholarly background in systems theory and evolutionary processes. Able to draw on his formal Western organizational and systems theory training and to integrate it with his knowledge of Eastern philosophy and dialectics, as well as with his early training in biological processes, he worked toward developing a formal theoretical model and a formal structure of activities to go with this model. The combination of experience and learning, input and feedback provided the ideal set of circumstances for the development of synergic inquiry.

In the spring of 1995, Charles Joiner and Susan Cannon, who had participated in the first synergy project, used the tentatively formed process of SI to address problems between an organization in the United States called World SHARE and its affiliates in Mexico. World SHARE is an international nonprofit organization devoted to stimulating community development and self-help projects in low-income communities. World SHARE's affiliates in Mexico had been failing in their mission, and, as a member of the board of directors, Charles Joiner proposed using SI to address these problems more creatively.

A team of five faculty members and students from the California Institute of Integral Studies (CIIS) was matched with a team of three leaders in World SHARE's Mexico project to form a core synergy team. The corporate president, three vice presidents, and the purchasing staff participated in this project as well. After preparatory work, the team spent 2 weeks visiting World SHARE affiliate sites in Mexico, and an additional 4 days were spent with corporate leaders.

One result of this work was total reorganization of the strategy and design of World SHARE's work in Mexico, with a culturally appropriate form being created for that effort. The board also reorganized the corporation as a whole, and there was a wholesale redesign of World SHARE's work internationally. This led to a revitalization of the organization as a whole and personal growth and change for participants in the inquiry (see Chapter 15).

With two successful projects under his belt, Yongming was able to rally support from the Chinese government, intellectuals, and business executives to use SI to search for new organizational forms for China, ones that would transcend the limitations of the systems in both Chinese and Western cultures. Yifu Yin, a professor in China, and Mr. Song, the CEO of Beijing New Building Materials (BNBM), invited Yongming to conduct an SI project with BNBM in the summer of 1995.

BNBM, a successful state-owned enterprise with 2,000 employees, produces new construction materials for the Asian markets. The company had an unusual amount of autonomy to develop a new organizational form that would fit the global market economy. Both the company and the government were looking for a new company system, one that would retain essential elements of socialism, while matching the needs of the fiercely competitive global economy.

In July, a group of 10 students and faculty members from CIIS spent 3 weeks in Beijing working with a complementary group of 11 key managers from the company (see Chapter 14). Organized into three teams—leadership, the human dimension, and marketing and technology—made up of people from both CIIS and BNBM, they interviewed BNBM employees, observed work settings, and went through the synergy process. At the end of the 3 weeks, each team had developed a series of recommendations to BNBM senior leadership.

All of the applications of SI to this point were at the organizational level. Responding to efforts to link CIIS with the Auroville community in India, Project India was an experimental application of the SI approach at the community level. This project took place in November and December of 1995. Under the leadership of Charlie Joiner and Susan Cannon, it worked with the international village at Auroville, India. Participants were also joined by nonstudents, including the president and the director of Latin American affairs of World SHARE, who wanted more experience with the process and more broadly based information about community development and self-help projects throughout the world.

An international community devoted to manifesting the sociospiritual vision of Sri Aurobindo, Auroville is an attempt to both transcend and honor the diversity found among humans and their communities. The intent of this synergy project was to see if SI could help the 1,100 people of Auroville find ways to more fully embody the community's framework of values and commitments in terms of the immense cultural diversity of its residents and relations with the traditional Tamil villagers that surround them.

The group of nine from CIIS met with a like-sized group from Auroville and organized into subteams around the themes of bioregion, economic structure, and community organization. These subteams spent 2.5 weeks clarifying the perspectives of all participants on these issues. A synergy day was designed to involve not only the Auroville synergy team but also major leaders within the community. Authentic dialogue emerged between the CIIS participants and the Aurovillians as they addressed their differing frameworks of assumptions and the issues surrounding how to synergize these frameworks to develop new strategies for community development.

An article in their community newspaper read, "Many of the Aurovillians who attended the afternoon session felt it represented something of a watershed: certain issues were being discussed openly for the first time in Auroville."

The first application of SI in a formal manner in the United States occurred in the winter and spring of 1996. Over the previous 15 months, serious racial tension had emerged in a cohort of doctoral students at CIIS that included 6 Blacks and 14 Whites. A project was initiated to address the issues of racism and intercultural differences as an integral part of their academic training (see Chapter 11).

As an instructor, Yongming established a diverse design-and-delivery team that actively collaborated during the whole process. Because of limitations of time and participant availability (the students met monthly for 3 days at a time), the SI process had to be highly structured to allow all to participate with the whole experience. Once the group had started the process, however, some felt that the experience was too rich to rush and decided to expand it from a 3-month to a 6-month project.

Dividing into a White team of 14 (including a female member of the faculty) and a Black team of 6, the students used the SI process to explore their racial consciousnesses within their own groups. Then, they used it for an intergroup exploration of the phenomenon of racism. Some of the experiences were intense, and the group in general dived deeply into these issues. The project produced significant, long-lasting effects on the group itself, as demonstrated in the full group's demonstration of learning for advancements to candidacy.

A second U.S. application took place with a small Japanese company in San Francisco in July and August of 1996. The purpose of this project was to improve teamwork, communication, and leadership. Yongming had been called to help the company at a time of crisis. Two symptoms stood out: the financial difficulties experienced by the company and the inability of managers and employees to work with each other to accomplish their tasks.

Yongming and six CIIS students worked for 4 weeks with the owner and his major team, interviewing employees, observing work practices, and engaging in synergy processes. By self-report, the owner was profoundly affected by the experience and has significantly changed his style of management. The inquiry team from the organization evolved a different work spirit, and a new, more nourishing culture developed for the organization as a whole.

Since then, there have been creative applications of SI in corporations and nonprofit settings. SI has been tailored to be delivered in various workshop formats and used as a strategy for coaching and consulting. Regular classes and public workshops in SI are now being offered on a year-round basis, and two organizations—the Global Synergy Network (nonprofit) and the Global Synergy Netlink (for profit)—have been established to promote this synergy work.

A number of former and present participants have begun to actively use SI in their research and publication efforts. These include Masaji Takano, whose dissertation research examines the effectiveness of SI, and Carole

Barlas, whose presentation describing the first application of SI in the United States at the U.S. Educational Research Conference in May 1997 received an award for the best presentation in the Human Justice domain.

Conclusion

Although we are inspired by its potential and timely development, we believe that our SI work is at best rudimentary at this point. This book only bench-marks our current reflections and learnings. For example, the writing of this book has helped us clarify a significant number of issues in ways we had not previously been able to articulate. This implies that there are opportunities for other theorists, methodologists, and practitioners to make contributions to the development of SI. It is in this spirit of sharing and inviting the participation of others that we present this book to you.

PART I

The Synergic Inquiry Methodology and Its Theoretical Foundation

This part of the book is devoted to introducing the synergic inquiry (SI) methodology and explicating its framework and theoretical foundations. It offers a presentation of the SI methodology, and it discusses SI in the context of major research paradigms and other prevalent methodologies. The purpose here is to provide readers with enough information about SI for it to be discussed knowledgeably by theorists and researchers and used by practitioners who are exploring the methodologies available to them, as well as to give fuller information to others who might use SI. The content of each chapter is briefly described in the following paragraph.

In Chapter 2, "Overview of Synergic Inquiry," the basic premises on which SI is based are described, and an overview of the methodology itself with a case illustration is presented. Chapter 3, "The Synergic Universe," discusses the theoretical foundations on which SI was developed. It presents our argument for a significant pattern we identified—the synergy principle—through various sources of cultural wisdoms, social sciences, and natural sciences. Chapter 4 places the methodology in the context of other research paradigms and major methodologies of change; the chapter provides a wider context from which readers can develop an understanding of the uniqueness of SI in its context of research and change methodologies.

The order in which the chapters appear is that which makes sense to us as authors, but it is not the only order in which this book can be read or used. We endeavored to keep each chapter sufficiently coherent and discrete so that they could be read in the order preferred by each reader.

Readers who are interested in only a taste of SI may prefer to read only Chapter 2, "Overview of Synergic Inquiry." This chapter is consolidated to provide an overview of SI with a specific case illustration. Those who are interested in understanding SI with an eye on SI methodology and practices may profit more by reading Chapter 2 and then immediately moving to the case studies presented in Part II. Those who are more interested in examining the theoretical core of SI in relation to its methodological processes may prefer to read Chapters 3 and 4 before a description of the method itself.

2

Overview of Synergic Inquiry

Scientists are further beginning to recognize that—like the artificial conflict between spirit and nature, between woman and man, and between different races, religions, and ethnic groups fostered by the dominator mentality—the way we view conflict itself needs to be reexamined.

—Eisler (1987)

The sage harmonizes with both right and wrong and rests in Heaven the Equalizer. This is called walking two roads.

—Chuang Tzu

I n this chapter, synergic inquiry's (SI's) methodological processes and phases are introduced by first defining basic terminology and then describing the steps involved in SI. This information provides readers with a basic overview of the method. A case, based on real experiences, is used to illustrate the process and phases of SI.

Basic Definitions

Consciousness and Its Dimensions

Because SI is about expanding human consciousness, it is important to understand the meaning of consciousness. Consciousness is an elusive concept, a notion that philosophers have debated for thousands of years. SI is more concerned with finding a practical way to expand human consciousness than with creating a new definition to compete with other definitions. Therefore, our definition is a pragmatic one; in this context, human consciousness can simply be taken as the essential structure of being that defines who we are and how we behave.

To facilitate the expansion of consciousness, SI uses three dimensions of consciousness, called the *visible,* the *logical,* and the *mythical.* The visible level of consciousness refers to immediate, visceral, affective, physical, and behavioral manifestations of consciousness. This is usually what we can see, feel, and taste. The logical dimension refers to the rational mechanisms through which we logically interpret the world. It manifests primarily in terms of our mechanisms for explaining how things work, including theory, concept, law, principle, and so forth. The mythical dimension of consciousness SI uses goes beyond the logical to encompass our deepest beliefs—such as myth, faith, spirituality, the unsaid, the unthought, and so forth—and includes all those symbolic and archetypal functions and processes that normally take place below the level of our conscious awareness.

These three dimensions of consciousness do not function each independent of the other; rather, they have mutual relationships with dynamic interaction (see Figure 2.1). Although we each tend to favor one of the dimensions over the others, it does not mean that we cannot also enter into each of the other dimensions. These dimensions of consciousness are better viewed as functioning in a foreground–background relationship that may or may not shift easily. We use this three-part understanding of the dimensions of consciousness to add both depth and breadth to our SI work.

The nature and orientation of our own individual consciousnesses manifest as significant differences in style between us. For example, some of us are more oriented to the visible dimension, and decisions are based on what things look like and what others do. Those of us with a natural focus on the

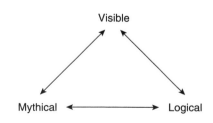

Figure 2.1   The Three Dimensions of Consciousness

logical dimension of consciousness may be more comfortable with reasoning and traditions of logic as a means to make decisions. Still others of us naturally focus on the mythical orientation of consciousness, and decisions are based on deep mythical or spiritual beliefs, which usually lie deep below the levels of our awareness.

These differences tend to cause difficulties among people. Often we simply are not aware that these differences are a matter of style and become frustrated or even angry when we cannot understand or when we are not understood. In other situations, people with one style may criticize or pass judgment on those with other styles, again causing conflict or confrontation.

Within the SI framework, we believe that we each tend to excel in our own consciousness style, but we are also limited by it. Our failure to recognize these limits is a major source of problems between us. To paraphrase Robert Vachon (1995), a serious obstacle to good human relations is that we are so rarely aware of the hidden assumptions behind our own style. Failing to recognize that which shapes all we think, state, do, or propose, we do not see that these assumptions are not necessarily the same as those of the people with whom we interact. The task of SI is to help us become aware of our hidden assumptions so that we can expand our consciousness from our own habitual preference for either the visible, logical, or mythical level, until our consciousness extends to all three dimensions. In addition, SI reframes what differences are and uses them as creative resources for human development, social problem solving, and conflict resolution.

Multiple Ways of Knowing

Corresponding to the three dimensions of consciousness are three ways of knowing to enhance the inquiry process. *Visible knowing* refers to inquiry into the visible dimension of consciousness. It tends to be unique and idiosyncratic. Because the knowledge obtained is mostly tacit knowledge, this kind of knowing can be hard to communicate to others. The visible knowing used in the context of self-knowing (SK) consists of using immediate experiences to know the self; these include sensory knowing through somatic reactions, perceptual understandings, and affective modes or emotions. When we engage with any situation, issue, or problem, there are immediate sensory knowings through our somatic reactions, perceptual understandings, and affective modes or emotions.

Each of us has cultivated an individualized capacity to understand, which comes to us through the experiences of our respective socialization processes. We can struggle to find words to express a specific experience, yet these words may end up being meaningful only to ourselves. This is part of the nature of visible knowing and should not be construed as a fault or deficit of the SI participant or the SI process. As Polanyi (1974) says, "We can know more than we can tell" (p. 4).

Likewise, *logical knowing* refers to the inquiry into the logical dimension of consciousness. It addresses the logical categories we use to interpret our experiences. These include the assumptions, values, and beliefs that are our primary logical mechanisms for interpreting experience. This logical dimension of consciousness is similar to what Mezirow (1991) calls "meaning scheme" (an assumption, value, or belief) and meaning perspective (a set of meaning schemes).

Mythical knowing means to generate knowledge about the mythical dimension of our consciousness. Encompassing our deepest myths, faith, spirituality, the unsaid, the unthought, and so forth, the powerful influences of this dimension of consciousness usually escapes our awareness. Raimon Panikkar (1979) uses the word *presupposition* to refer to the mythical dimension of consciousness. A presupposition is "something I uncritically and unreflectively take for granted. It belongs to the myth in which I believe and out of which I draw raw material to feed my thinking" (Vachon, 1995). This level of knowing is usually difficult to elucidate for ourselves because we are so unaware of it. Vachon asserts that the mythical dimension of consciousness can be discovered only by taking on a second mental plane or the perspectives of others.

Expansion of Consciousness

Expansion of consciousness refers to those transformative changes in the structure of our consciousness that enable us to engage the world differently. It is signaled by those subtle shifts that lead to new learnings and to additional awareness, skill, or capacity that occur in all of our lives. Expansions of consciousness, however, are different from changes in one's instrumental or technical skills and those changes that perpetuate one's habitual consciousness. An expansion of consciousness is the kind of shift that automatically leads to different ways of being and of behaving in the world.

It is important to recognize that an expansion of consciousness is an inward process that cannot be legislated. It can only be facilitated and nurtured. The intention within the SI approach is to expand our consciousness so that we can individually and collectively think anew toward reframing the world in ways that can healthily hold the whole together. As Buddhist teachings attest, major teachings reside in subtle shifts. It is the aim of SI to trigger, foster, nurture, and accelerate those subtle shifts that lead to the expansions of major teachings.

Synergy Cycle

SI presumes that the synergy process is cyclic and that the cycles of the SI process create an up-spiraling of expanded awareness and improved capacities to learn deeply and to be comfortable with complexity (see Figure 2.2). A synergy cycle refers to a complete cycle of the SI process. Within each synergy cycle, there are two major processes, one for differentiating and one for integrating. Each of these processes has two phases. Within the differentiating process are the phases of self-knowing and other-knowing. Within the integrating process are the phases of differences-holding and differences-transcending. Each step of the process is a context for learning, growth, and expanded consciousness and capacities. It doesn't matter whether the focal system is an individual, a dyad, or a larger collective; the steps and phases of this process are the same.

Action-Reflection Cycle

At the core of SI is an action-reflection cycle, which is embodied in every major phase of the synergy process. Just as the dance of inhaling and exhaling is required for life to continue, each phase of SI requires a dynamic dance between action and reflection. After one does some action work, a reflection process integrates the learning into oneself. Reflection is the key to expanding consciousness and capacities. After integrative reflection, we are more ready to engage in further action.

In SI, we include two types of reflection. One is reflection on the content of the exploration; this is to expand the awareness. When participants engage in inquiry within the SI process, many things that were previously unrecognized about the self will emerge, and it is important that participants reflect on what they are experiencing and what meanings they make of it. The other type is reflection on the SI process itself, which is used to develop or enhance skills and capacities. The specific experiences and insights that emerge for participants come out of the SI process. It is important to reflect on what led to the experiences, whether they are seen as positive or negative. Reflection on the process is what helps participants integrate the SI process into the natures of their own beings and into their behaviors.

Steps Into the SI Process

In what follows, a complete synergy cycle is introduced. The purpose of each phase and some guidance in conducting each phase are briefly described.

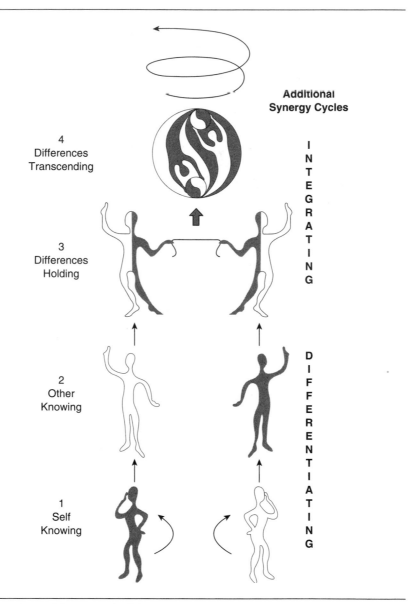

Figure 2.2   The SI Methodology

A case example is used after each step of the methodology to illustrate how these processes and phases have been used in relation to each other. This description uses SI to focus on solving problems or improving an existing situation. In other words, SI is used to focus on something specific. Additional synergy cycles can follow to focus on capacity building and the spiritual dimension of SI.

It is important to note that the case used as an example represents only one of many ways that SI can appear. In our experiences with applying SI to a variety of contexts, we find that SI tends to manifest differently according to both context and focus. (Ten case studies showing different ways that SI manifested are described in the case study chapters.) Here we use an example only to add a more concrete dimension to our description, in hopes of making the processes and phases as clear as possible. The complexity with which this essentially simple methodology manifests is explored in other chapters. It is also important to note that the case used for illustration was actually much more complicated than it appears in the description.

The SI application used as our illustrative example was one in which a business owner, who originally came from Asia, was having problems with subordinates who had been born and educated in the United States. Although all of them, the boss and the subordinates, wanted teamwork, they never managed to be successful at it. Their problems included frustration, lack of trust, miscommunication, and alienation. These were compounded by financial difficulties; although the business was growing, the problem of financial sustainability had become severe. It was clear to the owner, and to some of his subordinates, that if their team continued its "dysfunctional behavior," the whole company might collapse.

After some intense exploration with the owner and the key team members, we agreed to use SI to focus on improving teamwork. A team of SI facilitators was sent to the company to conduct an assessment and to interview the owner and team members. Then the facilitators developed the strategy to use SI for an intervention. This strategy included a series of off-site, intense learning experiences for the team members. Facilitators started by developing some basic norms to be used during the synergy process and securing a commitment from team members. A brief lecture was used to introduce the SI process to the team members. It is important to note that the SI facilitators also actively participated in the synergy process with the participants from the company.

Differentiating

Knowing self and others, succeed in all situations.

—Sun Tzu

Differentiating is extremely important in SI; thoroughness in differentiation is critical to the success of the inquiry. Designed to enable participants to cultivate different constructions of realities, this process helps them learn to authentically embody different consciousnesses. During the differentiating

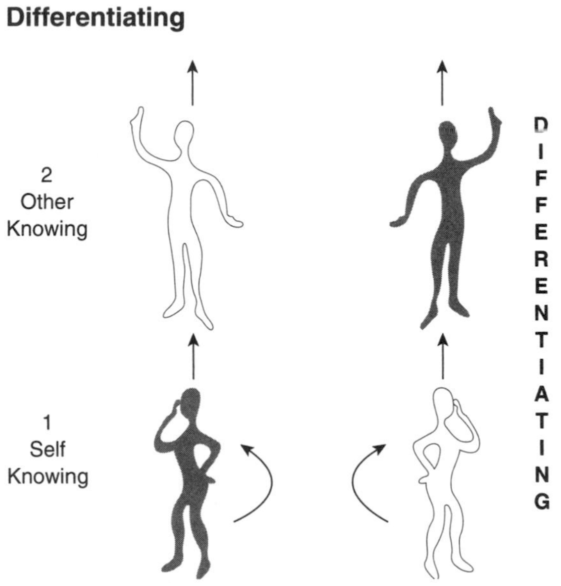

Differentiating

Figure 2.3   Differentiating Process

process, human consciousnesses are examined and reflected on. The two complementary phases within this process of differentiation are self-knowing and other-knowing. (See Figure 2.3.)

Phase I: Self-Knowing

The foot feels the foot when it feels the ground.

—Buddha

The first thing in the world is knowing how to belong to oneself.

—Michel de Montaigne

The inward-looking journey of SI starts, and ends, with self-knowing (SK). SK within SI is, by definition, to put the self as the focus of inquiry; it brings who we are and why we act the way we do, as well as the meanings and effects of our actions, more fully into our conscious awareness. Consciousness consists of a set of beliefs, presuppositions, assumptions, and values that are so completely taken for granted that we are usually as blind to our own consciousness as we are to the air we breathe. Although we are immersed in air constantly, and our very life depends on it, we do not usually see it. In a similar way, we are immersed in our consciousness. Always there, like air, within and around everything we see, say, or do, our own individual consciousness is usually so taken for granted that we are blind to it and to its effects. (See Figure 2.4.)

As a result, our interpretations of any phenomenon are always influenced by projections of our own consciousness. Without an understanding that this happens, what our own consciousness consists of, and how it links us to or separates us from others, it is impossible for us to expand beyond our own self or to truly include any other. When we are not aware of the presuppositions and precepts that our consciousness holds, it is also difficult for us to absorb anything new. However, once we learn to identify the lenses through which we see the world and to understand how those lenses construct reality for us, situations are reframed, deep learning can take place, and others can be included.

Not knowing how to know ourselves, we tend to define, evaluate, and judge others and the larger reality according to criteria, values, or standards that we unconsciously hold, and the fundamental beliefs that govern how and what we see tend to remain unexamined. There is a Zen story that illustrates the point we are trying to make. A disciple talked at much length about his desire for wisdom while the master was pouring tea. The master just kept pouring, even after the cup was full and the tea flowed all over. When the student was completely baffled and asked about this, the master replied, "You came as a full cup. How can you expect to take in anything new?"

Part of our predicament is that we usually do not know our cups are full, and we tend to lack the skills to find out. There are two basic conditions that need to be in place for SK to go well within SI. First, people need to have both willingness and commitment to reflect on themselves and on their own

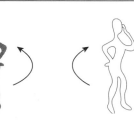

1
Self
Knowing

Figure 2.4   Self-Knowing

consciousnesses on a regular basis. Otherwise, that which they reject or are unwilling to address in their own consciousness could limit or even prevent true synergy.

The second condition that must be solidly in place before attempting to guide others through SI is cultivation of those specific skills that allow one to do SK well. Our socialization and educational processes have usually neglected these skills, and most of us end up beginning in SI with limited capacities to engage in SK.

SK Action. In this step, we begin to examine the inner structures of our consciousness. The purpose of this exploration is for us each to discover, clarify, and form knowledge about our own structure of consciousness. Three modes of SK—visible SK, logical SK, and mythical SK—are included in the design of an inquiry so that participants can examine all three dimensions of their consciousness.

With the purpose of SK clarified, SI participants are challenged to find ways to accomplish SK. As shown in the case studies in later chapters, different participants were able to create effective means to do SK. The following illustrates only one way of doing SK. In this case, participants decided to use a simple scheme of questions that is often used to get at the different dimensions of consciousness. These are *what* for the visible SK dimension, *how* for the logical SK, and *why* for the mythical SK. The following is a series of questions based on the scheme:

- *What* is your notion of teamwork?
- *How* might it work in your situation?
- *Why* do you think it would work better for you as a team? Why? And why? (Multiple why questions uncover deeper values, beliefs, faith, and so on, and participants are asked to use metaphors, drawings, and other modes to express their mythical SK.)

Starting with a self-reflective process that requires confidence in and compassion with one's own consciousness, each individual worked alone, using the questions to bring his or her consciousness into awareness and make it explicit. Participants were asked to follow the scheme and to get at all the different dimensions of consciousness. They were reassured that all consciousness is valid and legitimate and that any mode of knowing used to describe consciousness was entirely acceptable.

Once consciousness regarding the presenting issue—that is, teamwork—became explicit, each participant was asked to design a presentation that would teach other team members his or her consciousness. These presentations could take any form, and they tended to range from linear descriptions to storytelling, drawing, painting, and even dancing. Regardless of its form, the presentation should represent one's consciousness with an intention to make it explicit to others.

SK Reflection. Participants learn new things about themselves from this inner exploration. After SK action, reflection is needed for people to integrate the learning. The following questions, which encompass reflection on both content and process, were created to facilitate SK reflection:

- What are the key insights, if any, you have learned about yourself, and what do they mean to you personally?
- How are you feeling about this experience?
- What led you to experience the way you did? What have you learned about the process?
- What did not work for you? What would you suggest to make it work better for you?

After some reflection, most participants reported feeling good. Some of them felt it was very useful to do this exercise; this was the first time they had devoted time to examining what they are, how they view the world, and why they do things the way they do. Work had always seemed too pressing, and they did not have either the time or the intention to examine themselves before they acted. In addition, most reported that nobody in the company really cared about what they felt or thought. Thus, the experience was very different from what they experienced in their everyday work life.

Phase II: Other-Knowing

> *Through the Thou a person becomes I.*
>
> —Martin Buber (1958)

> *Knowing others is wise.*
>
> —Tao Te Ching

If SK is to know the inner world of oneself, other-knowing (OK) is to learn the outer world—the world of others' experiences, beliefs, and understandings and the world as it is in its own right. (See Figure 2.5.)

Why do we need to know the outer world? There are two very important reasons why we should. The first has to do with our shrinking globe. When people from different parts of the world actually lived apart—East is East

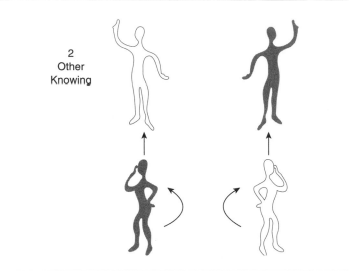

2
Other
Knowing

Figure 2.5   Other-Knowing

and West is West and never the twain shall meet—things seemed fine. Most of us could be comfortable within a collective consciousness that was fairly homogeneous and stable.

However, living as we do in a time of massive cultural interaction and change, we find that our constructions of reality are repeatedly challenged or put into question. It is also clear that no single individual or collective construction of reality could possibly suit every single person, place, and circumstance. In other words, every consciousness is limited, and every culture is limited. When these differences and their limits collide, all go through a crisis of myth (Panikkar, 1979; Vachon, 1995). To live in a peaceful modern world, we need to literally cocreate new myths and a new approach to reality that is inclusive and capable of transcending our differences (Panikkar, 1979; Vachon, 1995).

In addition to these differences between us, we all have underlying myths of which we are not aware. As was discussed in relation to SK, we always have presuppositions that we take for granted. In OK, we are able to take another mental plane to help us unveil those myths that we cannot see (Panikkar, 1979, p. 345; Vachon, 1995). It is important to emphasize that without these mirrors and help from others we cannot learn deeply about our own selves and our own deepest lenses on reality.

Without taking this learning to the mythic level, the most we can do is analyze and evaluate. Something very important happens when one activates one's own lens to evaluate or analyze new consciousnesses. This dynamic is significant and deserves serious attention. The outcome of analyzing any new consciousness is inevitably a process of externalization and objectification (Tang, 1994, 1995). In other words, the end result of analyzing and evaluating is to transform consciousnesses, or you as a person, into an *it*, or you as an object (Vachon, 1995).

This result is fundamental, core to the problems of our time. At the level of social dynamics, alienation occurs when one's reality is not recognized or accepted. Analysis and evaluation have many positive functions, but when applied to another's consciousness, they leave us with either the egocentric worldview—we are the only way—or the ethnocentric worldview—we have the better way (Adler, 1997). Neither of these is adequate to lead to harmonious relations with others or to address the complexities of our world and truly solve its problems.

Concretely, OK is the process whereby participants begin to explore these external realities from a more receptive and flexible place. In its early stages, this journey to genuine knowing of the other requires effort, new skills, and many levels of attention. The end result, however, will expand to a kind of effortlessness that is difficult to describe to those who have neither seen nor experienced it.

SI participants get to know the external world through a communicative process in which the consciousnesses of two or more individuals are brought to the surface and exchanged. To be more precise, OK is an attempt to understand other consciousnesses that are different from our own without distorting them. It requires a good deal of openness and capacity to empathize to be faced with viewpoints or consciousnesses that are different from our own and keep from judging on the basis of one's own perspective. This is especially challenging when SI participants are in a polarized or even confrontational situation. To create this openness, it is necessary to bracket one's own consciousness and to temporarily put it aside. As in the Zen story told earlier, we have to metaphorically empty the cup of our own consciousness to receive something new.

OK Action. In this step, we begin to inquire into the inner structures of others' consciousness. Again, the purpose of this exploration is for each of us to discover, clarify, and form knowledge about the consciousnesses of others. Three modes of OK—visible OK, logical OK, and mythical OK—can be used to gain insights into others' consciousnesses.

In our case example, during the OK phase the participants presented their SK to each other without judgment. The presentations took different forms:

Some were in the form of language, and others ranged from a drawing and symbol constructed with paper to a combination of language and images. The participants were allowed to ask clarifying questions, as long as these did not attempt to disagree with or evaluate the presentation. After having given attention to each other's SK presentation, a role-play exercise called deep listening was used to help participants embody each other's consciousnesses in terms of the visible, logical, and mythical dimensions. In this exercise, others tried to embody the presenter's consciousness in different ways, while being coached by the presenter. This process continued until the presenter felt satisfied, and every participant went through a similar process.

OK Reflection. After OK action work, another cycle of reflection occurs. This reflection focuses on learning and growth toward integrating new learnings into the self for another level of SK. Again, both content reflection and process reflection are needed. At the content level, participants are asked to reflect on their new experiences of the other and how that experience informs the self. At the process level, participants are asked to reflect on what enabled them to have the new experiences they had, what worked, and what did not. The process reflection again helps participants to develop and sustain the skills and capacities to embody the SI process in their own beings and in their behaviors. The following questions were used to facilitate the reflection experience:

- What did you learn about yourself through the mirror of others?
- What questions did you have about yourself and others?
- How are you feeling? And why are you feeling the way you feel?
- How is this experience different from other experiences?
- What made it work?

After reflection, some of these participants reported that the mirror of others helped them learn more about themselves. It was powerful to hear their own voices in the presentations of others, and trying to be the others also had a strong impact. The dramas played out in the exercise provided a different sense of boundaries and relationships. Some participants expressed the deep love, understanding, and connection they felt in this exercise. This seemed very different for them because the assumptions they made about each other got in the way of connecting and understanding. Some also felt they would now be able to go deeper into themselves because of the differences they heard in the presentations. Some were also struck by the different perspectives around teamwork and the deep passions associated with each vision of team. They all appreciated the opportunity to hear deeply and be deeply heard. They spent quite a bit of time talking about how this exercise helped them to understand other team dynamics that had occurred prior to this synergy project. The owner was emotional. He said that it was the first time he had been able to see a different perspective on things. He had always believed that everybody in his company ought to share his perspective because he was the most experienced. Now, he could be more open to new and different ideas.

> *The interplay of individuality and unity is not one of uniformity and unanimity imposed from above but rather of conflict among diverse groupings that reach a dynamic consensus subject to questioning and criticism.*
>
> —West (1993)

> *The great person holds harmony among differences; the small person holds disharmony with sameness.*
>
> —Confucius

Integrating

Once participants have completed the two phases of the differentiating process, it's time to begin the integrating process. As a result of the SK and OK work that has been done, different consciousnesses, or different constructions of reality, have developed. Now, it is time for participants in the SI process to learn to engage these differences so that they can eventually be used creatively for their own human development; for solving social, organizational, and environmental problems; and for transforming those schisms that lead to our great range of difficulties. In this integrating process, the differences that came out of the differentiating process begin to interact with each other with equality and fairness to produce new kinds of outcomes. This stage of the process also has two phases: differences-holding and differences-transcending. (See Figure 2.6.)

Phase III: Differences-Holding

> *Suppose we were able to share meanings freely without a compulsive urge to impose our view or to conform to those of others . . . would this not constitute a real revolution?*
>
> —Bohm (1991)

> *The sage harmonizes with both "right" and "wrong" . . . This is called walking two roads.*
>
> —Chuang Tzu

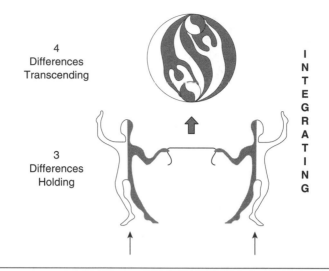

4
Differences
Transcending

3
Differences
Holding

I
N
T
E
G
R
A
T
I
N
G

Figure 2.6   Integrating Process

The first phase of the integrating process is differences-holding (DH), in which we further explicate the differences between different consciousnesses and learn to hold them as equals. It is not enough for us to know that the differences we have observed exist. We also need to hold those differences in such a way that the consciousness they represent is given as much weight and rights as our own. This is when the differentness of the differences that have been identified starts to hit home. Key elements of these differences start to come to the surface, and tension usually arises. This tension is a natural and expected part of the SI process. (See Figure 2.7.)

The tension represents energy that is not being well used. The energy of this tension has been purposefully generated and carefully contained through the preceding stages of the inquiry process. In DH, we start to use this tension as a creative resource, something that can lead to personal growth and transformation for individuals and to collective synergy for groups. However, if this tension is not handled well, polarization, conflict, or confrontation is likely to disrupt the SI process.

The goal of DH is to cultivate the capacity for a truly synergic consciousness. In other words, we are working toward changing the essential structure of our being to one that is more complex, inclusive, and capable of resilience and responsiveness to change. It is our experience that the synergic consciousness has a primary capacity that is inclusive, or both-and, which refers to the mental ability to transcend the limitations of both self and other by creatively using the strengths of each without being constricted by the limitations

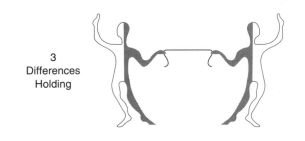

3
Differences
Holding

Figure 2.7   Differences-Holding

of either. This is another way of saying that we have shifted from a singular-value orientation to a multiple-value orientation.

It is here that the enlarged mental plane produced by OK begins to give one the capacity to move flexibly from inner self to an inner other that has been cultivated within the self and back again to inner self, a phenomenon that is portrayed in each of the two figures embodying two different (black and white) consciousnesses. When this can be done with ease, not only has one's consciousness been expanded, but also one's capacity for consciousness has been increased. This kind of expanded consciousness is then able to transcend apparent paradoxes, contradictions, and polarities between the different consciousnesses within oneself or between the self and other to recognize how they can fit together within a larger whole.

Our socialization processes have usually led to an either-or consciousness. We have been brought up to "know" one way is right, which means that other ways must be wrong. As a result, few of us are able to hold more than one consciousness as equally right. We haven't learned the skills or developed our capacities. And often we haven't even been given—or given ourselves—permission to do this. Within SI, we have a safe context and permission to try new things. In addition to the new skills we have learned and the new insights about ourselves and others we have gained, DH can give us the added mental capacity to transcend contradictions, polarities, and paradoxes that were barriers. This is what DH is intended to achieve.

An important reminder at this stage is that, within SI, every consciousness is believed to be incomplete and therefore limited. In this we agree with Kegan (1994) when he forcefully asserts that the presence of conflict caused by the inability to hold differences "is not the inconvenient result of the existence of an opposing view but the expression of your own incompleteness taken as completeness" (p. 320). We experience within each inquiry how our own individual incompleteness can become less limiting when we learn to enter the dance between the self and others that is the expression of a both-and consciousness.

We return again to Kegan (1994), who recommends that people "focus on ways to let the conflictual relationship transform parties rather than on the parties resolving the conflict" (p. 320). As we learn to hold our differences as equal, DH presents us the opportunity to reduce both inner and outer conflicts and become more complete by allowing ourselves to become more inclusive. The key to doing this is to always acknowledge our own incompleteness. The ability to do this suggests a fundamentally self-reflective attitude toward learning, an attitude that is qualitatively different from the traditional conflict resolution with which we usually approach tensions caused by differences.

Just as yin and yang constitute a whole with each including elements of the other, our consciousness is a whole with two sides to it: its completeness and its incompleteness. The way we can learn to find the incompleteness of our own consciousness by using the other as a mirror is extremely convenient. In this way, the differences that usually divide us can help us discover those holes in our being that cut us off from others.

It is, of course, critical that each participant be willing to look for the other side, the part of our consciousness that is in the shadow of what we perceive to be complete. Otherwise, we cannot avoid projecting our own shadows onto others. Doing this allows both sides of one's consciousness to become visible, and limitations become as obvious as strengths. Because it transforms our existing singular-value orientation to a multiple-value orientation, this process itself is a major reframing.

It is critically important here not to use one side (usually one's own perceived strengths) to subjugate, dominate, or oppress another's consciousness (usually the perceived negatives of others). Conversely, if one is normally insecure, has too often been a victim, or is a member of a repressed or marginalized group, it is equally important not to allow the other's perceived strengths to annihilate one's own consciousness by focusing only on perceived negatives. Both of these imbalances reinforce whatever racism, sexism, or ethnocentrism is hiding in the shadows of our own limitations.

DH Action. In the action cycle of this phase, key differences between the consciousnesses that have been presented are identified. This is to further differentiate the consciousnesses from each other. In our sample case, after some work, two significantly different perspectives, that of the owner and that of the rest of the team, were delineated along the dimensions of visible, logical, and mythical (see Figure 2.3). These participants were also asked to evaluate their own strengths and limitations, using the other as a mirror.

Thus, the major differences between the owner and the rest were captured as both strengths and weaknesses. (See Figure 2.8.)

Next, participants are asked to learn to hold their different consciousnesses as equals. It was apparent that the differences between the two radically different worldviews led to more tension between the owner and the rest of the team. The facilitators decided to break up the team and conducted several hours of individual coaching. This proved to be a necessary act, and participants came back with different energy and were ready to engage with each other again. Participants were again reminded that it is critically important in doing this not to use one side of consciousness, usually one's own perceived strengths, to subjugate, dominate, or annihilate others' consciousnesses, usually the negatives perceived. Participants in the example were

	The Asian Owner	Americans or Asian Americans
What	A good team functions in unison and succeeds in all situations.	A good team treats and respects all members equally, performs well, and has fun.
How	There should be only one leader. The leader functions as a head, and all others act like arms and legs. The head is the main headquarters, which gives orders, and the others are body parts that execute the orders. Individual minds are the problem, because they obstruct the communication process.	In a good team, everyone is a leader and facilitator. All problems should be discussed by the team members, and the team should take all responsibility. Voices need to be heard, and team members' ideas need to be respected. Whoever has a better idea acts as a leader, and the others follow.
Why	The universe is hierarchical. The best metaphor for a good team is the military team: One is general and the others are soldiers. Differences are the problem.	Everybody is born equal. Human dignity is God given. Everyone has ideas and can make contributions. The whole is always bigger than the sum of the parts.
Strengths	Decisions can be made quickly. The power of the owner is reflected.	People feel recognized. Better quality decisions are made.
Limitations	Wrong decisions can be made. Subordinates are alienated.	The decision-making process can be too slow to respond to market needs. If not done well, the owner may feel threatened.

Figure 2.8   Holding Different Consciousnesses as Equals

asked to act out two different consciousnesses without preferring one to the other; that is, they were asked to truly hold both consciousnesses as equals.

DH Reflection. After action work, another cycle of reflection on both content and process occurs. Again, this is designed to process feelings and experiences and to integrate new learnings and skills. The following reflective questions were used to facilitate the sample process:

- How are you feeling about yourself and the team now?
- What did you learn about yourself through this process?
- To what extent can you hold the different consciousness within you?
- To what extent can you not do this? Why?
- What made it work for you?
- What did not work? Why?

These participants felt great about the process. Most felt it was the first time that they could understand why there had been so many difficulties involving teamwork. A few felt that the experience created new space for them because they had rarely felt being held the way they experienced it that day. They could understand each other better, despite the major differences between them. This allowed them to hold each other's perspectives and respect their differing views. At this point, most felt that the energy in the room was changed, and participants were eager to create new possible solutions to the team problems they were facing.

Phase IV: Differences-Transcending

In the cauldron things are cooked together, and out of the things strange to each other, irreconcilable, something new comes forth. This is obviously the answer to the paradox, the impossible impasse.

—Jung (1984)

No problem can be solved by the same consciousness that created it.

—Albert Einstein

The last phase of each synergy cycle is differences-transcending (DT). This is the phase for practical strategies because only in this last phase does it become possible to take what has been learned into a full embodiment of synergy. Just as the function of DH is to help expand or transform

Figure 2.9   Differences-Transcending

consciousnesses, the function of DT is to manifest this change by developing strategies that express the synergic consciousness in the complex realities of our shared world (see Figure 2.9). In this way, the SI process is used to address complexity and can be creative in social and political contexts as well as in terms of the more concrete problems we face.

The DT phase occurs when, as suggested by Kegan (1994), "the conflictual relationship transforms parties" (p. 320), rather than when parties resolve the conflict. As Kegan recognized, if we depend on two parties to resolve conflict, the best that can be achieved is compromise. When differences are instead transcended, a higher order of consciousness has been reached through inner exploration, and this higher order of consciousness itself is the fundamental solution to, and usefulness of, conflict.

This new but very Western approach to difference is in accord with traditional systems thinking in the East, where it is called the yin within the yang and the yang within the yin. In Western terms, this same observation can be stated in a variety of ways: the masculine within the feminine and the feminine with the masculine, $E = MC^2$, form within function and function within form, and so forth.

Such a way of working with differences is believed to be highly creative. Alfonso Montuori (1992) stated the following idea:

> Creativity . . . involves precisely the ability to struggle with oppositions in a constant dialectic, and essential tension. These tensions seek release in a higher level of complexity and organization, and the ultimate "synthesis" must still be viewed as a process—not necessarily the elimination of oppositions, but the ability to learn to live with them in a creative, rather than a destructive fashion. The stress is on a continuing creative tension, rather than an either/or struggle between change and stasis, with its political analogy in the liberal/conservative polarity. (p. 197)

How does DT look in the individual context and in the collective context? In the context of an individual, DT refers to the phenomenon in which one transcends her or his own limitation of consciousness to become a synergic consciousness that is constantly evolving by dancing with differences. Behaviorally, the ways of engaging the world are new and different. One becomes more collaborative and creative and enjoys working with differences. Experiences and motivations that are based on the logical dimension of one's own consciousness can no longer be so unthinkingly projected onto another. With this change, expansions in our ability to listen to and recognize another consciousness as other are genuine. Although we may or may not recognize that difference internally, others with whom we interact will, and their responses to us will change.

At the mythic level, the very nature of reality comes to be understood differently, with effects that are more far reaching and durable than can be immediately seen. Evidence of these changes can arise from within us, sometimes seeming to come to our rescue in a situation that would once have been much more difficult and sometimes bubbling up like an intimate gift from deep within. Or we can see them externally through changes in our actions and choices that only seem new or unexpected in retrospect. These changes at the various levels or dimensions do not need to be sought or forced. They are a natural result of holding truly balanced differences until the creativity inherent in the tension between them is released.

In a collective context, participants are genuinely able to use our differences as resources for going beyond what the individual consciousnesses of participants can do alone to create something that is indeed new or even novel. Any energy that built up from the collision of differences during the preceding phases of SI has succeeded in piercing the boundaries of our limits, and there is a natural easing of tension and sense of relief and accomplishment. This is when we become genuinely able to move toward something new, and it is often important to do something concrete that incorporates this change. Because differences are no longer sources of friction, they can be, and now are, treated as sources of wisdom and insight.

DT Action. At this stage, participants move toward developing new, synergic solutions to the problems they address. In the DT phase, inner tension is usually produced within each participant by the differing views and perspectives they are trying to hold. It is important for them to allow this tension to be present, to hold this tension until they feel comfortable in both consciousnesses. This shift from discomfort to comfort channels the tension and turns it into a creative force. At this stage of inquiry, it is often useful to have participants separate into groups so that they can work together to develop new solutions to the focal problem.

In the case we are using to illustrate these processes, the participants had long conversations about how they could develop a new notion of teamwork that would work for all. Eventually a democratic-central team concept was created. In this concept, a democratic process was implemented to allow full participation of all individuals, including the owner. They agreed that the owner should have veto power over any major decision created by the team because it was his company. The owner expressed his commitment to using the synergic process in every major aspect of the company, including policy development, strategic planning, motivation, system redesign, and job improvement. These new concepts had gone far beyond the differences that had previously frustrated and limited the participants and the company.

DT Reflection. After the action stage, a cycle of reflection to continue learning and growth occurs. At this point, the participants in our example were generally excited about their new metaphor and the framework that followed from this metaphor. They felt that this new framework would work for the company and said that, in addition to producing the framework, the synergy process had also helped them learn how to communicate with each other and genuinely work as a team. The owner said he now had a gold-producing method. He saw the SI process as flexible enough for him to use to engage his team and individual employees on any issue that might emerge, and he felt that this approach could hold his team together and improve his company in many ways.

Additional Synergy Cycles

In these additional synergy cycles, participants are challenged to facilitate for themselves, using SI to solve other problems and to address other situations that concern them. They are also invited to use this process more broadly, in other aspects of their lives, whatever they do. Once participants are able to use SI to influence their own behavior, they see the world differently, act differently, and create new horizons for themselves and others.

The first synergy cycle is just a beginning; additional synergy cycles provide more opportunities for participants to learn the SI process and for them to go deeper into the expansion of their own consciousness. Eventually the skills and capacities that are cultivated through repeated synergy cycles start to become incorporated into the nature of the participant's own being. For participants to integrate the SI process, repeated synergy cycles are needed. Once one has truly embodied SI, the mechanics of the processes and phases can be transcended. Just like the successful tai chi or qi gong master who is no longer attached to any form of practice, these participants will have transcended the forms that helped them grow. In other words, they will think, act, and behave synergistically.

Returning to our case illustration, the synergy work did continue in the company after the first synergy cycle. The owner decided to use SI to work with his managers and key staff members on issues ranging from regular problem solving to strategic planning. He also said that he wanted to consider the possibility of restructuring ownership of the company so that the new team concept could fully materialize for everybody. He wanted his company to truly become a synergic organization, one with a high capacity for dealing with changing situations and rising complexities. He consulted with the SI facilitators on facilitation issues and occasionally used external facilitators to assist with an inquiry. Gradually these people became fully capable of carrying out SI without any external facilitation.

Reflection is equally important for additional synergy cycles. At this time, reflection on process should be emphasized more than reflection on content because this type of reflection helps participants focus on the inquiry process itself and learn how to make it work for them. The following types of reflective question were provided in the example we've used here:

- To what extent can you use the synergy process for problem solving?
- To what extent can you embody the synergy process in your personal and professional lives?
- What is the meaning of these changes and learnings for your life?

Most of these participants felt that they had learned the essence of the synergy process and that it could help improve their work. Most also felt that this intervention had influence for them beyond that of solving a problem. Some commented that SI gave them a tool they could use for their own personal growth.

The owner was very moved by this work and said that this process not only helped the company but was also life changing for him. Because he had been a practitioner of qi gong in Asia, many elements of this synergic process were already hidden in his consciousness. Through our inquiry, he reaccessed this wisdom. Having once again activated the synergy metaphor for his life, he behaved very differently. Although his situation was still full of great challenges, he stopped the habitual behaviors that had previously been so distressing for his employees, and an employee commented that his boss had indeed become a different person.

Conclusion

By now we have completed our presentation of the SI methodology as briefly as possible. Again, the purpose of this chapter is limited to introducing SI to such an extent that readers can understand its framework and basic steps. Those who are interested in learning how SI can be used in their own situations may want to consult Part II, in which many different applications of SI are described. Others will have different orientations and motivations and a whole range of questions about the theoretical foundations on which SI has been built and how SI fits in relation to research paradigms and change methodologies with which they are already familiar. Issues such as these are discussed in the next two chapters.

3

The Synergic Universe

The pattern which connects is a metapattern. It is a pattern of patterns. It is that metapattern which defines the vast generalization that, indeed, it is patterns which connect.

—Bateson (1979)

In our present age we need a worldview which takes into account the fundamental requirements of the age as well as the basic aspirations of man's evolving pysche. We need a worldview which shows how our deepest aspirations are related to the essential structure of the universe.

—Chaudhuri (1977)

S ynergic inquiry (SI) was in part inspired by calls from Gregory Bateson (1979) and Haridas Chaudhuri (1977) for new perspectives that connect to the essential structure of the universe. This chapter outlines our arguments for the grand universal pattern that we identify as the synergy principle of the universe and include in the theoretical foundation for the SI methodology. In doing this, we demonstrate the strong connection between the SI methodology and this principle that we take as part of the essential structure of the universe. We believe that the pattern this principle represents is both significant and pervasive and is what gives SI its power as a methodology for social action and change.

We believe that SI's grounding in a grand pattern is significant in terms of the momentum of our time and that the emergence of this methodology itself is part of the pattern that we call the synergy principle. In this chapter, we clarify the pattern that connects, which we see as underlying the evolution of reality, and we present support for our view from a variety of disciplines.

In seeking what Bateson (1979) called "the pattern that connects all the living creatures" (p. 8), we searched for and found metapatterns that do indeed "define the vast generalization" (Bateson, 1979, p. 8). This pattern was then combined with personal experience and used to design and develop a practical methodology that can guide action toward expansions of consciousness and greater capacities for addressing complexity and the need for human systems to change.

Our exploration of this aspect of SI's underpinnings has two layers. One layer is to show this pattern both within and in connections between the philosophical wisdoms of major cultures. The other layer is an exploration of a pattern that logically connects both the natural sciences and the social sciences. We start with the philosophical layer.

The Evolution of Consciousness and the Synergy Principle

Over the long period of human history, many have attempted to create definitions of the universe and reality, resulting in a wealth of divergent perspectives that compete with each other. In the text that follows, we do not focus on the definitions or boundaries that give us a snapshot to represent the immensity; instead, we focus on the dynamic processes within this immensity through which it has been seen to evolve. In other words, we explore descriptors of the basic process through which the universe evolves.

Our purpose here is to identify a significant pattern that is so important that it has the potential to integrate the divergent perspectives that normally compete and thus to eventually reexplain the world. The processes that emerge and result from this pattern have critical implications for human behavior and the effects people have on the world they share. People may ultimately have different perspectives on how the universe evolves, but this process, as described and used within SI, allows people to use the differences between their perspectives more productively.

By developing SI and sharing our work, we are reaching for a broader understanding of truth, one that has the potential to cut across boundaries of culture, class, beliefs, and experience. In this we share Panikkar's (1979) belief that there is no such thing as a private truth. If we want to identify a pattern that is so large and so powerful that we can claim its broad influence, this pattern must be one that connects to various cultural wisdoms.

In reaching for this kind of broad understanding, we explore literature from a wide range of sources, including Western theories of the evolution of the universe (e.g., Hegel, 1971, 1977; Laszlo, 1987, 1996; Wilber, 1995), Chinese Taoism and the philosophy of the *I-Ching* (Wu, 1985), Buddhism (Smith, 1991), the Indian integral philosophy by Sri Aurobindo (1992) and Chaudhuri (1977), and the emerging interculturalism as represented by the works of Panikkar (Prabhu, 1996) and the voices of a small group of Mohawk and non-Mohawk elders (Vachon, 1995). Because our attempt here is only to identify a metapattern across the range of these sources, we do not discuss the substance of any of this literature in depth.

We start with an old question: What is reality? Given all of the human intelligence that has been applied in attempts to explore this question, it seems clear that reality is elusive and that the totality of it is beyond our comprehension. It is full of mystery, and often it feels like pieces of cloud that are constantly shifting and changing. The *I-Ching,* one of the oldest philosophies of which we still have record and which heavily influenced the rubrics of Taoism, Confucianism, and Zen Buddhism in the East, states the nature of this mystery. As one translation into modern English reads, "The universe is an organic whole, a process of never-ceasing growth. All the existence within this growing context are organically interrelated and form a comprehensive continuum advancing into novelty" (Wu, 1985, p. 60).

This says that reality, in its totality, is in constant flux and evolution and therefore by nature unpredictable. Ordinary language, limited by its function to describing ordinary matters of life and our daily perceptual world, falls short in describing the mysterious nature of this totality (Wu, 1985, p. 29). In ancient Chinese belief, Tao is the origin of all things. As Lao Tzu elegantly expresses it in his famous saying at beginning of *Tao Te Ching,* "The Tao that can be spoken of is not the absolute Tao." The *Tao Te Ching* later continues,

> Tao, being a hollow vessel,
> Is never exhaustible in use.
> Fathomless,
> Perhaps the fountainhead of all existences. (Wu, 1989)

This belief is also shared by philosophers who belong to evolutionary schools of thinking in other cultures. For example, Sri Aurobindo, like his contemporary, Gandhi, is one of the modern-day saints of India. The core of his teachings address the ultimate unity of all beings and things in the Absolute or Divine. In Aurobindo's (1992) teachings, all that we observe as individuality is a manifestation of Divine consciousness. At that level, all is one, and all is part of an evolutionary process. Within this process, as seen by Aurobindo, first there was matter, then life, and then mind. Each arose out of the other and depends on these prior manifestations for its existence. Each of these steps is a progressive evolution of Divine consciousness. The universe is changing, but in a direction toward greater unity within the diversity of individual forms. Aurobindo sees the human race as being on the leading edge of this evolutionary process. Our purpose, therefore, is to participate in this evolutionary process and to prepare ourselves to be transformed and take on higher forms of consciousness. The consciousness that results from this kind of transformation experiences the unity in diversity, and this then becomes but another step in the evolutionary progression and expansion of consciousness.

Haridas Chaudhuri (1977), a student of Sri Aurobindo who founded a school to bridge Eastern and Western thinking in the United States, took a more philosophical approach in his writings, and he framed the evolutionary progression as a dialectic process. Chaudhuri, who sees dialectics as a process of resolving dualities back into One and advancing from lower to higher organized wholes, writes in *The Evolution of Integral Consciousness*:

> Reality's creative urge consists in the movement of energy from the relatively undifferentiated whole toward a continuously increasing self-differentiating of the whole. The human mind's quest for truth is the movement of consciousness from the dynamic tension between opposites toward more and more inclusive synthesis embracing the wholeness of Being. (p. 93)

Buddhism in general is also grounded in the notion that nature has its own evolutionary course and that problems are caused by the way we, as human beings, are stuck within our own constructions of reality, or egos, to such an extent that we are driven by them. Therefore Buddhist practices, especially those of Chan or Zen, have focused on teaching us to unlearn our constructions of reality so that we can participate more fully in the evolving process that we humans share with nature. When we align with nature's process, we will coevolve with harmony and happiness (Smith, 1991).

Emerging schools of thought in the West also share this perspective. In their book *The Universe Story*, Swimme and Berry (1994) explain that the origin of the universe is indeed a mystery, and they assert that we have to tell a new story, one that is refreshing and healthy. They also affirm the evolutionary process, which they say began 15 billion years ago and evolved from matter to life and then to mind. Wilber (1995), an influential integral philosopher, also takes an evolutionary approach in his explanation of the universe. He addresses the nature of the universe at the beginning of his influential book, *Sex, Ecology, Spirituality,* by writing, "It is strange to discover that the physical universe was manifested out of nothingness around 15 billion years ago; it is stranger that the life world evolved out of the physical world; even stranger mind arose out of life" (p. 1).

The evolving nature of total reality is also deeply rooted in the cultures of Africa. According to Marimba Ani (1994), African descriptions say that the universe is full of spirit that has its own course, refusing to be reduced to any rationalism. Recent voices of feminism also support this view of the universe as having an organic, relational, and evolving nature, saying that the masculine attempt to dominate this reality by confining it to static definitions is nothing but a product of human misconception and ego (Eisler, 1987).

This view, also shared by a concerned and articulate group of indigenous Americans, is described beautifully through the voice of Robert Vachon (1995):

> It is as if reality were refusing to let itself be reduced to any one principle, vision, experience, thought, concept, myth or symbol. Instead, it is inviting us to an awakening, to going beyond, to letting ourselves be moved, inspired, transformed—respectively—by an ever-new and more open myth that is trying to surface. Let us say that reality is calling us, each and all, to a deep mutation that we are still groping to see and to express, but which we are in the process of living, of discovering and co-creating gradually, together, every day. It is about an ever-open vision, synthesis and horizon. (p. 16)

What then is driving the evolutionary process of reality? If there does exist an underlying process for the evolution of the universe, is it even possible to decipher it? What would be a way to effectively move toward ever-open vision, synthesis, and horizon within this evolution? These questions too have long been addressed by philosophers.

According to the *I-Ching,* "All existences in the universe follow a definite order" (Wu, 1985, p. 50). Human beings are also said to have the capacity to understand this order or the principles and coherent patterns through which reality evolves. Part of our uniqueness as human beings is the ability to become conscious of the evolutionary process of the reality of which we are a part. In other words, although reality is vague and elusive, we can know its way of maintaining order or the principles behind the coherent patterns that form the manifestations of the totality.

A review of the literature from a wide range of Western disciplines shows that the dynamic nature of reality includes a fundamental pattern of differentiating and integrating that is inseparably bound in a cyclic relationship. (See the later section "Synergic Concepts and Phenomena Across Disciplines.") This contributes to our assumption that the processes of differentiation and integration are coherent patterns through which reality manifests itself and that the universe evolves through continuous processes of differentiation and integration. Although this perspective is informed by modern Western research, it is not new. It is implied in the *Tao Te Ching*, which says that the Tao manifests itself by differentiating and integrating; this idea is often expressed with a quote from Lao Tzu:

> The Way brings forth one.
> One brings forth two.
> Two brings forth three.
> Three bring forth all things. (Wu, 1989, p. 155)

In the *I-Ching*, the terms *yin* and *yang*—the two complementary cosmic forces—are used to describe the processes of differentiation and integration. All things are said to be brought forth by the differentiation and integration of yin and yang, and this process continues organically and indefinitely. This continuous interaction between yin and yang is the process of Tao. According to Ani (1994), in African cosmology there also exists a fundamental "twinness" of the universe, the complementary functions of opposites that cooperate to form the proper working of the whole (p. 77).

Through Chaudhuri (1977), Indian integralism also tells us that there is a law of cosmic balance:

> According to Indian philosophy, the Supreme Being, the One without a second, becomes many by producing dualities. Herein lies the most hidden secret of all creation and evolution—self-multiplication through polarization of energy. The nondual Being polarizes itself into the fundamental dualities of spirit and nature, mind and matter, God and world, light and darkness, heaven and earth, logos and eros. (p. 93)

A pattern of differentiation and integration is also found in the works of the great Western philosopher Georg Wilhelm Friedrich Hegel. In his encompassing dialectic system, Hegel describes existence as embodying multiple dimensions, which can be integrated into a unitary whole. According to Hegel, all human thoughts about reality are incomplete and therefore contradict each other. However, through a dialectical process, all human thoughts can complete themselves, resulting in a higher state of consciousness. Tarnas (1991) explains:

At the foundation of Hegel's thought was his understanding of dialectic, according to which all things unfold in a continuing evolutionary process whereby every state of being inevitably brings forth its opposite. The interaction between these opposites then generates a third stage in which the opposites are integrated—they are at once overcome and fulfilled—in a richer and higher synthesis, which in turn becomes the basis for another dialectical process of opposition and synthesis. (p. 379)

Hegel's dialectical philosophy has shaped the direction of Western philosophy (Tarnas, 1991), just as the philosophy of the *I-Ching* has influenced human thought in the East. In this way, Western approaches to understanding reality now appear to be converging with Eastern approaches called metaphysical philosophy. These processes of differentiation and integration as coherent patterns are also identified in matter, life, and mind:

These two processes are very obvious in the physiosphere (atom integrating differentiated particles, molecules integrating differentiated atoms, etc.) and in the biosphere (e.g., the progressive differentiation of the zygote and the progressive integration of the resultant parts into tissues, organ systems, organism), but they are also rampant in the sciences of the noosphere. Even psychoanalysis is on the board. Gertrude Blanck and Rubin Blanck, for example, pioneers in psychoanalytic developmental psychology, have persuasively argued that the aggressive drive is the *drive to differentiation,* and Eros is the *drive to integration,* and disruption of either one results in serious pathology. (Wilber, 1995, p. 69)

Futurist Charles Johnston (1991) has similar views and writes, "The creation of polarities is inherent to the workings of formative process" (p. 33). He asserts that creation is innately dialectical, that it cannot happen without separating the new from the old context. Within his creative system framework, integration is seen as the second half of the creative process. "Creation starts with unity, buds off new form—creating duality in the process—then with time re-integrates to a new, larger unity" (p. 32). As a result of this process, "polarities begin to bridge, and gradually a new, more integral whole comes to life" (p. 32). In other words, the polarities are integrated into a larger whole.

In a similar vein, the eminent systems thinker Ervin Laszlo (1996) summarizes both the classical disciplines and the emerging systems sciences into a general theory of evolution. In his model, which covers a period of 15 billion years, evolution starts with particles, atoms, molecules, and macromolecules, to evolve into protobionts, organisms, ecosystems, and ultimately social-cultural systems. The evolutionary process he describes is characterized by cyclic periods in which critical instability (i.e., differentiation) alternates with stability (i.e., integration). As evolution continues, the level of complexity increases.

Swimme and Berry (1994) tell a similar story in much greater detail, saying that in the process of differentiation and integration the cosmos evolves with increasing complexity and novelty. The outcomes that we call synergy are a product of these coherent processes of differentiation and integration as the universe evolves. First, newness or novelty is produced; this is the beauty of evolution. Second, in addition to the new complexities generated, our systems also seem to develop more capacities and abilities. New systems capacities, ones that would have been inconceivable in terms of the systems' parts, are generated. In other words, the combined effects that are developed go beyond what those parts could do alone. We call this process of differentiation and integration that leads to new and novel outcomes the synergy principle of the universe. In our view, it is a significant pattern that deserves attention, and we make it the underpinning of our methodological processes and practices.

Synergic Concepts and Phenomena Across Disciplines

The evolutionary process of differentiation and integration, or the notion of synergy, is a ubiquitous phenomenon. Although usually neither named that way nor recognized, it is an integral part of our personal lives. For example, many of the fruits, vegetables, and grains we eat are hybrids, or products of synergy. We also find it as a law within basic mathematics, as in the equation $(a + b)^2 = a^2 + b^2 + 2ab$. We have two different elements, a and b, that synergize with each other: The $2ab$ is a new outcome that did not exist before. It is because of this law that Einstein bridged the difference between matter and energy, making atomic energy available to us. Dozens of synergic phenomena have been identified in such scientific disciplines as systems dynamics, dissipative structures, and chaos theories, and Peter Corning (1995a, 1995b, 2003) asserts that synergy is a unifying concept for all sciences. We in SI use those synergic phenomena that have relevance to our practices to help us learn to embody natural processes in ways that improve our capacities to engage the contemporary world creatively.

In the following pages, we use examples from various theories and practices that relate to a variety of contexts and disciplines to demonstrate these patterns of differentiation and integration that have been addressed by philosophers. In doing so, we show the connections between practical applications and the philosophical exploration of the evolution of consciousness.

To be concrete, *differentiation* refers to a process in which an entity, perspective, identity, or whole is clearly distinguished from its context or environment (see Figure 3.1). *Integration,* on the other hand, refers to the

Commonalities
Differentiation refers to a necessary process in which a new entity—perspective or identity—is created, distinguishing itself from the other context or environment.

Biology: Griffiths, Miller, Suzuki, Lewontin, and Gelbart (1993)
Selfing is a process to produce different individuals with most homozygous state possible. In so doing, identical alleles at corresponding chromosomal loci are produced, which is a precondition for hybrid to happen.

Individuals: Kegan (1994)
"Before we can reconnect to internalize, or integrate something with which we are originally fused, we must first distinguish ourselves from it" (p. 326).

Relationships: Johnston (1991)
True partnership starts with two persons being independent, differentiated wholes.

Teams: Mouton and Blake (1984)
In assessing problematic situations, team members are asked to do ranking. Then, they are required to express the rationale for their ranking and to question each other's assumptions. In so doing, different mental models underlying different individuals' ranking are revealed.

Organizations: Lawrence and Lorsch (1967)
Successful organizations differentiate themselves in how they specialize their work to best respond to the demands of their environment: "As organizations undertake more complex tasks, they tend to complicate internally by differentiating new organization units" (p. 213).

Organizations: Savage (1996)
Effective organizations in the new era need to differentiate along three aspects—technology, information, and people—each having important function to successful management.

Societies: Ouchi (1984)
Japan was able to differentiate valuable Eastern wisdoms from Western strengths, clarifying the two alternatives.

Cross-/intercultural relations: Adler (1997)
In the cultural synergy process, culturally different individuals describe the problematic situation from their own cultural perspectives, that is, surfacing their cultural assumptions that drive attitude and behavior.

Globe: Thompson (1989)
A healthy ecology requires differentiated opposites to coexist. Otherwise, the ecology will be catastrophic.

Figure 3.1   Process of Differentiation Across Theories

process whereby differentiated entities work with each other (see Figure 3.2). The outcomes usually produced by these processes of differentiation and integration are characteristics and capacities beyond those of the individual parties involved (see Figure 3.3).

Integration refers to a process whereby differentiated
entities begin to work with each other.

Biology: Griffiths, Miller, Suzuki, Lewontin, and Gelbart (1993)
Crossing is a process between the two pure inbreds to produce hybrids.

Individuals: Kegan (1994)
Humans grow toward a higher order of consciousness via integration. There is an inner conflict. "[O]ne tries to restore one's sense of identity between the two views by finding some way to bring the views back into line" (p. 44).

Relationships: Johnston (1991)
True partnership results from linking or connecting differences. "Love is creative and rhythmic—a dance between the singular wholeness of our meeting and the separate wholenesses that we each are unto ourselves" (p. 58).

Teams: Mouton and Blake (1984)
After presenting differentiated perspectives, the team members work together to combine individuals' and reach a consensual statement that best describes the ideal position for the situation.

Organizations: Lawrence and Lorsch (1967)
Integration refers to "the quality of the state of collaboration that exists among departments that are required to achieve unity of effort by demands of the environment" (p. 11).

Organizations: Savage (1996)
Integrative process needs to happen between the three aspects—technology, information, and people—for collaboration and synergy to happen within organizational members and between organizations by completely breaking down the steep hierarchy that stifles organizations. Such integration is the key to success in modern enterprise and requires a both-and mentality rather than either-or thinking.

Societies: Ouchi (1984)
Japan learned to combine Western market and Eastern bureaucracy and clan to achieve a more powerful state.

Cross-/intercultural relations: Adler (1997)
"In the step of cultural creativity, members of different cultures work together to solve the problems" (p. 113).

Globe: Thompson (1989)
"The ecology of opposites requires differentiated identities such as marshes and deserts, oceans and continents, to balance each other" (p. 85).

Figure 3.2   Process of Integration Across Theories

In the process of creating genetic hybrids, differentiation is called *selfing*. This is a purifying process in which closely related individuals are bred with each other to create the most genetically similar (homozygous) inbreds possible. At the level of the genes, this process of inbreeding produces identical variants (alleles) of the same gene at corresponding chromosomal

> *Synergic outcomes* refer to the results of processes of differentiation and integration that go beyond what can be acquired by individual parties alone.

Biology: Griffith, Miller, Suzuki, Lewontin, and Gelbart (1993)
Crossing between the two inbreds produces many new, different combinations from which the best hybrid is chosen. Such a process simply produces more possibilities from which we can choose according to our needs.

Individuals: Kegan (1994)
Humans grow toward a higher order of consciousness via integration. "Such radical mental 'behavior,' dislodging one's identity with one's own categorical viewpoint, can lead to a whole different order of consciousness" (p. 44).

Relationships: Johnston (1991)
When different individuals come together, something harmonious and new will emerge.

Teams: Mouton and Blake (1984)
The team attempts to reach a consensual statement that best describes the ideal position for the company. In this process, a new statement that goes beyond—and embodies everybody's perspective—is developed.

Organizations: Lawrence and Lorsch (1967: 157)
"These conflicts must be resolved to the satisfaction of all parties and for the general goal of the enterprise" (p. 157).

Organizations: Savage (1996)
Integrative process leads to creativity, innovation, and a new broadened vision.

Societies: Ouchi (1984)
Japan learned to combine both Eastern and Western strengths to achieve a more powerful and healthy state than any individuals are capable of.

Cross-/intercultural relations: Adler (1997)
In the step of cultural creativity, members of different cultures create synergistic alternatives to solve their problems. "The answer should be compatible with, but not imitative of, the cultural assumptions of all represented groups. It should be novel and transcend the behavioral patterns of each of the root cultures" (p. 113).

Globe: Thompson (1989)
"There is, of course, conflict and disagreement, but like the relationship between the ocean and the continent that drives the gaseous clouds of rain that are neither sea nor land but both, the relationship of opposition, say between electronic Artificial Intelligence and neurophysiology, or between cognitivism and connectionism, is a creative one in which even the thunderstorms change the soil with the nitrogen the next generation requires" (p. 85).

Figure 3.3   Synergic Outcomes Across Theories

loci instead of the differing (heterozygous) variants that are more normal. This differentiation is a necessary precondition for hybridization (Jugenheimer, 1985); if the two parents are not sufficiently different, they will not produce a hybrid.

When two differentiated inbreds are crossed or mated with each other, hybrids, or new and novel variants, are produced. These hybrids variants have not existed before. The crossing of the two inbreds can produce hybrids with many new qualities. The variety of hybrids obtained is exponential, and most of them have qualities that go beyond those of their parents. As a result of this process of alternately inbreeding and interbreeding, new breeds of plants and animals are produced. We emphasize again that these are breeds that did not exist before.

According to Kegan (1994), something similar occurs within individual human development, and the act of differentiation is an important step. In Kegan's model of the developmental processes, the shift from a lower order of consciousness to one of a higher order starts with this process of differentiation. An example is the way an individualistic person differentiates himself or herself from others by having a strong sense of self-identity. Although Kegan sees this as a necessary stage, he believes this kind of consciousness is institution based and thus absolutistic. Individuals grow and move toward a higher order of consciousness by integrating different views. For example, in contrast to the absolutistic stance of the institution-based consciousness, an evolved person has the capacity of interpenetration of self and other and interpenetration of form and process.

Kegan (1994) proposes that the processes of differentiation and integration result in human growth and transformation. He also posits that individuals with a higher order consciousness are more capable of dealing with the demands of contemporary societies than are the individualistic identities of a typical Western adulthood. Moving outward from the level of the individual to that of interpersonal relationship, differentiation is found to be an important process, one that is necessary for true love or friendship.

In Johnston's (1991) creative system framework, we find something similar to Kegan's (1994) clarification of the processes of differentiation and integration. From Johnston's perspective, two parties (it doesn't matter whether they are lovers or friends) have to go through a process of differentiation. Otherwise, the relationship will not be meaningful and lasting. In other words, these two parties each have to know themselves as distinctive, separate wholes. As the relationship progresses, the two must continue to grow and to differentiate from each other. Without differentiation, the relationship falls peril to what Johnston calls the unity fallacy. This refers to the phenomenon of two persons in a relationship that does not allow them to have different individual identities. Within the unity fallacy, "love is being one together; girls are girls and boys are boys (and girls are better); all you need is love."

There is an interrelated process that produces the more integral view recognized as understanding. True love or friendship comes from people helping others to become what they want to become rather than stay who they are (Johnston, 1991). Thus, according to Johnston, the differentiated wholes of two lovers or friends also need a more integral whole between them. Integrated lovers or friends experience a new whole that is bigger than the sum of their independent, distinctive wholes, and the new whole continues to expand and transform; through this, the two separate wholes, or individual lovers or friends, continuously find new meaning in each other.

The process of differentiation is also critical to Mouton and Blake's (1984) team development theory. *Differentiation* here refers to creating different mental models or meaning perspectives. In one of their major educational designs, the clarifying attitudes design, team members are asked to make judgments about team or organizational performance and to use these to bring their underlying assumptions to the surface. In doing so, diverse perspectives about complex situations are differentiated. In this process, team members present and discuss their differentiated perspectives. They then work together to develop the consensual statement that best describes the ideal attitude for the team or the company in the future. During this process, majority vote is discouraged, and team members are encouraged to make the effort to reach a consensus.

Integration of all individual perspectives results in a consensual statement that goes beyond what could be made by any single team member. Once the team agrees on the soundest statement, the team members examine the differences between the actual attitude and the ideal one. Team members discuss how each wants to change his or her behavior to be consistent with the consensual description of the ideal attitude. The group then moves to develop a shared norm of conduct. In doing this, team synergy is achieved.

The importance of synergy as a team learning strategy was also addressed by Kasl, Marsick, and Dechant (1997). In their team learning model, the highest team learning mode is a synergistic learning mode in which "members have acquired a deep understanding of the creative potential in teams."

Moving still further outward, away from the level of the individual to the level of whole organizations, Lawrence and Lorsch (1967) find that organizations differentiate within themselves to respond to the demands of their environments: "As organizations undertake more complex tasks, they tend to complicate internally by differentiating new organization units" (p. 213). In response to increases in the complexity of their environments, organizations have to design and develop new departments; these contain the new job specializations that deal with the new levels of variety. Conflicts then arise, and the differentiated departments need to work together to integrate with each other.

Firms use differing methods to achieve integration. These may range from using the hierarchy or chain of command to creating integrating committees or teams to assigning individual integrators to managers using unofficial channels to achieve integration. The key is to find the approach that facilitates resolution of the conflicts. These conflicts must be resolved to the satisfaction of all parties and for the general goal of the enterprise. Those involved must have strong capabilities to deal with interdepartmental conflict, and resolution must take place at the level that has the required knowledge about the environment.

For Lawrence and Lorsch (1967), the processes of differentiation and integration lead to the satisfaction of all of the parties involved and to the achievement of the general goal of the firm. Differentiated functions deal with components of the organizational environment, and integration of the differentiated functions ensures that necessary collaboration will take place. Conflicts caused by differentiation are confronted and dealt with, rather than being allowed to escalate or to otherwise stifle change.

Although Lawence and Lorsch's (1967) work is not new, its value lasts. In his new book, *Fifth Generation Management,* Charles M. Savage (1996) continually exemplifies the pattern of differentiation and integration, despite arguing for more integration. In his thinking, modern enterprises need to differentiate along three dimensions—people, technology, and information—each of which is essential for effective management. Meanwhile, integrative process needs to happen between the three aspects—technology, information, and people—for collaboration and synergy to occur among organizational members and between organizations by completely breaking down the steep hierarchy that stifles our organizations. Such integration is a key to success in modern enterprise and requires a both-and mentality rather than the traditional either-or thinking. Savage calls for a new process—work as dialogue—which almost exemplifies the SI process in terms of steps and strategies. In his argument, companies with such an integrative process among three differentiated aspects are more creative, innovative, and effective.

Again addressing the level of whole groups, this time societies, Ouchi (1984) states that clarifying the unique strengths of each group is an important step. A more powerful state is achieved when different groups combine their efforts (integration), enhancing collaboration between groups. The integration of market, government, and clan leads to a powerful hybrid that can act in ways that transcend existing possibilities. Ouchi's studies of the Japanese show that they learned to use the strengths of both their own Asian wisdom and that of Western societies to produce the societal hybrid that made Japan one of the most powerful economic players in the world.

Looking at intercultural relations in a way that is similar to Mouton and Blake's (1984) synergogy, Adler (1997) describes the creativity that comes from developing and enhancing distinctive cultural perspectives. This is done by bringing to the surface underlying cultural assumptions, values, and beliefs. As a step toward cultural synergy, culturally different individuals work together to resolve problems. The first step is for people to describe a problematic situation from their own cultural perspectives. In this way both cultural similarities and cultural differences can be identified. According to Adler,

> the cultural synergy process involves role reversal—this approach assumes that all behavior is rational and understandable for the perspective of the person behaving, but that cultural biases lead us to misunderstand the logic of another cultural behavioral pattern. (p. 112)

In this stage of the process, members of each culture attempt to "wear" the cultural scheme of the other cultures and to behave in their cultural ways. In so doing, cultural differences and similarities surface. The different perspectives generated by this process are then treated as sources for cultural creativity, and culturally different individuals begin to genuinely explore with each other to find new alternatives, that is, creative solutions to the problems.

As a result of this integration of culturally diverse perspectives, members of different cultures create synergistic alternatives to solve their problems. According to Adler (1997), synergistic alternatives are new and novel: "The answer should be compatible with, but not imitative of, the cultural assumptions of all represented groups. It should be novel and transcend the behavioral patterns of each of the root cultures" (p. 113).

Moving still further outward to the level of the ecological vantage point, Thompson (1989) tells of how the four cultural ecologies of the West (Riverine, Mediterranean, Atlantic, and Pacific-Space) make their shifts when the new mentality differentiates itself from the old mentality. With a notion similar to Kuhn's (1970) paradigm shift, Thompson (1989) asserts that each shift requires a change in the structure of the world narrative, in the very manner in which a "world" is brought forth. In other words, each shift starts with differentiation. Likening this to the differentiation or complexity found at the biological level, Thompson (1989, 1991) further argues that differentiation will increase diversity, and thus innovation, to maintain ecological sustainability.

Linking human, cultural, and environmental ecology, Thompson (1985) tells us that ecology requires that opposites coexist. This ecology of opposites implies that the divisions between opposites are no more than artificial constructs. At a higher, more inclusive level, there is a larger whole made up of opposites that need each other:

An ecology requires the balance that comes from diversity, marshes and deserts, oceans and continents, and it is the same for an ecology of mind. If one single ideology were to triumph to become a monocrop, it would be monstrous and generate a "complexity catastrophe" that would be needed to maintain the openness to innovation that is basic to life. (Thompson, 1989, p. 75)

The differentiation and integration of opposites produces conditions the whole ecology needs to continue. Integration produces an ever-expanding ecological container in which creativity can flourish and possibilities expand. The small institute and the large institution should not be seen as yet another either-or dyadic set because the little and the large require one another. The little tends to be creative, and the large reproduces those innovations in a stable system (Thompson, 1991).

We believe that we have identified a significant process—the synergy principle—which drives the evolution of reality. It is a pattern that penetrates all major aspects of the known universe. We also believe that when humans are in synchronicity or alignment with the universe, they are also evolving with harmony, newness, and novelty. Conversely, when people are out of alignment with this universal pattern, they are stuck socially and ecologically. From our position, the challenge that remains is to learn how to embody the synergy principle so that people can coevolve with the universe. It is this challenge that SI sets out to meet.

4

Synergic Inquiry, Paradigms, and Other Methodologies

In this chapter, we contextualize synergic inquiry (SI) in terms of the currently prevailing research paradigms and other methodologies. We discuss at length where SI falls among the major contemporary paradigms on which most research methodologies are built, as well as how it stretches the horizons of these paradigms. In addition, we make a first attempt to relate SI to other major methodologies oriented toward change and transformation of human systems. It needs to be acknowledged that SI developed mostly out of practices in the real world. We did not begin to address the methodology literature until recently, and this is our first effort to give an account of SI as a research methodology and describe how it relates to other major methodologies.

Paradigmatic Questions

Egon Guba and Yvonna Lincoln (1994) developed a framework for examining the worldviews underlying various research methodologies and grouped these worldviews by paradigm. They define *paradigm* as "the basic belief system or worldview that guides the investigator, not only in choices of method but in ontologically and epistemologically fundamental ways" (Guba & Lincoln, p. 105). Guba and Lincoln identified four paradigms—positivism, postpositivism, critical theory, and constructivism—and they claim that these are accepted by researchers as the foundations on which all major research methodologies are built.

61

A fifth paradigm—the participatory paradigm—was recently proposed to differentiate this approach from the other four dominant paradigms (Heron, 1996; Heron & Reason, 1997). In this chapter, we use the following four questions—the first three from Guba and Lincoln's (1994) work and the last from Heron and Reason (1997)—to guide our evaluation of methodologies. First, we discuss these questions in the context of the SI methodology; then we compare methodologies:

1. Ontological question: What is the form and nature of reality, and what can be known about it?

2. Epistemological question: What is the nature of the relationship between the knower or would-be knower and what can be known?

3. Methodological question: How can the participant (would-be knower) go about finding out whatever he or she believes can be known?

4. Axiological question: What is intrinsically worthwhile?

Ontology

We believe that there exist two worlds—the inner world (i.e., consciousness) and the outer world (i.e., reality)—that are in a dialectical relationship. As demonstrated in Chapter 3, we believe that there exists a primordial reality that surrounds and includes existence and human awareness. The mysterious whole of this reality is constantly evolving with infinite diversity and novelty. This evolution started with matter and then rose from matter to life and to the human mind, and the journey of this evolution continues.

We humans come to understand reality through our consciousness, that is, through subjective constructions of the external reality. In other words, the consciousness that we critically or uncritically construct in our inner worlds is qualitatively different from reality because reality actually is in the outer worlds and at levels beneath and beyond our capacities for awareness. Because of the elusive and infinite nature of reality, all descriptions of reality, even those we carry unseen within our respective consciousnesses, are at best maps rather than the territory. As Chaudhuri (1977) writes, these too are inevitably partial:

> Since a map is not a territory but a sketchy guide chart indicating possible lines of movement and action in the real world, no ideological scheme, whether theological or metaphysical or scientific or political can be said to exhaust the multidimensional fullness of the universe. It should be clearly recognized that the universe, essentially different from all conceptual maps, necessarily transcends

all philosophical, religious, scientific and political ideologies. The universe is the ground and the comprehensive unity of all thought systems without itself being a determinate system. (p. 87)

In light of the dynamics between human consciousness and reality, we seek a shift in focus from constructing what reality is to learning new ways of exploring how reality evolves. This is a fundamental shift from viewing reality as "things" to approaching reality as process. We believe that humans have a unique role in terms of our participation with the evolution of reality. On the one hand, humans are the products of this evolution. On the other hand, humans have developed unique evolutionary qualities that appear to them and that are seen as being beyond those of most other forms of life and matter on earth. People have the potential to become conscious of evolution itself (Wilber, 1995).

With that critical realization, we seek to describe what we see as the basic process that underlies the evolution of reality and also to use this same process to expand human consciousness. In Chapter 3, we identified a significant pattern that we and others have found to lie beneath the evolution of reality. We believe it is a fundamental pattern of differentiating and integrating inseparably bound in a cyclic relationship that drives the evolution of reality. The outcome of this pattern is the manifest world we experience though our senses and through our participation with it.

The underlying process itself cannot be seen directly any more than we can directly see the air that moves as wind. And yet reality, like the wind, manifests itself. We see the wind indirectly through the things that it moves. We can feel and use its movements, hear the sounds its passing makes, and perceive its different temperatures and the smells that it carries, but unaided by these externals or sophisticated tools, we cannot see the wind itself. In much the same way, we can interact with, use, and observe the effects of this process we see as moving the evolution of reality, but we cannot see it directly.

This fundamental process, the pattern of differentiating and integrating inseparably bound into a cyclic relationship, is what we call the synergy principle. It appears to drive the evolution of reality and to be a metapattern that cuts across all domains of reality, whether in the form of matter, life, human mind, or human society. Because humans too exist within this larger, ineffable, but evolving reality, people are all products of this same fundamental principle. Thus, within SI, as we have experienced it, unity comes in the form of this unified principle that produces all the diversity of all our worlds, the ones represented by our consciousnesses and the matrix within which our lives and consciousness exist. The differences produced by this pattern of differentiating and integrating are then used to create the new.

The universe started with a few forms of matter, which gradually evolved with increasing complexity. Intrinsic to this evolution is the way that different forms of matter and of life have played major roles in creating new forms of life and being.

Like many before us, we believe that when humans fail to recognize and honor this full process of differentiating and integrating, they obstruct not only their individual evolutionary processes but also the evolution of reality itself. (Evidence in support of this assertion is discussed later in the chapter.) These obstructions in the processes of evolution create deep pathologies that manifest as problems and crises for both human beings and their ecology.

It is evident that despite all the wonders humans have created, they have also created some big problems for themselves and for the planet. The kinds of symbiosis often observed among the various other living species is not well reproduced in relationships among human beings and between humans and nature. Within our experiences of synergy through inquiry and from our understandings of the synergic processes of the reality in which humans live, we can only agree with those who say that the source of people's failure to relate in an ecologically sustainable manner lies in their own human ignorance and their inadequacies of consciousnesses. These lead to humans' attempts to dominate others and nature in ways that create deep pathologies. We believe that we can come to a more productive relationship among ourselves and our surroundings by learning to embody and use the same kinds of synergic processes that characterize universal evolutionary processes.

Epistemology

We know most truly what humans can experience deeply and observe for themselves. SI evolved by the same means it uses to expand consciousness: synergic transformations that came about through the genuine meeting of self and other. Thus, the knowledge and purpose that first informed it were pragmatic; experiences of painful dilemmas resolved themselves through spontaneous occurrences of qualitative shifts in awareness. These shifts did more than remove the limits that had been painful; they were powerful transformations that rippled inward and outward with effects that went far beyond what could have been predicted from the original dilemmas. Transformations that could be both experienced and observed, initiated, assisted, and enhanced with conscious direction and focus—these are what led the current purpose of SI: to design transformative approaches to learning by creating conditions, processes, and contexts that enable these expansions to occur. Within this framework, knowledge is based on experience and observation, and a transformation of consciousness is an integrated qualitative shift in perspective that increases the capacity to experience and to use experience to derive knowledge.

Change tends to be incremental and quantitative, but transformation is not. It causes beings to engage with themselves and the world in qualitatively different ways. Although change may come about as the result of new evidence or different facts, humans can always interpret these facts in ways that fit their existing consciousness. It is therefore essential that the structure of consciousness itself be changed before people can say that transformation has occurred.

The synergic worldview requires that the relationship between the knower and the known be a dialectical one. The knower comes to understand the known through an exploration of self with varied reiterations and reintegrations until barriers release and consciousness expands. As is implied by the presence of the known, these inner explorations are coupled with an outer exploration with the intention of understanding other. Reality comes to be understood through the meeting of self and other that leads to the expansion of consciousness.

The knowledge and knowing within what we call consciousness can be concretely described as having two dimensions: an inner dimension that focuses on exploration of self and an outer dimension that focuses on the interplay of self and other. The inner dimension involves the three dimensions of consciousness that we characterize as visible, logical, and mythical knowings. Because it is inner, the process through which it is acquired is a contemplative one, and this process produces both internal and external forms. The external forms include knowings in the social, behavioral, and communicative domains that become accessible or manifest by means of the differentiated knowings of self and other as these combine with the integrative knowings of holding and transcending differences. These forms of knowing constitute an expanded base that provides latitude and cuts across both inner worlds and outer worlds.

These inner explorations discover, clarify, and form knowledge about one's own structure of consciousness and are thus in alignment with Jack Mezirow's (1991) claim that human beings acquire knowledge by actively organizing and reorganizing their own experiences. The schemes that conduct this organizing process include the visible knowing that is obtained from immediate experiences. They also include the logical knowing of the assumptions, values, and beliefs contained in our rational mechanisms for interpreting experience and are similar to Mezirow's meaning scheme and meaning perspective. These schemes define or influence visible knowing in both overt and covert ways, and they include the mythical knowing of those deep dimensions of consciousness that influence and determine the structures of our logical and visible knowing and which we usually take for granted without reflection or critique.

In SI, the nature of the relationship between the knower and the known is dialogical rather than dialectical. In differentiated knowing, the knower and the known differentiate from each other by coinquiring into each other's realities. This requires them each to reflect on their own realities first before they engage with each other. Coparticipants use the three dimensions of knowing to make more explicit their own constructions of reality and then engage with each other's realities through self-disclosure and empathic receptivity. In this dialogical process, participants are able to uncover their own underlying mythic knowing by entering into the other's mental plane and reflecting on the self. This is of critical importance because humans' own mythical dimensions cannot be accessed directly; they can be discovered only by taking on a second mental plane (Vachon, 1995).

In integrated knowing, coparticipants learn to dance with self and other and to use their differences as constructive resources. In this way, participants gain access to an order of consciousness that allows them to interpenetrate self and other and form and process (Kegan, 1994) in ways that lead to an expanded capacity for dealing with complexity.

The foreground of differentiated knowing is directive, separating, and generating. It requires strength to differentiate realities and can therefore be seen as more masculine. In contrast, the foreground of integrated knowing is connected, integrative, and harmonizing and is consistent with the feminine and with women's ways of knowing. The cyclic process of alternating differentiated and integrated knowings makes it possible to fully manifest positive outcomes without going to extremes. In this way, there is balance between the masculine and feminine aspects of our processes of knowing.

Methodology

The combination of a unique ontology, which fundamentally believes in an underlying principle that drives evolving reality, and a unique epistemology, which takes transforming consciousness as a primacy, also demands a unique methodology. Synergic forms of inquiry are aligned with a large family of participatory methods that presuppose that researchers are subjects and subjects are researchers. In so doing, the traditional dichotomy between researchers and subjects is eliminated and coparticipants are equally empowered to inquire into each other's realities within their mutual intentions to expand consciousness.

The process of this research is collaborative and synergic. Coparticipants use a focal question to differentiate and integrate their respective realities through four phases to achieve their synergic outcomes, and specific learnings can take place from each of these phases as well as from the full cycle of the inquiry.

In the self-knowing phase, the nature of the inquiry is self-reflective, and coparticipants use an inner focus to explore their immediate experiences, their thinking and reasoning processes, and their underlying myths via visible, logical, and mythical knowing. One outcome of this process is learning about the essential structures of the lenses through which the external world is viewed, and an important transformative outcome for many is that reality is no longer seen as only objective and external. Instead, participants see that the lenses of their consciousness interpret the external world. Because people tend to take these lenses for granted, new behaviors usually accompany this clarification of their own consciousness in terms of its logical and mythical dimensions in ways that expand their awareness and enable them to detach enough to examine their consciousness.

In other-knowing, coparticipants attempt to get to know and be with each others' realities by "wearing the shoes" of the other, which requires them to take the reality of the other as a truth. When the reality of the other can be experienced and accepted without judgment, evaluation, or distortion, something significant again emerges. Participants may experience a new and different way of constructing reality, and this alone can be transformative.

In differences-holding, coparticipants explore the possibility of holding multiple realities until tensions between the differing realities are transformed into a creative resource. A major outcome here is the capacity to keep one's own singular consciousness from subjugating, dominating, or even automatically critiquing other consciousnesses. This is by far the most challenging step to achieve, but once achieved, significant changes again occur.

In differences-transcending, the transformative journey that was generated by the tensions in differences-holding leads to the development of new and practical strategies that manifest expanded consciousness, which in turn enhances the transformative journey. This allows participants to practice new ways of being and behavior to sustain their new, expanded awareness.

Additional synergy cycles, each with a different emphasis, also enhance this transformative journey by extending it and by helping participants to progressively embody the synergic process.

When one embodies the synergy process, a new, qualitatively different consciousness develops that is both-and and process based. In addition to this development and the acceleration of one's own journey of consciousness expansion, embodying the synergy principle enables the power-with dynamic to fundamentally transform the power-over dynamic that lies beneath racism, sexism, and anthropocentrism.

Because the action-reflection cycle within each phase unravels layers of self that are usually hidden, coparticipants often find themselves reforming their research questions in ways that expand and include the initial questions as the research process unfolds. This leads to the necessity of going through several complete cycles of all four phases to complete the research.

Axiology

The question of what is intrinsically worthwhile is of critical importance because of the different approaches humans have developed to address their problems, which seem to have created more problems than can be solved. The quote by Einstein that begins this book indicates that this is because so many of these approaches have come out of the same mindsets that created the problems or out of the polar opposites of these mindsets. Because of this, we believe there is a need for established criteria to evaluate people's approaches to problems.

First, the value of an approach depends on how well it corresponds to reality in its totality (Vachon, 1995). A sound approach ought to embody or reflect people's best understanding of the wisdom of the universe, which can be understood in the form of its principles:

> . . . the value of a statement does not come primarily from the number of individuals who subscribe to it, nor from its official governmental or professional charter, but from its foundation in the reality of life itself. In other words, we believe that our mandate to live and speak does not come primarily nor ultimately from any government, nation-state, religion or culture, nor from Man alone, God alone, or Nature alone, but from the whole reality. It is to the circle of the whole reality that we are ultimately accountable, and not only to any government, expert, culture, religion, man or god. (p. 127)

The value of an approach can also be judged by whether it contributes to the inherent purpose of the whole of reality, which is, in our belief, the evolution of consciousness:

> In the ultimate analysis it is the human factor which counts most. No matter to what extent the economic and political structure of a society be drastically overhauled, until and unless there is a real transformation of inner consciousness—a genuine change of heart, as Gandhi would say—exploitation of others and the environment and injustice can hardly be eliminated from society. (Chaudhuri, 1977, p. 95)

Our working hypothesis is that the universe suffers from an underlying pathology that manifests itself in the form of the problems and crises that we experience today. Therefore, from our viewpoint, to effectively solve problems, people have to eliminate this underlying pathology by transforming their consciousness. This does, of course, presuppose that evolution of reality and transforming the essential structure of human society are two sides of the same coin.

Finally, the value of an approach depends on whether it is equipped with an adequate methodology for human action. To be adequate, a methodology has to satisfy two conditions: It must correspond well to reality, and it must work to eliminate pathology. Furthermore, it ought to be heuristic, or able to be applied to all levels of human systems, from individuals and relationships to groups, organizations, communities, and whole cultures.

In our view, what is intrinsically worthwhile is fundamentally a question of what transforms consciousness. Our experience enables us to feel comfortable with the assumption that transformation of consciousness occurs only in two of its three dimensions: the logical and the mythical. When transformation happens at the logical level, the result is a set of rational-logical values, assumptions, and beliefs like those that constitute Mezirow's (1990, 1991) meaning perspective and lead to a logical reinterpretation of experience and possibly even a new or more complex paradigm, worldview, or meaning perspective. But this transformation in one dimension is merely an exchange: One consciousness is traded for another. Such a transformation is important because it helps one to take different mental planes and evolve to a different consciousness.

The type of transformation that enables a shift from a perspective-based consciousness, which is essentially static, to a process-based consciousness, which essentially evolves, is something of a different order. This magnitude of change requires a shift at the mythical level. This argument is akin to Dean Elias's (1997) approach to transformative learning, which brings Jung's notion of collective unconsciousness to theory and practice.

It is the myth that reality is static, knowable, and definable that lies beneath all normative perspectives, and in our view this myth must be transformed to include an understanding of the constantly evolving nature of a reality that is only partially comprehensible and can therefore never be completely or definitively described. With this can come the understanding that the more limited truths of the perspective-based consciousnesses can interact within us to give us more access to the whole. Such a transformation is evolutionary in nature. It allows one to dance with different perspective-oriented consciousnesses with the intent to evolve rather than to get stuck in any single perspective.

Again we assert with Einstein that humans cannot solve a problem from within the same consciousness that created it. Nor can people solve one by rebelling against that consciousness and trying to do the opposite. Therefore, within the structure of these beliefs, the ultimate purpose of transformation within SI must be to use human differences as catalysts for the purpose of changing consciousness. Within this pattern of belief, people can avoid generating unneeded problems and crises—and find better ways to solve those that do arise—when they accelerate the evolution of their own consciousness and help evoke transformation in others in a way that enables human flourishing.

Assuming also that human bodies are tightly linked to human consciousness, people must also use SI to facilitate the evolution of planetary consciousness by consciously embodying the evolutionary patterns found there. As we all know, bodies often fail to honor those changes made at the logical level. Change must go beyond the logical dimension to transformation at the mythical level to become embodied. This is where those deeper kinds of change occur. When this deeper level of change happens, one's presuppositions about oneself and the nature of reality also shift.

Panikkar (1979) and Vachon (1995) assert, sometimes forcefully, that the underlying causes for all of the problems and crises facing people cannot be cured unless humans transform at the mythical level of consciousness. The precise transformation that Vachon and Panikkar see as needing to occur is the movement from a content-oriented consciousness driven by ideology to a process-oriented consciousness that is constantly evolving. Our experience with SI indicates that Vachon and Panikkar are correct in their assertions that lack of appropriate myth constitutes one of the most significant obstacles to achieving world peace and social harmony, and this should both alarm and awaken people as transformative theorists, researchers, and practitioners.

Most other paradigms within which transformation is expected to take place are based on perspectives, concepts, or theories that reflect reality as static, definable, or knowable. These theories seem to operate from an either-or mentality that inherently manifests a power-over dynamic, whether this is their intention or not. As implied earlier, no definitive perspective about an evolving reality can stay true for long. The logical assumption that automatically comes out of this is that no definitive perspective can fundamentally solve problems and crises.

It is our position that a worthy methodology must reflect the same pattern that guides the evolution of consciousness. Focus on the evolution of consciousness is a qualitatively different perspective from that of logically recognized needs and problem solving, and SI has developed the criterion for worthiness just mentioned. With SI, people recognize the dynamics and complexities of human consciousness and approach problems and crises holistically and ecologically by means of the same pattern that guides the evolution of consciousness.

At the mythical level, SI embraces the myth of evolution because people believe this myth is the best available match for the complexity of the world as they experience it. At the logical level, SI crystallizes the synergy principle that has been found at so many levels of reality and through so many different modes of exploration. With this use of the synergy principle, which allows pathologies and fallacies to be addressed at their foundations, SI attempts to go beyond those levels of consciousness that have created humans' problems. People use this process because it inherently breaks ignorance and outdated patterns (Fuller, 1981) to expand human consciousness and capacities.

How SI Relates to Other Paradigms

As a methodology, SI does not automatically fit into any of the four predominant Western paradigms—positivism, postpositivism, critical theory, and constructivism—that are, according to Guba and Lincoln (1994), the basic underpinnings of most methodologies developed in the West. Nor does the new participatory paradigm that Heron and Reason (1997) propose include SI fully. This is in part because SI did not emerge from any of these five paradigms but, as previously discussed, emerged out of experimentation with observations of personal experience, our practices of SI, and the synergic worldview we developed.

SI's relationship to these paradigms is complex. What follows is our first serious attempt to account for the similarities and differences between paradigmatic SI and the five research paradigms most similar to it. We again use the four dimensions—ontological, epistemological, methodological, and axiological—to guide our discussion.

The Ontological Dimension

Looking at the ontologies of the five recognized paradigms from our standpoint, we can identify significant similarities and differences. The positivism paradigm argues that (1) there exists an external reality that is real and that (2) the real reality is an apprehensible reality because it is driven by immutable natural laws and mechanisms. Knowledge "is conventionally summarized in the form of time—and context-free generalizations, some of which take the form of cause-effect laws. . . . The basic posture of the paradigm is argued to be both reductionistic and deterministic" (Guba & Lincoln, 1994, p. 109).

Postpositivism also implies that human beings have the capacity to fully understand reality through mastery of its fundamental and immutable laws. In essence, postpositivism is quite similar to positivism in most of its arguments, but though an external reality is assumed to exist in postpositivism, it is understood as only imperfectly apprehensible because of limits in human intellectual capacity. Under the label of critical realism, it calls for a wide critical examination of apprehended reality.

The SI paradigm agrees with positivism and postpositivism that there is a reality that exists "out there." But there are limits to that agreement. Although we do believe that there are absolute, immutable laws about which time and context-free generalizations can be made that apply across all domains of known reality, we do not believe that such laws can be deterministic. Up to this time, we have not found any deterministic law or principle that is genuinely time- and context-free across all realms of matter, life, and human experience.

SI also recognizes and constructs laws about the nature of reality, but these laws differ in kind from deterministic laws. Within SI as a paradigm, we believe that the laws that exist underneath the evolution of reality are totally different from context-specific laws such as gravity, which work only in the material realm. The SI law—the synergy principle—is not deterministic; it is a process that, so far, appears to stay equally true within all realms of reality as it is known. This law of evolution refers only to an underlying process that drives the evolution of matter, life, and mind. The effects "caused" by this law cannot always be determined in advance. In other words, we can predict to the extent that the universe continually evolves, but the forms of diversity that evolve within this law are essentially unpredictable.

There also seems to be confusion within both positivism and postpositivism about the distinction between consciousnesses and reality. These two tend to be fused together by the assumption that all that exists in reality can be known. Because these two paradigms are intrinsically nonreflective, what is real out there cannot be separated from the projections of one's own consciousness. In addition, they fail to address the evolutionary nature of reality and how this invariably overwhelms people's capacity to comprehend the totality. These paradigms attribute difficulty and holes in people's understanding only to the limitations of the knower, whereas SI allows for the possibility that reality is also changing in its most basic forms.

Critical theory posits that reality, which was once plastic, has over time been shaped by many social, political, cultural, economic, ethnic, and gender factors that have crystallized into a set of factors that now can be taken as real (Guba & Lincoln, 1994). The attention of critical theorists therefore seems to be focused on those who are dominated and using what these critical theorists find true to get dominators to recognize these truths and thus change reality (Kincheloe & McLaren, 1994).

SI agrees with the view of reality that sees our human realities as full of domination, subjugation, and oppression and that these have been part of our evolutionary processes. However, within SI we believe that human participation with this view is part of why people are stuck. One of the purposes of SI is therefore to liberate all those who suffer from the domination dynamics that are driven by the either-or mentality.

Although SI posits that both dominators and dominated have different consciousnesses, it sees both of these as partial and different from the totality of that which is real. It is our belief that humans can neither truly liberate nor be fully liberated unless they all evolve new orders of consciousness. The larger challenge is for both dominator and dominated to recognize the larger processes of evolution that take place within consciousness so that people can evolve without the continuous power-over dynamics that paralyze them as individuals, groups, and social systems. The narrower view of critical theory schools of thoughts does not see a reality that includes the possibility of coherent, dynamic patterns behind this apparent structure that has been shaped over time by cultural factors. The danger, then, as Freire (1970) forcefully argues and as people have witnessed so often in human history, is that those who are emancipated may also become dominators.

Constructivism sees reality as relative; reality consists of multiple, intangible mental constructions that are socially and experientially based. Some schools of constructivism seem to go too far in that they tend to overemphasize the subjective nature of the construction of reality. Some of them, such as the radical constructivists, even go so far as to deny the existence of an external reality (Heron & Reason, 1997), which we also see as a confusion of the distinctions we make between consciousness and reality. SI affirms that humans construct their understandings of realities, but it also proposes that an external reality exists. This larger reality is bigger than people and is the matrix that contains both humans and their evolutions of consciousness, and people must relate to this reality for evolution to be healthy.

The constructivist paradigm also fails to acknowledge that a unity of principle might underlie all manifestations of the totality. Within the SI paradigm, there is the belief in a larger purpose behind the evolution of reality and that this larger evolutionary process has great wisdoms to teach humans. For people, therefore, it is imperative to recognize that humans' realities are all limited and that everyone has a responsibility to help these constructions evolve. The danger within constructivism, or for that matter postmodernism, is that it has a tendency to unreflectively make every construction seem as valid as any other and through this to either purposefully or unconsciously ignore social and ecological perils.

In Heron and Reason's (1997) recent critique of these four dominant paradigms, they proposed a new worldview, which they call the participatory paradigm. Central to this paradigm is the belief that "there is a given cosmos, a primordial reality, in which the mind actively participates" (Heron & Reason, 1997, p. 279). They even go so far as to say that "mind and the given cosmos are engaged in a cocreative dance, so that what emerges as reality is the fruit of an interaction of the given cosmos and the way mind engages with it" (Heron & Reason, 1997, p. 279). The crux of their ontology is that reality is both subjective and objective. It is subjective because people make meaning with their own frames of reference. It is objective because the cosmos exists in ways that go beyond humans' constructions of it. "Worlds and people are what we meet, but the meeting is shaped by our own term" (Heron, 1996, p. 11).

SI is well aligned with this paradigm's view on the dynamics between consciousness and reality, and we agree with the ontology of Heron and Reason (1997), in that we believe that humans are indeed part of the cosmos and that people actively participate in its cocreative processes. Implicitly, then, both paradigms seem to agree about the evolutionary nature of a constantly evolving cosmos, with the human mind actively participating in the evolutionary process.

Although the human mind has the unique potential to become conscious of this participatory process, all other forms of being, matter, and life also participate in the cocreation process. Where the participatory paradigm, as now framed by Heron and Reason (1997), seems to fall short is in the failure to recognize the existence of patterns or principles that could guide healthy human participation in this evolution in ways that could prevent the occurrence of existing patterns of social and ecological evils. Within SI, participation cannot be an end in itself because it does not get to the core of why things keep falling apart in spite of people's best efforts and intentions.

Within SI, when the synergy principle is obstructed in social and ecological systems, pathologies continue in spite of participation. In other words, we believe that there are both healthy and unhealthy forms of participation and that it is healthy when people dance with differentiation and integration to participate in such a way that they break free of their "stuckness" and accelerate evolution. On the other hand, it is unhealthy when people indulge the separation fallacy by differentiating without adequate integration and when people overbalance in the opposite direction with a unity fallacy that integrates without adequate differentiation.

It is important to note that activities pertaining to differentiation and integration also exist in the cooperative inquiry methodology of Heron and Reason (1997). For the differentiating process, participants collect individual data, and in the integrating process they collectively identify common themes in their collected data to develop shared knowledge. Because the purpose for SI relates to expanding consciousness and capacities for flexible responsiveness and organic resilience rather than to developing shared knowledge, the focus of cycles of differentiation and integration is on using differences that are found as creative resources for transformative changes.

The Epistemological Dimension

In positivism, the relationship between the knower and the known is dualistic and objectivistic. In the postpositivist view, the notion of dualism is abandoned. However, the investigator and the object of the investigation are assumed to be independent entities. Thus, an objectivist view is still effectively maintained through a system that places emphasis on external experts and critical traditions within critical communities, such as the academy, editors, and professional peers.

In the SI paradigm, all participants' realities are assumed to be true to those whose consciousnesses manifest them. Knowledge is constructed through the lenses of all participants, even when these seem to produce mutually exclusive views of reality or perspectives that cannot logically coexist. The dichotomy between researchers and subjects breaks down further because all subjects must become coresearchers for an inquiry to be fully synergic. When the focus is on developing reflective consciousness and on the differentiation and subsequent integration of self and other, knowledge expands and is prepared for usefulness. In this process, participants learn to incorporate the synergy principle into consciousness of the nature they share with the rest of reality.

In critical theory, investigator and subject are also assumed to be interactively linked. This relationship is transactional and subjective; the values of the investigator are normally assumed to be higher than those of the investigated, and the human interaction between them is used to raise the awareness of the other to this value orientation. All findings are therefore value mediated. SI differs from this approach in that no values are discarded, but neither the values of the initiating or lead investigator nor the values of those who become coinvestigators are given higher priority. All values are considered equally, and the synthesis that is sought must transcend all value orientations as synergy.

In constructivism, the investigator and the object of investigation are assumed to be interdependent, and findings are created as the investigation proceeds. In this way, the line between reality and investigator disappears; the interaction itself creates its reality. This perspective is shared by SI as well. However, in SI the focus is on constructing inner knowledge, through which one comes to expanded awareness and capacities, and inquiries are designed to help one learn to consciously incorporate the synergy principle into the deepest possible levels of one's being.

The participatory paradigm includes critical subjectivity in participatory transaction with the cosmos. "Critical subjectivity means that we attend both to the grounding relations between the forms of knowing and to their consummating relations" (Heron & Reason, 1997, p. 282). In this way, there is the basic capacity to self-reflect and to continually examine underlying assumptions, which is quite similar to the intention of SI. Within the participatory paradigm, several modes or levels of knowing—experiential, presentational, propositional, and practical—are used to enhance critical subjectivity.

SI also uses experiential, presentational, propositional, and practical activities for knowing, but, in contrast, these are in service of three dimensions of knowing—visible, logical, and mythical—for the inner reflective process and two dynamics of knowing—differentiating knowing and integrating knowing—for the social and communicative domain. Within this, the visible dimension relates to what the participatory paradigm calls experiential and practical; the logical dimension relates to its propositional knowing, and mythical to its presentational.

What is more to the point here is the way SI differs from existing participatory paradigms in its paradigmatic commitment to enter into the mythical dimensions of knowing to reflect on and transform the mythical dimension of consciousness. It seems to us that SI has a deep commitment to the focus of the mythical dimension of consciousness in ways that the participatory paradigm does not. It seems that the participatory paradigm's use of presentational knowing is limited to use as a strategy to honor the intuitive and imaginal knowing that is different from the logical knowing. Within SI, however, in part the intention is to transform the mythic self.

In addition, SI also uses differentiated knowing and integrated knowing to address the meeting of self with other. What seems to extend the participatory paradigm further is SI's focus on consciousness, which contrasts with existing participatory focus on mind. Our experiences as SI practitioners lead us to see mind as tending to fall into the logical dimension of consciousness. We therefore differentiate these two aspects of the human self and see consciousness as embracing more of human nature than mind.

The Methodological Dimension

In positivism, the knower goes about finding new knowledge by identifying questions and making hypotheses and then subjecting these hypotheses to empirical tests. In postpositivism, the emphasis shifts to using multiple views or triangulations as an approach to prove a hypothesis false. SI contrasts with these paradigms in that it is not designed to verify any hypotheses, nor are manipulative experiments conducted.

The nature of an inquiry in critical theory involves a dialogue that is dialectical in nature and that attempts to transform perceived ignorance or misapprehension into what is perceived as a more informed consciousness. This approach has similarities to SI in that it is assumed that consciousness is not static and can be raised. However, because of SI's intention of preparing the inner self for the exchange of inner realities to expand one's consciousness, SI's methodology is more akin to dialogue as described by David Bohm (1996). Therefore SI is better characterized as dialogical than as dialectical. The difference in this regard is that the SI process is designed to let participants experience each other's realities without critiquing, evaluating, or analyzing them as is often done within the approaches of critical theory. Another difference is the way in which SI dialogue begins with the assumption of two valid viewpoints and uses these differing viewpoints as resources for the development of a new, transcending consciousness. In this way, all participants, including facilitators and researchers, gain insights.

The different constructions that emerge within constructivist research are interpreted by the researcher, who uses hermeneutic techniques. These differing constructions are compared and contrasted through a dialectical exchange. The aim is to then distill them into a more informed consensus construction. The synergy process has similarities to this too, but there are still important differences. The key difference in SI is the absence of an attempt to reach a consensus or the pulling out of common themes toward that end. In SI there is, instead, a blending of attitudes toward an appreciation and celebration of differences, the goal being a synergy where the outcome goes beyond the construction of any of the individual views that went into it. This goal is often achieved by means of an insight that was not part of any of the original constructions and that brings in a totally new view.

In the participatory paradigm, there is cooperative inquiry among a group of individuals, and the line between researcher and subject breaks down. Coresearchers collaborate to define the inquiry questions and specific strategies for the exploration. Common themes and consensus are often sought and specific actions are deployed to this end. SI includes most of these components, but with two significant distinctions. One is that the SI paradigm is to intentionally seek differences and to use them as resources so that transformative change may occur. In this way, SI focuses more on transcending differences to have new and novel solutions as a strategy for achieving a common group and consensus. Second, the SI paradigm includes the assumption that participants will benefit from embodying the synergy principle and encourages participants to learn the method and to use it to help them continue in a journey of expanding consciousness. In other words, with transformation consciousness, rather than local benefits as the primary goals of the SI paradigm, the local benefits—which in our experience to date invariably accompany this kind of expansion—are side effects. It is this larger purpose that enables participants to create a container for their inquiry that is large enough to hold all their differences in history, belief, experiences, conflicts, fears, and talents with objectivity and safety and use whatever comes up to achieve a matrix of understanding that genuinely includes all that is in this container.

The Axiological Question

Returning again to what are effectively our ancestral paradigms, in both positivism and postpositivism, propositional or logical knowing is an end in itself. Building on this, both critical theory and constructivism add transactional knowing to propositional knowing as the means to social emancipation, which then is an end in itself. On the foundations of learnings that the preceding paradigms brought—and often continue to bring forth—the participatory paradigm uses the practical knowings of how to arrive at a balance of autonomy, cooperation, and hierarchy to flourish within a culture, and this is an end in itself.

Although SI has clearly benefited from the ways in which the aforementioned paradigms have contributed to the matrix of content processes and contexts that have allowed it to flourish, its primary motivations have come from pragmatic attempts to bridge intolerable gaps and the pragmatic delights of sharing something that has worked unexpectedly well and continues to work well. It did not begin as a paradigm about which an axiological question could be asked. However, the power of the concept of paradigms is that they appear to emerge regardless, seem to exist, and can be found through observation and analysis.

With this caveat in mind, we perceive the paradigmatic purpose of SI to be embodying the basic synergic process of evolution to help people learn to consciously manifest—in the always unique ways of their individual consciousnesses—the evolutionary wisdom of the universe. Within SI, this is what is intrinsically valuable, and it is an end in itself. We acknowledge that the auxiliary outcomes, such as increased skills and capacities for dealing with multiplicity and complexity and the emancipation of human beings by means of collectively informed but individually self-generated expansions of consciousness, are also valuable and needed in this era. But we also recognize that these are still auxiliary outcomes and merely signs of the larger alignment of individual and collective human process with the synergy principle of shared totality. We seek them, but we seek them as signs, not as our primary purpose. During those times in some inquiries when the focus of purpose shifts too far from the largest level of alignment to the more local purposes of these auxiliary outcomes, it is our experience that these desired signs do not appear. They remain submerged as potentials until the larger purpose can effectively be reestablished.

Based on this cursory overview of differing methodologies, we have to conclude that SI belongs to a paradigm that is different than the four identified by Guba and Lincoln (1994). Although SI appears to be closer to the participatory paradigm in many ways, it has also developed in other ways that the participatory paradigm does not yet, and may never, include. We can hope that SI will eventually be viewed as an important extension of the participatory paradigm. But that still lies in the future.

How SI Relates to Other Methodologies

In what follows, we attempt to relate SI to other methodologies. Because SI is a methodology in its early stage of development and because this is our first effort to connect SI with the predominant methodologies, this account must be viewed as initial and tentative. Our intention here is to use this opportunity to initiate dialogue that will surely inform and refine SI.

We chose to compare the methodologies based on the following criteria: (1) being participatory action oriented and (2) being transformational in nature. These are both qualities that characterize SI. We begin by relating SI to some participatory action-oriented methodologies.

Other Participatory Action Methodologies

SI compares best with highly participatory methodologies. In our judgment, action science (AS), action inquiry (AI), cooperative inquiry (CI), and participatory action research (PAR) are the more highly developed and influential of these methodologies. These have therefore been chosen in this attempt to fully contextualize and differentiate SI, and they are compared in terms of purpose, level of focus, theoretical foundations, and major strategies (see Figure 4.1).

AS (e.g., Argyris, 1982, 1993; Argyris & Schon, 1992) and AI (e.g., Tobert, 1991) are similar enough to be combined for our purposes here. These methodologies focus primarily on individuals in organizational settings. Each of them proposes to solve problems by cultivating leadership's capacity to create organizational change. A key characteristic of their strategies is critical reflection on how espoused theories influence actions and how espoused theory differs from theory-in-use. With its base in scientific rationalism, AS also emphasizes objective observations and facts.

	Action Science/ Action Inquiry	Cooperative Inquiry	Participatory Action Research	Synergic Inquiry
Purpose	Problem solving, leadership, organizational change	Empowerment, shared knowledge	Social change, empowerment	Transformation of consciousness, capacity building, problem solving
Level of focus	Individual, organization	Individual, group	Individual, community	Various systems from individual to organization to community
Theoretical foundations	Rationalism, experiential learning theory	Constructivism, participatory universe	Dialectics, critical theory	Evolutionary processes and the synergy principle, sciences and social sciences
Major strategies	Critical reflection, diagnose	Critical reflection, group consensus building	Critical reflection, consciousness-raising strategies	Action-reflection cycles, differentiation-integration processes, synergy cycles

Figure 4.1   Some Contrasts Between SI and Other Participatory Action Methodologies

CI, as exemplified by Heron (1971, 1996) and Reason (1988, 1994), empowers individuals in a group context. Its theoretical foundations include the assumption of a participatory universe (Heron, 1996; Heron & Reason, 1997; Reason, 1994), and its major strategies are critical reflection and shared meaning making. These strategies are used to break down the dichotomy between researcher and researched while exploring the knowledge and meanings that influence behaviors. Within this framework, noncognitive modes are used to help develop and refine knowledge. A major focus of the methodology is enabling colearning and consensus building among participants.

PAR, as exemplified by de Roux (1991) and Tandon (1989), was developed to create justice and social change by empowering individuals to participate in improving their own situations. Within this method, a group identifies a problem and then collectively develops strategies to solve it. The group also acts as a resource for individuals to receive suggestions and critiques as they explore a common issue. The theoretical foundations of PAR lie in dialectics and critical theory, and its major strategies are consciousness raising and critical reflection.

By way of contrast and comparison, the purpose of SI is to help people align with larger evolutionary processes in a healthy way, and, as a natural result of doing this, problems are solved and capacities to create healthy changes and transformations are developed. The level of focus for these changes and transformations can range from focus within a single individual through a focus on social collectives, such as groups, organizations, and communities. The theoretical foundations of SI include both Eastern and Western theories about evolutionary processes, the synergy principle, and a pervasive, grand pattern found in both the natural and the social sciences. The major strategies used by SI are action-reflection cycles, processes of differentiation and integration, and repetitive synergy cycles that include the smaller cycles within the two processes in ways that are systematic and thorough.

With an intention to integrate the strengths of these other methodologies without being confined by the kinds of limitations that SI recognizes, this methodology differs from AS and AI in that it does not rely on scientific rationalism. Although it does not reject rationalism, SI recognizes it as being a manifestation of the logical level and rejects the limitations that come from focusing on only one of the dimensions of consciousness. SI also posits that transformation needs to occur at the mythical level to be both fundamental and sustainable.

Like AS and AI, SI also cultivates leadership capacity. However, the leadership capacity that SI endeavors to cultivate and foster is qualitatively different. This central leadership capacity, which has been described as Kegan's (1994) fifth order of consciousness, Wilber's (1995) vision-logic, and Tobert's (1991) ironist leadership, consists of the ability to embody the processes of differentiating and integrating. These more-developed people have been described as able to copermeate "self and other" and "process and form" (Kegan, 1994, p. 315), "hold in mind contradictions" and "unify opposites" (Wilber, 1995, p. 185), and create conditions for the possibility that "intersystemic development awareness rules process" (Tobert, 1991, p. 43). These provocative schematic models assert that those who know how to differentiate and integrate would be in much demand for leadership roles in the larger societal and global contexts and that few people actually reach this stage of development. Thus, SI can be viewed as a transformative process that may accelerate the kinds of development of higher order consciousnesses that are said to be much-needed capacities for functioning well in relation to the systems of complex contexts.

Whereas CI tends to focus on developing consensus among participants, SI's more inclusive approach encourages full participation from the full individuality of each participant. SI achieves its synergic outcomes from this diversity and does this in a way that allows everybody to gain from the process. Furthermore, the outcomes achieved are often more powerful than those that can be achieved by a consensus approach. Merely identifying major themes that are shared by participants excludes their equally real and informative differences. When participants go beyond shared themes and pay as much attention to identified differences, these rejected differences can then be used as valuable resources.

SI goes beyond the participatory aspect of the universe that is assumed by CI to look at the grand patterns of evolution in which the whole of the universe participates and then crystallizes these patterns into a few deceptively simple steps that can guide human action to accelerate the process of human evolution. Although SI does solve problems and cultivate the capacity for human growth, creativity, and social problem solving, it is this larger, essentially spiritual aspect of our efforts that has proven to be the most profound.

The pragmatic effects of SI's nonreligious but ultimately spiritual approach can, like PAR, address the deep-rooted problems of domination, oppression, and social injustice, if participants elect to focus on such issues. However, in our experience, even when these are not the focus, manifestations of these problems frequently arise during an inquiry and must be addressed in the concrete terms of that context. In this way, SI goes beyond more traditional ways of seeing these issues and also "promotes a politics of differences that refuses to pathologize or exoticize the Other" (Kincheloe & McLaren, 1994, p. 145).

In our inquiries, we repeatedly saw how domination, subjugation, and injustice, which are caused by power-over and either-or mentalities, cannot be resolved by these same power-over and either-or mentalities. Through our continuing experiences with SI, we have also seen that, at a metalevel, power-over is the essential penetrating thread underlying all "-isms." In other words, all "-isms" are indications of problematic power dynamics. It has also been our repeated experience that when one suppresses differences, whether intentionally or unintentionally, the power-over dynamic manifests itself. In those hierarchies where people foster stability, control, and power, power-over is the weapon they use. Thus, power-over dynamics and their either-or mentality constitute significant obstacles for humans.

SI both covertly and overtly addresses the problems of this dynamic by requiring all participants, oppressors and oppressed alike, to examine their own consciousnesses and to begin to interact with each other to expand their consciousnesses. In the way that it does this, SI provides a new context in which people can learn to interact with each other toward creating contexts and cultures in which power-with dynamics and both-and mentalities prevail. This, we believe, is transformative and of value.

Other Methodologies Oriented
Toward Change or Transformation

In this section, we discuss SI in relation to heuristics, appreciative inquiry, strategic assumption surfacing and testing (SAST), interactive planning (IP), and soft systems methodology (SSM) as related methodologies that are oriented toward change or transformation. Heuristics relates to SI through its emphasis on self-knowing. As another new form of collaborative inquiry, appreciative inquiry (Cooperrider & Srivastva, 1987; Srivastva & Cooperrider, 1999) also frames organizational situations from a positive, intuitive, and appreciative angle and tends to liberate people from situations that are seemingly problem driven and paralyzing.

Heuristics is an approach that focuses on an internal search in which the researcher experiences a growing self-awareness and self-understanding through the research process. In this way, heuristics can be related to much of the kind of self-knowing that is done in SI. According to Moustakas (1990), "heuristic research involves self-search, self-dialogue, and self-discovery" (p. 11). However, it does not focus on knowing other or on purposefully engaging a differing perspective as something that can help clarify one's self-understanding.

In heuristics there is an intentional indwelling, or turning inward, to seek a deeper and more extensive understanding of the question being investigated (Moustakas, 1990, p. 24). There is also a focusing in that inner space where one can tap into thoughts and feelings necessary to help clarify a question. Both of these processes are useful in the reflection aspects of SI to gain clarity in terms of knowing the self, but there is in SI the careful work to clarify the differences between views, which also facilitates this process.

Key to the heuristic process is immersion, also true in SI, with applications that range from momentary and limited to traveling long distances to be immersed in vastly different contexts for significant periods of time. Whether a specific expression of this tool is limited or global, long-term or brief, like those using the heuristic process, an SI researcher lives the question intensely for that period of time. These two methodologies are also similar in their final phases. For the heuristic process, this is called a creative synthesis, and it takes place after the researcher has mastered all the material that illuminates the question and has attempted to put it all together. However, SI is a more formal process that also involves differing perspectives that are first gathered and then held in one's mind as if both were true to generate energy through inner tension that can push participants toward a higher order insight or synthesis that transcends both of the original perspectives.

Appreciative inquiry is a new form of collaborative inquiry that frames organizational situations from a positive, intuitive, and appreciative angle. The results of working in this new framework tend to liberate people from situations that are seemingly problem driven and paralyzing. By taking an appreciative frame, situations can be reframed as positive, an act that lifts both the spirits and energy of participants (Cooperrider & Srivastva, 1987). This has similarities to the other-knowing processes of SI, and, although underdeveloped as a whole, the set of approaches and tools in appreciative inquiry can be used to enhance the other-knowing of SI.

SAST is a systems approach based on the philosophical thought of Churchman (1968). It includes the beliefs that (1) all organizational problems can be better understood by inquiring into opposing perspectives, (2) all members of an organization need to participate in the problem-solving process, (3) differences must be brought together so that a higher order of synthesis can be used to produce action plans, and (4) managers' views are expanded by understanding the opposing worldviews and the various constructions of the organizational problems. This methodology has four parts: group formation, assumption surfacing, dialectical debate, and synthesis (Flood & Jackson, 1991, pp. 123–124).

It is not difficult to see that SI shares many aspects of the philosophical foundations and methodology with SAST. The two major differences are that SI is designed to achieve a broader purpose and it has an epistemology that goes beyond that of SAST.

IP, the influential process for organizational planning developed primarily by systems thinker Russell Ackoff (1999), also has basic principles underlying its methodology that are similar to those of SI. These three principles are presented as participation, continuity, and holism. The participative principle asks all stakeholders to participate in the planning process, because, as Ackoff emphasizes, the process of planning is more important than the actual plan produced. Ackoff claims that in the process of planning, organizational members come to understand and learn to work with each other. Ackoff's continuity principle suggests that situations change, and thus plans always need to be revised, and these revisions must be timely. His holistic principle requires all parts or functions of an organization to interact with each other in the planning process. Methodologically, this holism is expressed in the IP steps of mess formulating, ends planning, means planning, resource planning, and design of implementation and control.

In the ways that this is accomplished, IP shares two major characteristics with SI: It motivates all perspectives to be surfaced, and it uses differences as creative resources to develop a plan of action for organizational changes. Designed to deal with differences of all kinds, SI tends to have a broader range of application than IP, which is basically limited to organizational systems, and SI also has a broader and deeper purpose.

SSM, which was pioneered by Peter Checkland, was developed to deal with "ill-structured or messy problem contexts where there is no clear view on what 'constitutes the problem,' or what action should be taken to overcome the difficulties being experienced" (Flood & Jackson, 1991, p. 168). Its four major principles are learning, culture, participation, and two modes of thought. The learning principle is essentially an inquiring attitude toward explicating and defining problematic situations, which is significantly different from some systems approaches that seek to achieve preset goals. Culture is an idea that powerfully guides SSM practitioners in identifying the key social rules and practices that constrain an organization. The participation principle is so important to SSM that without the participation of all involved, an application is considered invalid. SSM's idea of two modes of thought refers to polarity between ideal systems thinking and real-world thinking. The experienced practitioner moves easily between these two worlds for realistic interventions.

Again, there are both similarities and differences. SI is aligned with SSM's learning principle, cultural principle, and participation principle, which are inherent within SI processes and actions. SSM complements SI in its two modes of thought when SI is applied to organizational problem-solving situations. Part of this complementarity comes from the contrast between SSM's focus on messy problems and contexts and SI's focus on inquiry itself within a larger purpose and the deep connections that come from how the synergy principle allows us to participate with enduring aspects of universal process.

We therefore want to make it very clear that we in SI recognize and acknowledge that a myth lies beneath the SI framework: the myth of the evolution of consciousness. It is not the aim of SI to create yet one more logical alternative that competes with other logical alternatives but to create an intelligent and effective process framework through which people can learn to embody the synergy principle for their own evolutionary journeys.

As a process framework that enables individuals as well as social systems to engage with each other on more level playing fields, SI has already made it possible for participants of different cultures and traditions to interact in extraordinarily rich and meaningful ways that are not opportunistic. The power and ramifications of these experiences within SI have concretely shown that intercultural exchange like this is imperative if human consciousness is to evolve, because nobody—not governments, political parties, cultures, religions, leaders, or the common folk—has the whole of truth. If it is as true as it seems to be that all people are limited, then they all need to evolve and expand, and they each need the other to do it. A myth that says that consciousness evolves and that this evolution both means and does something in relation to larger realms than the individual, group, or local beliefs and issues, help form a container that can hold the tensions and energies generated in the intercultural, organizational, familial, and personal exchanges. This is documented in the case studies in Part II of this book.

Conclusion

Although it is still in its early stages of development, SI has already established itself as a powerful methodology for research, action, transformation, and change. The synergic worldview on which SI was built distinguishes its paradigm from the predominant research paradigms of positivism, postpositivism, critical theory, and constructivism. SI is akin to the newly proposed participatory paradigm, but this does not yet stretch far enough in a few important dimensions to fully include SI. The methodology that we introduce in this book does have important similarities to some of the prevailing methodologies for action, change, and transformation, but its differences point to SI's unique value as an action or transformative methodology.

In Part II of this book, we focus more concretely on the practice of SI to demonstrate both its similarities to other paradigms and methodologies and its individuality. The case studies represent a current sampling of those cases for which we have documentation. We hope that reception of this approach and these case studies both encourages and fosters continuing analysis and synthesis of documentation from other SI cases.

PART II

Synergic Inquiry Practices

Part II addresses how synergic inquiry (SI) can be practiced in varied settings; it includes a discussion of the key issues involved when considering or starting the practice of SI and a set of selected case studies that covers a wide range of settings and issues. In Chapter 5, we provide the outlines of a basic map for applying SI in different contexts. We also briefly describe the contents of the case study chapters (Chapters 6 through 15) to provide readers some direction for their differing interests. In Chapter 16, we reflect on the case studies in terms of some of the central themes and their implications for future SI work.

5

Practicing Synergic Inquiry

I deally, it would be wonderful to have a multifaceted map to take synergic inquiry (SI) participants through each step, procedure, and choice of
the inquiry process. It is important, however, to keep in mind that synergy
is an organic, emergent process; too detailed a map limits the creativity of
the participants. The purpose of this chapter is to provide instead signposts
and directions to help participants conduct SI, rather than a map of such
detail that it freezes out creativity of synergy for practitioners.

There are two parts to this chapter: The first outlines the basic elements
necessary to organize an SI inquiry, and the second provides a road map for
the case studies that follow. One can gain further ideas about how to use SI
in practice to conduct an inquiry by studying these cases.

Section I: Elements of SI Inquiry

Initiating SI

In our experience, applications of SI have been initiated in two ways: by an
SI facilitator or by a group experiencing a need. Often, the impetus comes from
an individual initiator. In these cases, the initiator plays a key role in engaging
others in the process by explaining the method and effectively communicating
the benefits of using SI. In many instances, an experienced facilitator can help
artfully frame the benefits of using SI in ways that make these benefits clear to
others and with the kind of authority that experience provides.

The other way that SI has been initiated happens when an existing group
calls an experienced SI facilitator to help them deal with a problem that they

collectively face. Normally in this kind of instance, someone in the group has learned about SI through a personal referral or by reading about it. In these cases, it is important that the SI facilitator first attempt to understand the group's situation as fully as possible and then to design a series of synergic activities that fits their needs. In other words, there is no magic formula or boilerplate for SI that can be applied routinely in every situation. To achieve true synergy, information about the purpose, needs, history, issues, makeup, expectations, and personalities of a group must always be included in the design of an inquiry.

Contracting

This is an important step in conducting an inquiry because it is where participants arrive at mutual agreements about how to use SI as their method of inquiry. It is not unusual for participants to have fears and concerns about engaging in this kind of work. Participation in a process that involves working with differences can be threatening, especially when there already exists a situation in which participants experience confrontations or polarizations around differences. The resulting fears and concerns must be addressed before the process begins.

Even though SI is a process that treats everybody equally, and thus should not be threatening, it still requires some contracting of the basic preconditions for participation. It is important for each set of participants to determine its own conditions for entering into the process. During this activity, concerns and fears can be addressed directly, and a safe container for the entire group can be created. It is during these activities that commitment to the entire process can also be gained.

Once participants have come to an agreement on these conditions and the other norms to be honored, they are ready to begin the SI process. What follows is a list of basic conditions that must be present for all inquiries:

- Use nonjudgmental dialogue
- Maintain an openness to others' viewpoints and feelings
- Hold a learning and growth attitude
- Commit to going through the entire SI process
- Respect the role of the facilitator

Planning

It is important to come up with an inquiry plan that includes several major components. The basic categories of a plan are identifying the focus question and outlining the activities.

Identifying the Focus Question

The first task in planning is to conduct an inquiry that defines the focus for the larger inquiry. After this, a specific question or questions are formed around this agreed-on focus. These questions help a diverse group hold the necessary level of coherence of focus during the inquiry, which allows them to attain their desired result.

Because SI is a collaborative process, it is important for participants to engage with each other in the development of these questions. In this way, the issues and concerns of those whose voices are normally excluded can be included in the inquiry. By developing a clear focus and formulating specific and relevant questions at the beginning of an inquiry, trust and confidence are built among the participants.

Outlining the Activities

The next step in planning is to outline the specific activities that will carry the inquiry forward. The complexity of inquiries will vary. Factors that affect this complexity include the purpose of the SI application, the size of the group, the differences involved, and the amount of time available. The key to a successful application of SI is planning activities as carefully as possible and then keeping an attitude of openness and flexibility that makes room for the organic, emergent nature of the SI process. The case studies that follow this chapter present rich descriptions of this complexity, as well as some of the specific strategies that may be useful for a given application.

SI has four intrinsic phases—self-knowing, other-knowing, differences-holding and differences-transcending—and none of these can be treated superficially or omitted. This means that some pragmatic negotiations among participants is inevitably required as far as time and energy are concerned. During each of the four phases there are activities that require the joint engagement of all participants. Times and places for all of these activities need to be determined so that each participant can make plans to have the time and resources to engage in the entire process. It is especially important to define sufficient time for reflection and closure at this early stage.

Facilitating SI

In most cases, it is helpful to use a facilitator to get the SI process started. This is especially true when a group wishes to address an issue of conflict. Members of an inquiry group need to learn about the process and to take enough time to formulate the necessary norms for their inquiry. Effective facilitation of this initial activity is very helpful.

The role of the facilitator is to guide participants successfully through the SI process. This guidance includes maintaining a balance between the content of the inquiry and the processes through which this content is addressed. It is important to remember that each facilitator needs to respect where the members of the group are, balancing content and process in such a way that the necessary outcomes of resolution and synergy can be met. The facilitator provides guidance through each of the steps in such a way that balance is maintained. After a group masters both the mechanics of the SI process and an understanding of this balance and the need for reflection, they may be able to function without an external facilitator and facilitate their own process.

Content Facilitation

Part of the facilitation has to address the content of an inquiry, that is, the intrinsic experiences of participants. Once the SI process starts, participants tend to get excited about others' perspectives and real-life stories and excited by their interactive and emergent experiences. It is important for the facilitator to help participants go deeply into their own processes, rather than rushing to quick resolution. It is therefore important that the participants' capacities for SI are treated as a priority equal to the need to resolve the presenting issue.

Process Facilitation

The other major part of facilitation involves the processes and phases of the inquiry itself. Several cautions must be included here. First, the facilitator needs to make sure that the group actually goes through all of the phases of the SI process, including both the action and the reflection parts of cycles within each phase. Second, the facilitator must pay attention to how well participants are learning the process. Participants tend to swim in the content of their experiences without paying adequate attention to the process itself. The facilitator also needs to help participants go through each of the reflection cycle steps so that they can learn to develop capacity and skills to sustain the practice of SI without a facilitator's presence.

Working With Emotionally Stuck Participants

Differences often cause stress, and a group may find it difficult to handle the emotional issues that emerge during its inquiry. It is not unusual for individual participants to become emotionally stuck during the process of an inquiry. A good facilitator needs to know how to break open this kind of emotional stuckness for the group. To do this, facilitators need the ability to coach, to counsel, and to help specific individuals deal with the emotions that arise as part of the inquiry process in a manner that expands consciousness and promotes synergy.

Two skills are often helpful in moving through emotional stuckness. One is to have participants express their feelings in the form of "I" statements so that they remain in their own experiences rather than speaking for or about others. This creates a space for each to be open and for the other participants involved to receive. Facilitators need to catch those forms of statements that sound judgmental and thus offensive. The other skill needed is the ability to have respondents acknowledge and validate their feelings, instead of rushing to solving the problem.

Follow-Up

After their intense experiences together in SI, it is important for groups to have one or more follow-up sessions with each other to reinforce learning and to offer the support that is often needed. These types of activities are of critical importance in the follow-up sessions. One way to do this is to reflect on the actions taken after a synergy cycle and to process participants' learnings and challenges. This is important because new consciousness and new behaviors need support at the beginning to be sustained. Otherwise, one too easily falls back into old consciousness and habitual behaviors. Thus, helping participants learn to continually develop new strategies for change or transformation is essential. The group can also use the SI process to develop new action plans for sustaining change or transformation.

Second, it is important to make sure that participants do not neglect the content reflections, during which they process their feelings and thoughts sufficiently to move on. This allows them to continue to sustain the emotional filter necessary for their own learning and growth. Finally, it is critical to the development of skill that participants also repeatedly reflect on how they have used the SI process. Participants are encouraged to discuss their skills as well as their difficulties during their experience with the SI process.

Qualifications and Characteristics of SI Facilitators

A good SI facilitator has gone through many personal experiences of SI and, through personal learnings, has mastered the SI process and understands how to balance both this and the content of an inquiry. It is important to point out here that SI is not just another instrumental technique that can be learned quickly and applied mechanically within a short time. Facilitators need to internally master the SI process in practice, not just in theory. Good facilitators therefore use SI regularly as an integral part of their own processes of personal and professional development. The following are other key conditions a person must meet to become a good SI facilitator.

Tolerance for Ambiguity

Facilitators must have a high tolerance for ambiguity. The SI process is organic and emergent, and the way it manifests depends on the individuals participating and on the specific cultural setting. A facilitator must be able to pay attention to the steps that each specific group of participants needs to take and to not impose structure or beliefs on an inquiry from a personal perspective. Facilitators also need to be able to separate their own synergizing from the processes of the group being facilitated.

Empathy

SI facilitators especially need to have a capacity for empathy. Our experience shows that this characteristic is essential for the synergy process to actually take place. When participants feel that they have been received and are understood empathically, they feel supported and are willing to go more deeply into themselves and the issues of an inquiry.

Balancing Content and Process

A good facilitator needs to have balanced knowledge and experience of both the content and the process involved in a particular situation. Although SI is designed to deal with all types of differences, adequate knowledge pertaining to the kinds of specific content issues, such as culture, race, or gender, that tend to arise during an inquiry is essential. On the other hand, mastery of content issues without an adequate grounding in the SI process tends to allow facilitators to fall back on other traditional forms of working with differences. Therefore, it is critical that an SI facilitator be skilled at maintaining balance of content and process. This balance can be enhanced by using a team of facilitators who complement each other.

Creating Openness

Skills that foster openness are also key to successful SI facilitation. When participants are open and honest within an inquiry, they are able to go more deeply into their subconscious than is normally possible for them. This creates the preconditions for genuine expansions of consciousness, not simply incremental learning.

Empowering Participants

The ability to empower participating participants is another important skill a facilitator needs. In addition to general empowerment skills, a good SI facilitator knows when and how to let participants create their own processes and activities, as well as when and how to provide guidance without disempowering them.

Issues of Validity

The issue of validity criteria and procedures for qualitative research has been hotly debated among qualitative and interpretative researchers. One extreme position holds that the obsession with identifying criteria for ensuring validity is a product of objectivism and that we should have a "farewell to criteriology" (Schwandt, 1996, p. 58). On the other hand, most qualitative methodologists, including those from the participative inquiry schools, argue that concern for such criteria is indeed relevant for qualitative and interpretative research but that different types of criteria are needed for validating research outcomes (Heron, 1996; Reason & Lincoln, 1996). Reason (1988) argues that the question of validity is of extreme importance because "we must counter the charge that our work is mere subjectivism" (p. 228). Following this line of reasoning, some emerging criteria for qualitative and interpretive research have been developed (Lincoln, 1995).

When we say that a research is valid, we mean that the research findings or outcomes are true, trustworthy, or well grounded (Heron, 1996). In terms of SI, validity has to do with whether the knowledge and capacities developed through SI are trustworthy. Concretely, SI produces visible, logical, and mythical forms of knowledge in each of its four phases: in self-knowing, knowledge about self is increased; in other-knowing, there is a similar increase in knowledge about the other; from differences-holding comes knowledge about embodying multiple realities within oneself, and an understanding of implications for the collective is formed; in differences-transcending, new and practical knowledge is acquired about how one (individual, collective, or both) can change and transform through access to different behaviors or alternative solutions. In addition to these increases, SI also produces or reinforces skills during each phase of SI and the overall capacity to practice SI in the situations of everyday life.

To address the question of validity for SI, it is necessary to be aware of the ontological and epistemological underpinnings for this methodology. The synergic worldview posits that a larger reality than that which humans perceive and project does exist, that this reality is constantly evolving, and that humans come to know this reality through a dialectical process of constructing their own versions of reality, engaging with the different versions of reality constructed by others, and then working to synergize these toward a new construction that embraces the wisdom of both participating realities.

In addition to resolving a presenting issue or focal question in an inquiry, we endeavor to help participants learn how to consciously embody this evolutionary process in an ongoing way so that they accelerate the evolution of their own individual consciousnesses. In our experience, it is through this conscious embodiment of a universal process that people continue to develop skills and cultivate a capacity for dealing with differences of many kinds.

To ensure that the outcome of a specific inquiry is trustworthy, critical strategies need to be developed by participants. The following sections detail what, at this stage of the development of SI, we have found helpful.

Critical Self-Awareness

Critical self-awareness refers to the quality of awareness about all three dimensions of consciousness: the visible, the logical, and the mythical. To develop this awareness, it is important to examine one's own consciousness in terms of all three of these dimensions of knowing.

In practice, we have found that most people gravitate to one dimension more frequently than to the other dimensions. For example, some people are primarily logical, and logical knowing receives their primary focus and more of their energy. We argue that, whatever the personal preference is, it is critically important to engage in all three levels of knowing because the dynamic interconnection of all three creates the desired qualities of awareness. What often happens is that participants start with only one level in full use—usually the visible or the logical—and stop the process of thorough self-knowing before it has gone as deep as it can.

Another tendency often found among participants is difficulty sustaining enough focus on self to complete the work of self-knowing. This may be a result of cultural upbringings that provided no education about inner development. Participants need to attend to and acknowledge such a tendency when it happens, and over time it becomes easier for them to do the self-knowing. Many of the tools and exercises in Chapter 3 are helpful for achieving high-quality outcomes of self-knowing.

Critical Subjectivity

The term *critical subjectivity* is already in use by other qualitative and interpretative researchers (Lincoln, 1995). This term refers to the capacity to enter a state of awareness "for the purpose of understanding with great discrimination subtle differences in the personal and psychological states of others" (Lincoln, 1995, p. 283). This capacity is precisely what is needed in the processes of other-knowing and, to some extent, differences-holding.

During the work of other-knowing, participants need to learn how to bracket their own consciousnesses to such an extent that they do not automatically translate, reframe, or distort the consciousnesses of others. Participants are asked to receive a total perspective on reality without distorting or transforming it.

Critical Action-Reflection Cycles

Critical action-reflection cycles are another way to ensure quality outcomes for the SI process. Action-reflection cycles are designed to enable participants to move between reflection and experience for the purpose of expanding both awareness and capacities. The reflection work here is what enables participants to process the new awareness and learnings that come to them through the full, intense experiences of the SI process.

Within the self-knowing phase, reflection is designed to help participants reflect on their experiences of self-knowing and on the skill set of self-knowing. This is to cultivate a high quality awareness of the multiple dimensions of self. Reflection cycles in the phases of other-knowing, differences-holding, and differences-transcending are designed to expand self-knowing. These reflections on self that are initiated by meeting and taking on the consciousnesses of others lead to a deeper knowing of oneself than can be accomplished without these differing mirrors. Panikkar (1979) and Vachon (1995) argue that one can discover one's own mythical knowing only by taking on the mental planes of others. At the end of each complete SI cycle, there is a metalevel reflection—an overall reflection on the experience of the entire cycle—in terms of content and process. This is important because it enhances capacity for incorporating the SI process into the fabric of one's own being and behavior.

Critical Reciprocity

Reciprocity is a term used by many interpretative researchers (Lincoln, 1995) to refer to the importance of studying the ways in which people relate with each other and how the self changes through intense mutual sharing with another. Through most parts of the SI process, such mutual reciprocity is the norm. We include it here under critical reciprocity because it is important to pay attention to how the self-knowing of each participant is shaped through the intense mutuality of this process.

Starting with the process of other-knowing, SI participants intensely interact with each other. Often this interaction generates a field in which different consciousnesses interpenetrate and initiate a journey of expanding awareness. It is because of precisely this mutuality that SI as a process creates the conditions and contexts for transformation of consciousness that it does.

Critical Novelty

Critical novelty refers to the new or novel ways of being and of behaviors that arise in the phase of differences-transcending. Although expansion of consciousness and capacities is essentially for developing high-quality awareness, this kind of awareness does not automatically and invariably lead to different ways of being and of behaving. The exhilaration of insight can sometimes entrance one in such a way that the changes are not integrated deeply enough to manifest as synergy. To ensure that the outcome of an SI process has been genuinely transformative, it's necessary to double-check each new way or solution to see whether it is indeed new and novel. Sometimes what appears to be new may, through further examination, actually prove to be a subtly cloaked repetition of the old. When this happens, participants need to return to the cycle and deepen their work.

Critical SI Cycling

Finally, multiple SI cycles are needed if capacity building is to be enhanced. This is especially important if the purpose of an inquiry is to have participants learn to incorporate SI deeply into themselves. One of our primary intentions in developing and communicating the SI process is to incorporate these core principles into our very beings and spontaneous behavior so that we may use them freely and easily in everyday life. Experiencing multiple cycles of SI followed by metalevel reflection on each helps those of us who use this kind of inquiry to achieve that purpose. The experienced driver no longer needs to consciously monitor the individual steps and procedures initially learned for handling a car because those driving skills have been mastered to such an extent that they slip into the subconscious. In a similar way, we find that some participants are able to gradually master and embody the essence of SI to such an extent that these too become automatic. They no longer need to mechanistically follow its steps.

Section II: Applications of SI

Case Studies

SI has many possible applications, only a few of which have been documented. Through the cases that follow insight can be gained into some of the varied possibilities for using SI. The cases included here have been categorized by the level of complexity of the human system to which SI has been applied. The least complex level that has been documented to date is the individual level, and the level of the international organization is the most complex.

These levels of human systems also intersect with the many issues that these cases represent, issues that include personal development, leadership, racial differences, gender differences, teamwork, communication, conflict resolution, strategic envisioning, organizational development and transformation, and cross-cultural exchanges. We expect that different readers will be interested in different kinds of cases, so we have tried to offer a range of examples. The following summary of cases may help in the selection of which to study.

Individual Level

In "Geisha and Cowboy: Synergizing Inner-Life Differences Through the Mythic Realm" (Chapter 6), organizational consultant Joanne Gozawa shows how the principles of synergic inquiry can be applied at the personal level. Joanne was wrestling with questions about how she could use her mythos to develop depth. She identified two significant mythic symbols—the geisha and the cowboy—that, as part of her being, drive her behavior.

Joanne observed how these symbols relate to her behavior and undertook a program of reading to better understand each of them. Through the process of synergizing these two mythic symbols, she found a way for them both to dance with each other synergistically. As a result, she increased her capacity for dealing with differences and conflict. In this study, she also tells of integrating the SI process into the nature of her being. Because she now embodies it in both being and behavior in terms of these two mythic processes, SI is no longer a formal process that she has to consciously follow.

Relationship Level

Chapter 7, "Husband and Wife Synergizing" documents how a wife and husband used SI to improve their relationship in a harmonizing and sustaining manner. In this study, Venus and Eric demonstrate how nagging difficulties between a husband and wife can be resolved through SI. The focus of the inquiry in this case revolves around the preparation of meals. To do their self- and other-knowing, Venus and Eric each wrote from their own perspectives using a what, how, and why structure. After these reflections were shared, they engaged in reflection on what they had learned about the other.

To hold differences, they read their reflections on each other's perspective. This was followed by more reflection. What emerged was deeper understanding and appreciation of each other. As a result of their inquiry, their feelings about buying food and preparing meals were transformed. Although they still have to prepare meals, there is a new balance in this and a greater source of enjoyment for both of them around the issue of mealtime.

In Chapter 8, a mother and a daughter describe how they used SI to deal with their difficulties involving housecleaning. Lien found herself obsessed with her daughter's lack of cleaning, and neither mother nor daughter wanted the distress of this conflict to continue. They used an external facilitator to help them while they engaged with each other in the SI process. During this process, Lien found something deep in her psyche that was contributing to the difficulties. The process turned into a bonding experience that has had a long-lasting impact on both mother and daughter.

Group Level

In Chapter 9, "Developing a Community Through Synergic Envisioning," Elisa Sabatini describes how SI helped a group overcome tensions that threatened to block progress in forming a new intentional community. This group began by identifying common questions and then preparing individual mandalas, or symbolic drawings, and sharing them. After trying to hold each mandala as their own, they then created a group mandala together that reflected their consciousness as a group. In the sharing of this process, group members realized that they were on different timetables for changing residences to join in the physical community that they were building. This realization allowed the project to move forward, and shortly thereafter a major land purchase was made and the homes in the community were started.

In "Using Synergic Inquiry to Resolve a Group Conflict," Chapter 10, Lien Cao describes how SI was used to resolve some deeper issues that were challenging a group. The focus this time was on changing established study groups at the beginning of a new work cycle. Because of some of the sticky issues involved, it had been difficult for the group to come to their previous agreement, and they were struggling to find a way to organize their work that would be satisfying to all. The members of the group decided to use SI to help them tap into the deeper dimensions of self that were driving their behaviors. After using SI for sharing, tremendous understanding and empathy were achieved. As a result of these new understandings, the group members no longer had any attachment to the form of their study groups, and the issue that had once been such a source of conflict among them disappeared.

In Chapter 11, "Synergic Inquiry in Action: The Expansion of Racial Consciousness," the authors document how another group used SI to deal with racial differences that seemed to generate unwanted power imbalances within their group. These participants split into a Black subgroup and a White subgroup to clearly differentiate perspectives. Their process was codesigned and cofacilitated by participants from each subteam, with Yongming Tang acting as their adviser. Two synergy cycles were used for this inquiry, one for within the subgroups and one for the group as a whole.

In the first cycle, intracultural synergy, each subgroup, through an intense process, developed a collective perspective on the cultural consciousness of their race. They used all three levels of consciousness to express their collective consciousness and various exercises to hold the differences that emerged. In the second synergy cycle, intercultural synergy, the subgroups engaged with each other synergistically. In an intense 6-month process, they engaged in SI with each other to expand their individual as well as their collective consciousnesses, both as two racial subgroups and as one collective whole. The result of their inquiry was the dissipation of many racial issues and the emergence of a new level of teamwork.

The study in Chapter 12 describes an inquiry that was designed to address gender issues in a 2-day workshop setting. The process was codesigned and cofacilitated by five facilitators who had different degrees of experience with SI prior to the workshop. This group first used SI to focus on the design of the workshop itself, an experience they believe was critical to the success of this inquiry.

Three synergy cycles were conducted during the workshop. The first of these was designed to help participants learn about SI and to give them some basic skills for effective participation. For the second synergy cycle, the men and the women separated into gender-specific subgroups toward understanding and synergizing as a group. Each subgroup went through the synergic experience, using exercises and activities that were tailored to their own gender.

In the final synergy cycle, both men and women, as subgroups, engaged with each other; this resulted in further expansions of consciousnesses, and the workshop turned out to be a powerful and healing experience for both facilitators and participants. A unique aspect of this workshop is that the facilitators became participants from time to time, and some of the participants organically moved into the role of facilitator for the process. This shifting of relationships and roles was found to contribute greatly to creating a deeper and more meaningful experience.

Chapter 13 describes the application of SI in a high school classroom setting. Roma Hammel tells of her experiences using SI as a new pedagogical approach for working with the ethnic and cultural diversity of the students in her classes. She offers several examples of how she integrated SI into the subject matter she was teaching.

In one of these she tells of dividing students into two groups along gender lines and using Ibsen's "Doll House" as part of a process of exploring gender issues. The students did self-knowing and other-knowing and then decided that they preferred to share in an atmosphere of mutual respect and community. This class engaged in a second synergy cycle, using art and movement to help them explore gender issues more deeply.

In another application, racial and cultural differences were chosen as the focus of the inquiry. In this case, each student paired with another of a different cultural background and then prepared synergistic cultural presentations. In a third application, her class combined SI with a reading of Ralph Ellison's (2002) novel *Invisible Man* to explore how experience shapes worldview. Roma ends with some powerful student reflections.

Organization Level

Chapter 14 documents an international cross-cultural use of SI in business. In this case, a project team from the United States was organized to interact with a project team from Beijing New Building Materials (BNBM), a large, successful, state-owned manufacturing business in China. The purpose of this project was to use differing cultural perspectives to help expand the perspectives of BNBM's management team and their capacities for the kind of creative problem solving they would need in the future. They wanted to maintain current levels of success and social responsibility and at the same time improve their level of economic performance in the increasing competition of the global marketplace.

The complexity of this project required participants to organize into three subteams, each with participants from both cultures. One subteam focused on leadership, another concentrated on motivation systems, and the third focused on marketing. The U.S. team members engaged intensely with their Chinese counterparts, as well as with other parts of the company and the larger society, through conversations, shared meals, site visits, and interviews. Several synergic outcomes came out of this experience, among them new views on motivation and new organizational ways to support cross-disciplinary cooperation. The performance of this company has improved, and the Chinese executives consider the project successful.

In Project Mexico (Chapter 15), a team from a doctoral program in the United States worked with a team from a San Diego–based international community development organization called World SHARE for a two-layered project. Part of the project focused on difficulties World SHARE was having in taking its program into Mexico. Using this focus as a context, a subteam also explored the transformative processes and effects of the SI process on themselves as participants.

The first stage of differentiation was achieved through reading, interviewing corporate executives, and participating in a food-distribution day in the United States. A field team then visited several affiliates in Mexico, interviewing their leaders, leaders of other community development projects, and participants in local food programs. Two perspectives were developed for this project, one representing corporate World SHARE and the other representing the Mexican affiliates.

After clarifying these two perspectives, a session for differences-holding and differences-transcending was held in which both corporate executives and Mexican affiliate leaders participated. Both views were presented, and specific issues were identified around which to synergize. The end result was recognition by corporate management of the magnitude of differences between their cultural environment and that of their start-ups in Mexico. When corporate management no longer demanded that all programs operate like the U.S. program, an innovative, culturally responsive program could be developed for Mexico.

6

Geisha and Cowboy: Synergizing Inner Life Differences Through the Mythic Realm

Joanne Gozawa

As a practitioner of synergic inquiry (SI) in my profession as an organizational consultant, I find that I also hold principles of SI in my personal life. I recently became intrigued by the potential of applying SI to the paradoxical differences that abound in my inner life. It also occurred to me that it is difficult to access the mythical dimension of self, that is, one's personal myth. This is where, I believe, the opportunity for profound change lies. What I mean by personal myth is much aligned with Lauter's (1984) conclusion that "myth is that belief which seems sacred to the holder and reconciles life-baffling oppositions."

This chapter is about my own personal synergy journey into the mythic realm of myself. It shows how I, as an individual, embody synergy in the nature of my behavior and being and describes a journey that was profoundly transformative to me.

Self-Knowing and Other-Knowing

In its phases of self-knowing, other-knowing, differences-holding, and differences-transcending, SI seeks to use the tension that emanates from polarities to transcend them into expanded consciousness. I find that the processes of self-knowing and other-knowing can be applied to my own inner life by using polarizations within myself as self and other. When I allow this tension of inner opposites to surface, insights about myself, my self-knowing, is deepened, and my ability to engage in knowing another is enhanced.

What has helped this inner journey is, what seems to me, my natural propensity for indwelling. In that place, I stumbled onto a process that took me deeper into self-knowing through the mythic realm. My indwelling had me exploring the ideas of what I call my personal survival mythos—that which symbolizes how I cope with feelings of danger when I engage with what feels to me like an oppressive other or others. The nature of the feeling is a sense that the other is crushing an essential part of who I am and what I am about.

In my case, I felt safe when I sensed that my being was in harmony with the other, and I felt in danger when the harmony of the relationship was threatened by what seemed to me to be differences between us. Although I had already surfaced psychological and cultural reasons for this, these had not been significant to my self-knowing on the mythic level. Because the mythic is beyond the intellect, to access this realm, I had to rely on a way of knowing that could be supported by intellect without being initiated by it.

In my self-knowing and other-knowing processes, I noticed that two figures often came up in my consciousness. They were the geisha and the cowboy. Their obvious differences intrigued me. One was Eastern and the other was iconoclastic Western, particularly American Western. One was female, and the other was male. Geisha exuded inclusivity, empathy, and concern for the other, whereas Cowboy symbolized fierce independence, individuality, and stoicism. In contemplating the relationship between these two figures by continually asking how they showed up in a survival moment, I was able to deepen my knowing about my mythos and the beliefs that informed how I acted when I was in survival mode.

To get into the shadows of my own consciousness, I began reading about geishas and cowboys and looking at art that depicted them. I compared the societal symbology of each with my own sense of what they were, always holding a specific question: What do these tell me about myself that is hidden to myself? Next, I tried to surface their positive characteristics and then their negative ones.

As I began to associate these with my own self, Geisha told me that I was empathetic, feminine, and caring about others, while at the same time I sensed that my empathetic nature was at the cost of losing some other part of myself. In a stressful situation, where my brand of danger was at hand, I mediated the situation by taking on an empathetic posture, but sometimes I took this posture to such extreme measure that I was at risk of going along with anything, even that which might diminish my own spirit. In survival mode, I then reflected, I took on what I thought to be the negative characteristics of Geisha. Another shadow characteristic also occurred to me. Geishas are part of what, in Japan, is called the floating world, a world of magical illusion that is designed to support the intangible spirit, is at the periphery of society, and is not grounded in the practicalities of everyday life. There was, therefore, a certain unreality about the Geisha, and I too would at times feel inauthentic, a persona designed to please rather than as a person with her own agency.

Cowboy too had his message for me. This message came from a movie I had once seen in which a cowboy rode into a town with revenge on his mind. He had been a young sheriff in this town long before. At that time, the town had set him up to be attacked and left him for dead, so they could capitalize on some illegal plot. When he rides into town, now unrecognized by the townspeople, he finds that they are threatened by the gunslingers who had been complicit in the town's past illegalities. Those gunslingers, who had engaged to kill the young sheriff years before, were later deceived by the townspeople and sent to prison. The gunslingers were now being released from prison, and they too had vengeance on their minds. The movie ends with the cowboy, who first makes the townspeople think he will save them from the now-freed gunslingers, riding into the sunset and leaving the "upstanding" citizens of the town to their own fate.

The Cowboy, as depicted in this movie, revealed another side of myself to me, the one that balances the vulnerability of Geisha. Geisha risks herself in her giving, but she is balanced by Cowboy, who can simply walk away with no regret. This system of perfectly complementing mythos, however, kept me locked in the same consciousness and minimized my own agency.

Differences-Holding

Differences-holding for me means to hold different ways of being as equals and to learn to dance with them to such an extent that they are to my advantage. In my case, Geisha and Cowboy were initially held sequentially. That is, when Geisha could no longer keep me safe, Cowboy would take over. In contrast to this, the differences-holding phase of SI holds opposites as equals in preparation for what logicians call the inclusive third and what SI calls differences-transcending. I found that after I surfaced Geisha and Cowboy metaphors of my psyche, I began to hold them simultaneously. I did not consciously will this holding. Instead, it seemed to just happen. My "will" in the process was passively expressed, and I merely received the images of my own indwelling and imaginal processes.

Space does not allow me to speak of all of the insights I have had since allowing the figures of the Geisha and the Cowboy to dance together within me. Briefly, however, one very significant insight was that as Geisha I saw the other as always "good," whereas as Cowboy I always saw the other as "bad." The ability to hold Geisha and Cowboy within me simultaneously allowed me to see that others are also simultaneously good and bad, whole in their imperfection and necessarily complex in their need to survive both in the physical and spiritual realms.

My indwelling allowed me to use the metaphorical language of Geisha and Cowboy to explore my survival mythos, the one that said if I were emphatic, safety would prevail, and as a last resort I should get up and leave disharmonious situations. I could see how my survival mythos played out in my two marriages, which ended with me leaving my husbands.

I have also been able to reassess my sense of danger regarding the lack of permanent equanimity with another or a group. I am now able to see that without imbalance there can't be balance, only stagnation. Geisha and Cowboy complemented each other. They were in balance, but they had kept me locked in a survival system that retarded my evolving sense of self and prevented my consciousness from expanding.

Differences-Transcending

Differences-transcending has to do with how I transcend the limitations of Geisha or Cowboy in my behavior and in my being. I believe this particular application of SI, for the differentiation and reintegration of my internal life, has been transformative. A situation that comes to mind to demonstrate this change relates to the doctoral program in which I am enrolled. It is set up in a cohort structure that explores the notion of learning in a diverse group.

Recently, my group was to submit a proposal for their group demonstration of competency. A small group of us sat down to write this proposal while trying to hold everyone's consciousness. I took responsibility for the background section and sent it out for cohort-wide review. The people of color in the cohort took offense to what I had written. After a lengthy cohort discussion, we tried again to rewrite the background and, incidentally, the entire proposal. A feminist and a Jewish woman in the cohort both spoke adamantly against our second draft.

We were under a time constraint and had to submit our proposal to the faculty within a couple of days to comply with the department's scheduling requirements. Here was the kind of situation that normally triggered my survival mythos; it particularly played on my fear of diminishing time and disharmony in my relationships with faculty members, not to mention the obvious disharmony in the cohort. It was usual for me to become overwhelmed by everyone's need in such a situation and, in this state of lost energy, to project my survival fears onto those who were so "divisive," those who just couldn't go along with things. My energy would, in such a situation, usually be oriented to giving up and leaving. In the simplified terms of my mythos, Geisha would want to please and, finding that she could not, would become Cowboy, who would want to ride into the sunset, leaving the others to their own foolishness.

I found that I had transcended the initial dilemma caused by these characters in my mythos. I felt neither overwhelmed by the cohort situation nor disdainful toward those who were speaking out. I was in a space of being able to receive the other, of getting into their consciousnesses and holding their differences in such a way that I could include their voices in the proposal. I could hold their complexity without judging them as "bad."

In mythic terms, I had transcended the polarization of being either vulnerable or strong and found I could be both. I was able to engage with the feelings of the other, to make myself vulnerable, while, from a centered place, I could explain my thinking and suggest effective revisions. I was not defensive. Rather, I was open and receptive to the emotions that threatened the proposal writing process. Geisha was empathetic, yet strong. And Cowboy stayed instead of leaving. He stayed to listen and be affected so that his actions could be informed by compassion. In my cycle of personal synergy, I seemed to have transcended my need to be empathetic, at the cost of losing myself, and transcended my need to be stoic and overly independent, at the cost of hardening my heart.

With the differences transcended, three elements were simultaneously true: The Geisha, the Cowboy, and the included middle that surpasses both were all real in me all at once. Geisha and Cowboy provide the creative tension that allowed the inclusive third to come into being. In the understanding that comes from differences-transcending, I now know that all three, both of the poles and the middle, are required. Instead of being bound by the limitations of either Geisha or Cowboy, I am paradoxically freed by their boundaries.

Before the insights from this cycle surfaced, Geisha and Cowboy conspired within and complemented my unresolved polarization of wanting to be empathetic and wanting to act with my own agency. When held as a duality these constrained me. When held in the domain of what Basarab Nicolescu calls ternary thinking (Baker, 1997, p. 66), they freed me.

After 8 months, I've noticed that the images of Geisha and Cowboy do not come up in my consciousness as often. What does come up is a figure that resembles myself, a figure who has found her own sense of self in relationship with others. I feel more of a groundedness, a lack of timidity and temporalness. This gives me a solid lightness of being that is no longer paradoxical to me. And I now find myself able to know the other better, because, in disharmonious situations, my survival is less at stake.

With this inner cycle of SI completed, I find I can better hold differences and transcend them in my outer life. Part of this increased capacity stems from understanding the place that tension plays in my own unfolding. Geisha and Cowboy will always be with me, but they now hold a place in my mythos that engenders growth rather than stagnation. By using SI for my inward journey, I have deeply learned how my survival mythos, while effective as a system for avoiding my own felt sense of danger, kept me hostage in its predictable strategy of using Cowboy or rescue Geisha. In maintaining this status quo, I had also maintained my sense that disharmonious situations were actually dangerous.

If I had languished in that consciousness, I would continue to avoid diversity. I would continue to judge people as good or bad according to whether Geisha or Cowboy was evoked when I related to them. With my expanded consciousness, situations I had previously seen as issues of survival are now apt to feel less dire. When survival situations are thus diffused, one is able then to engage with less fear. When the other is allowed to be both bad and good, this paradox is no longer a paradox, and transformation is more likely to happen.

7

Husband and Wife Synergizing

Venus Bobis Jendresen and Eric Bobis

As a couple, my husband and I usually live and work well together. We do not have chores that are assigned by gender roles: taking out the garbage, doing the laundry, washing the dishes, servicing the cars, taking care of our daughter, paying the bills, and so on, are tasks done by whomever is available. But there was one place where we would always get stuck. Shopping for groceries and preparing our evening meal proved to be our downfall.

We had many heated and intense arguments, usually at dinnertime, about what we would eat, about the lack of food in the house, about who should prepare it, about why one or the other of us didn't think about supper earlier in the day (after all, it is a meal that comes around each day like clockwork), among others. The arguments usually ended in bitter frustration. Recently, I threw a bunch of asparagus at him and walked out of the room, returning to the kitchen later to fix a scrambled egg for our daughter's supper, but ignoring our own.

We both consider ourselves fairly enlightened people, but it occurred to me that I might not be ready to effect transformative change in others if I could not even get supper peacefully to the table of my own house. So my husband, Erik, and I agreed to put the synergic inquiry (SI) model to the test and dig into what had become the bane of our existence.

We sat down together one evening after a great day together—rollerblading with our daughter, visiting a street fair, and peacefully managing to prepare a nourishing supper. I mention all of this because we were in no way stressed when we embarked on our journey of inquiry together. We were both receptive and attentive. We had no matters immediately pressing and could offer each other our conscious and undivided attention.

Self-Knowing

We started first with the self-knowing portion of the model. I read Erik the questions we were to consider, and then we agreed to write our answers individually within a set period of time. After we completed our answers, we followed instructions in the model by taking time to reflect quietly on what was being revealed: "What were your reflections, each of you? Please include your revelations here. Briefly, of course."

Other-Knowing

I then read Erik the section describing other-knowing so that we would both be clear as to how we should try to listen to each other. I asked him to go first, to read what he had written and then elaborate on it. This is what he wrote:

> *What:* Meals themselves are not difficult. The difficulty manifests with the contemplation of the meal—the need to make choices—to anticipate the procuring of ingredients, to then prepare the ingredients.

> *How:* It is nearing dinnertime. Neither of us has shopped with any specific menu in mind or both have picked up this and that sort of stuff—we have a cupboard and a refrigerator full of staples. The question arises: "What are we going to do for dinner?" I make a suggestion and Vennie expresses either apathy or distaste for the suggestion. I make another suggestion—another idea that is by no means unique or original, or it might be too unique. Soon we are expressing frustration and anger with each other. Appetites are being lost like ships in the Bermuda Triangle. . . .

> *Why:* I am approaching mealtime in a practical way. I know the options and am pursuing them. For me, meals are either functional (i.e., fulfill the need to eat wholesomely to get on with the rest of the evening) or experiential (i.e., sensual, contemplative, and fulfilling, spiritually as well as organically). A lot of the time, too much of the time, I feel that there is only time for the first brand. But I know that Vennie is dissatisfied with such eating because of what it could be. I cannot help but agree and regret that neither of us has taken the time to provide for the other—to anticipate the need or the desire that we both have for a fuller experience. For we seek the fuller experience in all that we do.

This issue like so many others is reflective of a much larger dynamic that exists in the space in between us—the place that is created when we focus our intentions and desires on creating our reality. I find her willingness to allow the rest of the subtext to bear on a meal frustrating, yet I am utterly sympathetic to it. We cannot, I know, wait for our lives to accommodate our desires; rather, we must fulfill our desires and accommodate that which we need for and from each other.

It was then my turn to share what I had written:

What: The preparation of meals beginning with the question of who will go to the grocery store and bring the food home.

How things work: I buy the food, then I prepare it. Because there is no help or interest from Erik, I become disinterested. The meals end up being routine, undistinguished. I then end up buying the same things at the store, again and again. I become frustrated with the lack of creativity and interest and I resent cooking, I finally lose interest and just don't want to do it.

Why: I would like the evening meal to be a team effort—a creative event. I would like from Erik a genuine interest in food. I don't want to feel like I am "doing for" Erik but that we are each "doing with." I want the meals to be appreciated genuinely—something that we can both find satisfaction in, but because of Erik's upbringing I know that he will express appreciation whether he likes something or not. I don't trust these expressions because he won't say if he doesn't like something, and then I am left guessing, based on what's left on his plate or in the refrigerator, what he likes and doesn't like. Grocery shopping becomes extremely frustrating because of my unsure knowledge of his tastes. I end up not knowing what to buy and what to avoid. I would much rather he say, "I won't eat this because I don't like it," rather than politely, time and time again, avoiding it silently.

I am also plagued by the concern that the meals I prepare aren't good enough because I do know of his upbringing, so I finally give up and don't even try. His mother took great pains to craft a perfect dinner for the first 16 years of his life. Every evening was an event, and dinners were affairs that went on for hours at a time.

I am also aware that I feel like there is a "right" way to prepare meals and that I feel like I am falling down on the job—that I am failing. I am aware that meals are not important for him, but I feel like it is something I should be attentive to—I feel like it is my role as a "good" wife, but I really would like for it to be a cooperative, collaborative venture.

Good wife, good mother—what does that mean? It is important to me because of where I come from, to have an alive, vibrant, warm home—I see cooking and eating as a part of that—but I don't want to be stuck doing it alone.

Erik asked only one question after I had finished presenting. He wanted to know what I meant by a "collaborative" meal. I explained that I thought perhaps there was a middle road for meal preparation, something other than the two examples he had presented. Maybe one of us might find the perfect tomato or some fresh basil and bring it home because it looked so good, and maybe the two of us could build a meal around that. A meal didn't have to be a presentation that was reflective of the talents and intentions of the cook. It could be a collaboration that emerged from the tastes and interests of those who would be sharing and eating it.

Erik and I then took some time to reflect on the other-knowing presentations. Again, we wrote our answers to the questions from this part of the model. The first set is Erik's answers, and these are followed by my other-knowing reflection:

What did you learn about yourself? I learned that my responses to Vennie's cooking are colored by my experiences as a child—in a home where appreciation of other's efforts was important and almost prompted. I feel sorry for my mother right now. I learned that I can be lazy—easily relaxed into a "provided for" state, yet in this case I am consciously aware of guilt for allowing Vennie of all people to prepare something for me. I don't expect her to do anything that she doesn't want to do.

I wonder why I am still susceptible to double thinking my responses to food— to sustenance. My willingness to admit that something is fulfilling when it is not. Hmmm . . .

Feeling thoughtful, impressed by Vennie's shameless honesty—shameless? Does shame have anything to do with my relationship to food? I was subtly shamed into "feeling" things that I hadn't had time to feel.

What did I learn about myself? I learned that I have issues about what a house should and could be—that I see cooking and eating together as a communal experience that I want everyone to care about and be involved in. To me, it means warmth and vibrancy and home. I learned that doing it by myself does not fulfill this desire because I want us all to be interested—not because we "should" be but because we want to be.

What questions do you have about yourself and others? Why is this such a problem? Why does his disdain for meals cause such a deep emotional reaction from me?

How are you feeling and why? I feel some clarity into my own feelings about meals. I am concerned that some of what I voiced Erik might have found offensive and that when we go into the next round of discussions he may shut down somewhat.

What did I learn? I learned that meals can be fun and interesting and that they don't have to be a chore. As I write this, I am having memories of looking through cookbooks when I was a little girl. I used to look at the pictures of people enjoying each other and the food and I think I really longed to be part of a family like that. Of course, my reality was very different from the posed holidays in the cookbooks.

Differences-Holding

Erik and I moved into the differences-holding stage. We first read that section from the model, and then we read aloud to each other our written reflections. It was obvious to both of us that we had already moved into a deeper level of conversation than just discussing who should buy the groceries and who should cook the chicken.

We realized that we had been brought up with two opposite extremes: he in a very formal, traditional home and myself in a catch-as-catch-can environment. His mother was the "perfect" housewife of the time. She read all the right magazines, and her whole identity was wrapped up in making her home a showplace. The family dressed for dinner, and every night, without exception, she presented to Erik and his father a meal that consisted of several courses.

My mother divorced my father when I was very young, and, as an only child I spent a tremendous amount of time alone. Meals on weeknights were leftovers from the weekend that I reheated and ate alone. My mother, who was building a private practice and had to work late every night, ate when she arrived home at 9:30 p.m. I prepared the plate for her and put it in the oven to warm at 8:45 p.m.

Sundays were a big deal for me as a child because it was then that we would visit my grandmother for lunch. This was always a big and festive affair with several main dishes and many vegetables served in the style that can only be found in the southern United States. I lived from Sunday to Sunday and was always sad at the end of a Sunday afternoon when I realized that a Monday morning was looming, with another repetition of our weekly routine of leftovers.

We also reflected on the differences-holding exercise. For me, it was obvious that the ways that Erik and I had been conditioned to experience mealtimes were very different. He had been showered with presentations and expected to appreciate them. I had been alone, wanting the warmth of the pictures I saw of families in the cookbooks. I realized that, when Erik spoke with such disdain for the way mealtimes were performed in his house, I was actually jealous. I would have loved to experience some of what he had come to feel imprisoned by and hate. This jealousy was my deep emotional response to his apparent apathy for how we now ate.

Erik experienced the difference-holding as being "very powerful." He realized that indeed he was a prisoner of the past when it came to meal planning and was surprised at how quickly the exercises of action and reflection took him to a very deep emotional place. He felt cleansed by the experience of looking so deeply at this issue.

Differences-Transcending

As we moved into the differences-transcending phase of the model, we realized that we didn't have a new and practical plan about how we would approach meal planning. What we had instead was a new way of looking at the whole situation. We both felt like a lot of the air around this issue had been cleared.

We decided to wait until the next day to share our reflections. We wanted to let all of the intense, in-depth work we had done sift and simmer in our mutual consciousnesses. Erik reported feelings of empathy for me and my position. He really liked that we could talk about this calmly and that there was actually something to talk about. He had doubted this when we started. He was genuinely surprised at how quickly work with the SI model had uncovered deeper issues, and he wondered earnestly why he had ended up feeling sorry for his mother. Was this an issue that needed to be explored more deeply? He proposed that we use this model for other issues that may surface between us.

For myself, I too was delighted by the clean nature of this model. There was absolutely no acrimony or need to be right involved in any of our dialogue. I attribute this to the clearly defined parameters we created. We both knew that each would have a chance to speak, so the kinds of interruptions that can lead to destructive tangents were unnecessary. The reminder from the model to "bracket our individual consciousnesses" was instrumental in our being able to listen to the other. We were not asked to forget our own points of view; they were not invalidated just because it was time to listen to the other.

Because of the action and reflection cycles, both of us were able to recognize and share things about ourselves. Rather than reacting from a purely emotional place, for once, I simply noted on paper that I was feeling a strong emotional reaction. That note helped me to pay attention to the emotion, to become a witness to it rather than being driven by it. Rather than feeling accused, which is often the case in a charged, argumentative situation, both of us were left feeling validated. There was now a spark of excitement in each of us about preparing meals together.

I also think that setting aside a specific time to move through the model together did us a world of good. All of our previous discussions about the apparent lack of interest in food had occurred at 5:50 in the evening. At that time, it was just too late. There is a little girl to think of, and we had to eat. As a result, we had never been able to get past the apparent resistance. Finding a nonthreatening time and place to work this issue through was just as important as listening attentively.

Two-Month Check-In

The changes in attitude for both of us around meal preparation are astounding. A major shift has occurred. Erik has engaged in meals with the sort of exuberance that follows relief from strain. He feels as though he has honestly met and discarded a part of his past that was clinging to him and perverting his experience of the present. His discovery, at age 37 years, of the possibilities and joys of food preparation is almost comical.

As for myself, there is no longer any stress or tension around mealtimes, regardless of our eating plans. I am cooking some, and Erik is cooking a lot—wonderful, creative meals. One of my greatest pleasures as a result of this test of the SI model is going to the grocery store with a list that Erik has given me of items to get for the evening meal. What a switch!

8

Synergizing the Mother-Daughter Relationship

Lien Cao

In my first synergic inquiry (SI) class, my final assignment was to find a situation in my life where I could apply SI. The first situation that came to mind was a problem I was having at home with my 17-year-old daughter, Mary, about cleaning up the kitchen. I had tried talking to her many different ways but to no avail. A classmate of mine, Dacy, volunteered to facilitate an SI process for Mary and me. I presented the activity to Mary as an exercise for class, and she agreed to participate. Dacy and I designed the intervention together, specifying the questions and the different steps.

Self-Knowing

For self-knowing, we were to think about the issue of housecleaning and to explore our feelings about it on the visible, logical, and mythical levels. Mary and I agreed to spend time alone to go deeper into ourselves and then return to engage with each other for the next step of the inquiry.

Other-Knowing

After our time alone, we came back together and shared our self-knowing with each other. I started by relating how much the "messy house" situation had affected me at the visible level. Each time I arrived home, the first thing I did was check the kitchen, expecting that it had been messed up. At a deeper level, I discovered something important about myself. It wasn't that I was a cleaning nut but that I had not been a good role model for my daughter when she was younger. Now I was determined to teach her to keep the kitchen clean. That was my goal, and I was obsessed with it. I got angry and complained to my husband in frustration, sometimes even blaming him for the problem, and built up resentment and anger toward Mary.

I reflected on how this issue had cropped up in our life. Mary was about to leave for college, and I felt like I had not taught her the basics of being a self-respecting, independently functioning young woman. I wanted her to be ready to face the world and life outside our home, and I wanted people to respect and accept her. I felt deeply sad and disappointed in myself for not having done enough, not having talked to her enough, or been close enough to her when I still had time. I was not feeling at all like a good mother.

At another level, I was aware of deeper feelings relating to her departure. Mary had just been accepted at an Ivy League school far away from our California home. Although I had agreed to give her every chance for success, my memory was flooded with images of what had happened when I left home for college. My mother had died of cancer while I was away. I had recently had a bout with cancer myself, and I just could not let Mary go. Maybe that was why I was constantly "in her face."

Sharing my own self-knowing was strikingly powerful for all of us. At that time in the session, I choked up and could not continue. My daughter also felt the impact of our exchange, and tears ran down her cheeks. Dacy could not help but cry. We passed the tissue box and stayed with our emotions for our own healing.

Then it was Mary's turn to share her self-knowing. She talked about how I had stressed "education for survival" for so many years and how she had been conditioned to think that academics was the most important thing in life. She had set very high academic goals, and was doing well in school. Now she was suddenly expected to clean up, too. If she agreed to clean up the kitchen, what else would she be expected to do? More chores? Babysit her brother? She felt her parents, who both had professional jobs outside the home, were neglecting her younger brother. It hurt her to see this, but she was not willing to be a parent to him either.

All her friends were looking for what they wanted to be and do in life, discovering the kinds of friends they liked, exploring lifestyles, and trying different career paths. To do this, they needed to hang out, discuss things, and try out new ideas; they didn't have time to stay home cleaning. She usually meant to clean up after cooking a dish or baking a cake. But one of her friends would call, and out she had to go. Mary felt she was at a disadvantage because she was younger and did not have much life experience to report. She was starting to think this exercise was a setup by the adults to get her to agree to clean.

I tried to empty myself to listen to her. I felt that I understood her and mirrored back most of what Mary said. But I noticed that I also resisted showing any agreement. Apparently, I was afraid this would mean that I had conceded my "bottom-line position." Then I remembered that SI requires a flexible attitude open to learning. This reminded me about how the SI process is different from typical conflict resolution processes. In SI, it is not a matter of finding a happy medium but a matter of seeking out each person's viewpoint and letting the other in and becoming the habitat for another person without dissolving that person, so both can be maximally transformed. This is how I dealt with my habitual response to conflict and maintained the attitude that SI requires. When it got late, Dacy suggested we all think about this more and come back another day.

Differences-Holding

At our next session, it was clear to me that the problem of cleaning was just the tip of the iceberg. The air had been cleared, and Mary and I could now go deeper. To promote learning and hold our differences together, I suggested that we explore our beliefs about the developmental tasks of a teenager. This helped us bring more of our differences into our exchanges.

I was born in Asia and was raised with strong traditional family values. The purpose of raising a child was to develop a self-in-group, a person whose sense of self was derived from her capacity to live harmoniously in a group and whose value and norms were sanctioned by the group. The task of the teenager, as she prepared to leave the home and represent her family and community, was to stay close to her elders and to learn the subtle codes of conduct that are ascribed by roles and status. In my view, Mary would demonstrate her maturity by abiding by those rules. Independence did not mean separation; it meant acquiring skills that allowed her to become autonomous, to contribute, and to return gratitude to her family and society.

Mary was born and raised in the West. Like her peers, she had been encouraged by Western society to become independent, to separate and individuate as soon as possible. The task for her was to know herself, independent of family and community, to develop a critical mind, and to take a critical stance toward established rules and roles. She needed to discover her truth from her own experiences, without the influence of authority figures. In short, Mary's development followed the basic individuation principle that underlies Western psychology, guided by the ultimate goal of individual independence and freedom.

These were two completely different, at times opposite, life tasks and experiences. We had to be cautious in looking at each other through the other's lens. We both tried to recognize each other's life experience in its entirety and in its own right and tried to imagine growing up in one culture, then in the other. It was easier for me to hold two sets of values in true equality because I had lived in both cultures, but Mary tried hard to also hold both views. After a while, she said that she was no longer interested in this activity, and we stopped the process.

Differences-Transcending

After Dacy left, Mary asked me for the first time in a long time if I would go for a walk with her. This was very significant to me. I was very touched and delightedly agreed to go. As we walked in the neighborhood, enjoying the flowers and the cool breeze, Mary put her arm through mine, a gesture we never used in our family. We did not talk, but I felt very close to her and realized that this sense of closeness had been my real need behind all the conflict. The problem had disappeared for me, and I was no longer attached to seeing Mary clean up the kitchen. We were at another place in our relationship.

Mary left for college, and we talked by e-mail every day. She was sharing a suite in the dorm with three nice girls. One of them, Olga, was very naturally neat and organized, but the other three had no aesthetic sense of orderliness. One day Mary called me on the phone to let me know that Olga had called a meeting. She had taken everyone to dinner and reported that she could not continue living with them if the other girls did not commit to cleanup. It had been an emotional conversation with some initial blaming and an intense moment. Deeply affected, the other two girls started crying. "What happened to you?" I asked Mary.

She responded, "Oh, didn't I tell you? I have become the cleaning lady in the suite!" Excited and curious I asked how that had happened. Mary responded that she cleaned up because she respected Olga's needs. I was overwhelmed with joy. Flashes of our synergy session came back to me, and I realized that Mary had gotten a lot more from that experience than I had ever imagined.

9

Developing a Community
Through Synergic Envisioning

Elisa Sabatini

In December 1996, six other people and myself gathered in Blacksburg, Virginia, to explore the possibility of developing an alternative community. We were seeking a way to live in greater harmony with nature and spirit. This idea had been developing for a year when five of us participated in a synergic inquiry (SI) project in India.

That SI project took place in the community of Auroville, where people from 37 nations live with the intention of being part of a global transforming force of humanity by seeking the unity of human consciousness. The five of us were profoundly affected by our experiences in Auroville. After returning to the United States, we were confronted with such culture shock that we began to make significant changes in our lives.

This group continued to be woven together by shared experience. We came together on several occasions during the year, including a spring journey when our spouses joined us on a trip to Central America. There we put into writing our desire, as a group, to change our way of living. This took the form of a simple vision statement. During the process of writing this statement, the dream emerged of forming a community that truly cared for the welfare of all.

All of us participated in developing the clear purpose, mission, and objectives of this vision and felt ownership of both the idea and purpose. As we came together in Blacksburg, however, we felt tension among us. This tension emerged when it became clear that each person in the group held a somewhat different idea about where to locate our envisioned community and when to start buying property for it. At that time, no decision had been made as to location, but several sites had been visited. Some in the group expected immediate agreement to buy land in a specific place. Others weren't quite ready to make such a major decision. These differences seemed to overshadow the greater ideals for forming the community.

The vision we had so carefully crafted was not strong enough to overcome this tension, and we could not move forward. We needed to find common ground before investing more emotional energy in this dream—let alone the funds to purchase a piece of property. But how could we find common ground without understanding much more clearly each member's position, personal motivation, and personal life situation in relation to our dream?

To put it simply, we were stuck and unable to move forward with our dream. This case study briefly describes how we used SI to move through our stuckness to build a stronger shared vision and the impact this had on us both individually and as a community. This case was documented 1 year after the 1996 meeting and includes interviews to reflect on and capture the SI experience.

The SI Application

Those of us who had participated in the synergy project in India felt that SI could help us discern the differences that blocked us and allow us to move forward. We began with a question about the intention of this new community and identified the following questions for individual reflection: What kind of community do I want to create? How do I want to do it? Why do I want to do it?

Self-Knowing

To do self-knowing, we decided to use an individual reflection that would eventually be expressed in the form of a personal mandala (a traditional spiritual art form, usually made in a circle to symbolize the unity of life). The mandalas we created had five parts to them. Four were sections around the outer part of the circle that consisted of questions: Where am I now? What do I want to create? How do I want to do it? Why do I want to do it? At the center of our mandala, we each symbolized the higher purpose of the community as we envisioned it. Each participant had a large sheet of newsprint and crayons, pastels, and markers to work with, as well as representatives of nature that had been gathered from the garden for constructing the symbols and drawings of our mandalas.

Before starting this process of individual differentiation, we gathered as a group to focus ourselves on this task and to share our recent experiences. This took the whole morning. The afternoon was used to create our mandalas. This work felt sacred, and the process of working quietly to create our own mandala brought a sense of harmony to each of us.

Other-Knowing

To engage in other-knowing, we sat in a large circle in the living room and shared our mandalas with each other. Each person was given as much time as they wanted to present his or her mandala and explain it to the others. All listeners were encouraged to ask clarifying questions but to withhold any judgment on what was presented. This experience of creating a mandala to develop and express a personal vision about community was powerful. A year later, the following comments were collected from participants:

Working on our mandalas forced me to reflect on what was really important to me. We could only use crayons and were supposed to draw symbols. It was difficult at first, but then I found that I shifted into another kind of mind, and the time flew by. When the time was up, I looked at what I had drawn and was amazed at the clarity of my vision about community and why it was so important to me. Later in the synergy process, it gave me a vehicle to share my deepest thoughts with others. The pictures spoke for themselves and prompted me in sharing my personal feelings. One of the most significant aspects of the drawing was the center, or my purpose in life. Here I found a bright sun with rays radiating out and piercing through all the sections of the mandala. I felt like another person analyzing the finished mandala. It was as if I were looking at what another part of me had done. I realized how my desire for community was another step in my spiritual quest for unity with the Divine.

I think the mandala was helpful for me. It served as a security blanket, it made sense, and it expressed how others and I were feeling. I think it brought out the truth, even in families. I liked that clarifying. I could see where each person was coming from, and I could accept it. There is no right way to do anything. We all grow by doing this.

The mandala has always been a motivating element for me. I still carry elements of the mandala with me.

I don't remember my mandala. I can remember others' clearer than I can remember my own. I found it hard to make it more concrete. Mine was more abstract. It is like the writer's block on a blank page. I have the artist expectation of creating something beautiful, not necessarily concrete. The difficulty in doing it was a learning experience about self.

The time to do the mandala seemed short. Presenting our individual mandalas to others was a very revealing process of each individual's inner beauty.

The mandalas were a way to speak the truth. The people in the group had more of a tendency to hold back from expressing deep emotion. The mandala created a way to communicate.

Differences-Holding

For differences-holding, we were asked to walk around the room alone and concentrate on each mandala as we came to it. We were to try to hold each one as our own and to observe the feelings that arose when we did this. In this way, we could experience others' perspectives and learn to hold all of them within our own consciousness. Our feelings were then shared.

To enhance the process of holding differences, we held dialogues in pairs, and each of us tried to restate the other person's perspective. This process required reflection and questioning to gain a deeper understanding of the other person. This exercise provided an important step to help us develop a shared perspective.

The differing viewpoints were revealing. The members of the family who lived in Blacksburg had become very clear about their intention to remain in that location. Others in the group gained new insights into these deep feelings and the reasons behind them. One member of this family was torn between the power of the vision to create a new community and honoring the needs and desires of his family to remain in that place.

Another couple was by now fully committed to finding a place and beginning to build the new community. For them it was a calling from God, and they felt a need to make a leap of faith and to act on this calling. The specific place was not that important to them, but the timing was. Another couple also saw this as a Divine calling, and they too were ready to move forward.

I felt a strong desire to be in community with these people, but ongoing work in international locations needed to be completed first. This process helped me see where I was and the role I could play in the formation of our community. However, I knew that it would be some time before I could make any commitment to actually live in a new place. In all cases, there was a deeper acceptance and understanding of each person in the group.

The differences-holding experience had a lasting impact on the participants, and the following statements were made during a recent interview:

I felt I could hold the differences and be comfortable with it, but I was sad, and I still wanted others to be in the same place I was. Now a year later we have all moved forward in diverse ways. Now I feel supported and united.

I was making assumptions about everyone, so the clarification helped me accept the differences. You could then go past the differences. The relationship was no longer about the differences, and they were no longer irreconcilable. Conflicts were diffused. The process was not arguing with one another or to convert but to fully share of self with expanded awareness and consciousness.

When we could spend enough time on the differences, the process kept us in it long enough that we arrived at a place of acceptance. The idea was not to judge or change the other person or come to a common denominator solution. Taking the time on this was very important. We often try to hide differences, put them aside to move forward, bury them. When differences are not spoken, there is no place to go. In the process, it is safe for them to come out.

I remember trying to reach out and diffuse the differences. I saw others being able to live in this tension. Things don't have to be my way. It was a real lesson. You have to honor people's positions.

Differences-Transcending

As we engaged in differences-transcending, it became clear that even though we all shared the same ideals, we had different constraints and different views about when or how to contribute to this project. There was consensus about searching for property initially in the southeastern part of the United States in or near the Appalachian Mountains. We realized that, when the community began, some of us would have to remain in different locations with the possibility of joining up later as personal circumstances changed. This gave these members freedom to participate without feeling they would have to give up what they held to be critical to their current situation and needs. The group was now free to move forward.

Shortly thereafter, the group purchased 210 acres in South Carolina. By June 1997, four members were in residence and beginning to carry out the mission and objectives that the group had developed. In July, we assembled as a group at the new site and made a personal commitment to the development of the community. Since then all have contributed in some significant way to the development of this community, even though not all were in residence at this early stage.

When asked what was helpful in the SI process and why it was important for them, participants commented as follows:

Not only did the clarification of others' perspectives happen, but I clarified my own. The process allowed real deliberate time for that. In many meetings, some speak, others do not—with the synergy process this was the purpose. You really got to see where each of the people was coming from. Before that process, I may have assumed what each person meant, but with the process, the extended time, things were brought more into view.

It led to the group taking the next step. It has formed and shaped the direction of the group. The underlying tension was dealt with, and we moved on.

Coming to clarity on the group was key. At the beginning, I was feeling that we all spent time and energy, and they seemed to be off doing something else. I began the experience with a complete lack of understanding of the motivations of others. It was revealing that everyone held very individual positions. It freed up energy to move forward. There was always a reason prior to the process of why we could not move forward.

It took a lot of time, and it accomplished a lot. It was in a nonlinear way. The process was more holistic. It seemed to bring in all the appropriate issues.

I felt so certain that we should move forward from my perspective at that moment. My heart would have hurt if we had just gone ahead and left others in the group by going our separate ways. Now we can stay in relationship.

The most important thing to me was the deepening of the relationships. It led to this group staying together in a new form. The synergy let me hold open the chance that community initiatives could emerge in various places across the country with a similar spirit.

Conclusion

The importance of the synergy process in this case was its capacity to remove tensions that potentially kept the project from realizing its vision. The SI process did not bring everyone to the same place; instead, it legitimized the position of each person at that moment so that the differing needs could be properly considered in future decisions. SI did not transform in the sense of generating new ideas; rather, it opened a space for greater love and trust in each other.

10

Using Synergic Inquiry to Resolve a Group Conflict

Lien Cao

I am part of a group of 11 adults involved in a doctoral program titled "Learning and Change in Human Systems." This program is based on a cohort model in which we use the text of our own group life to learn about transformative change and the ways to midwife change in the world.

We had just completed 1 year of study together and were planning the 2nd-year program with a weeklong intensive session. As the meetings approached, I had much anxiety about dividing the larger group into small study groups. Because the program was designed in such a way that the whole group met face to face only once a month, many class discussions and assignment preparations were expected to be done in the small groups.

The previous year, in our first experience of study-group formation, intense interpersonal conflicts erupted, revealing strong incompatibilities in working styles. One problematic issue was that, after only a few days of group interaction, one group of women wanted to form a study group without other members of the cohort. This decision was met with discomfort and resistance from the rest of the group, but these women felt strongly about staying together. After much discussion and after trying out different configurations for study groups and brainstorming on strategies, these women stuck with their initial decision, and the rest of the students agreed to divide into two other study groups.

By the end of the 1st year of course work, each study group was responsible for delivering one section of a group research project. At the last class meeting, two of the study groups brought papers, but the women in the group described earlier did not complete their portion of the study. They had discovered that they could not continue to work together and had been planning to change study partners at this meeting. This came as quite a surprise to the other two groups, who had finally adjusted to the working styles of their group members and did not want to change study group configurations.

My classmates and the professor in charge asked me to teach synergic inquiry (SI). Because the 2-day class had gone well and all participants were excited about the method, we agreed to apply the SI process to the issue of forming study groups. In consultation with our faculty advisor, I was asked to design the process and focus question. Because I would also participate, I asked a faculty advisor to help facilitate when needed. As a result, I became both a facilitator and a participant.

Self-Knowing

I was aware of how much apprehension and anticipation of conflict and tension there had been during the informal discussions about study group formation. I was also aware of the different strategies that we had tried the previous year and how all our efforts ended in more intense, conflicted situations. We needed to design a focus question that could contribute to building a safe container for the group, one that would allow strong emotions to be expressed in responsible and respectful ways and that would move the initial focus from the concrete final configurations to each person's sense of vulnerability and deepest needs.

I discussed my concerns with our advisor, and we began to coexplore some of the possible questions to deepen self-knowing. We decided to explore the feelings, thoughts, and beliefs each person brought to the cohort as we approached the study-group formation. With this focus, attention could shift from people trying make sure they did not "lose out" in the process and lose their "individual rights." We worked on the focus question individually overnight and returned the following day prepared for other-knowing.

Other-Knowing

We started the day with a group meditation. Then we agreed that after each person shared his or her self-knowing, we would reflect back with firm discipline what we had heard so we could truly embody all that was expressed.

We also agreed to hold each sharing mindfully and to make a special place in our hearts for the person who was sharing. A lot of deep and heavy feelings were uncovered, ranging from anger, frustration, resentment, and disappointment to fear of being picked last, fear of not having done one's share, fear of being blamed, and so forth. There were hidden and overt issues of control, fairness, personality, and working styles. We listened to each other reverently.

We agreed to empty ourselves of our own knowledge and issues while listening to others. However, this was not easy. We had spent lifetimes developing our personal lenses to make sense of the world. Our challenge was to hold these lenses so lightly that we could let in new information that did not fit in the frameworks created by these lenses. At times, we slipped into feelings these lenses created, disagreeing with a viewpoint or discussing an issue instead of undertaking deep listening on a viewpoint. Each time we helped each other by identifying those moments for what they were and getting back to deep listening.

Once, after a man shared deep feelings of discomfort and frustration, a woman comforted him instead of reflecting him. When it was pointed out that she was trying to make him feel better instead of reflecting his feelings, she realized in a flash that her feedback was a form of judgment. Later, she commented that becoming aware of a deep pattern within her was a breakthrough moment, and she shared her total appreciation for the opportunity for self-correction and profound learning.

Another person commented that the process helped "surface some very personal life issues around fully 'belonging' in a group." She said:

> I imagined that interpersonal challenge and confrontation would be necessary to break through the dynamics that had led me to pull back, and it was something I was not looking forward to. I was surprised to find that, instead, the synergy work helped to simply dissolve some of the emotions that held me back, and I naturally felt myself belonging more.

Another commented later:

> The other-knowing that we did as a group was incredibly powerful as it opened my heart and allowed me to see each of you as incredibly precious and achingly vulnerable. I couldn't help but feel tremendous love for all of you.

The process of other-knowing took longer than expected; we needed more than 6 hours to deeply listen to and reflect on the views of nine people. However, at the end of the self-knowing and other-knowing steps, the group moved to a different place. Interpersonal conflicts were melting and deep compassion emerged as the overall feeling within the group.

Differences-Holding

We took a short break to reflect on how much had happened in those 6 hours. We felt that the other-knowing step had been so deep that people were no longer attached to any specific configuration for study groups. We started to talk about the differences we held regarding our needs in study groups and to brainstorm about the different types of study groups we might have. Against the backdrop of the deep sharing that had taken place, each idea that was put out was considered reverently. Instead of being intellectually debated, it was probed for the deeper personal need it represented. Those who had expressed discomfort in the self-knowing phase checked out each item of discussion, each movement toward decision. There was not a single major issue that could not be worked out.

Differences-Transcending

Eventually the logistics of study-group meetings seemed to emerge as the most important consideration for good functioning of the groups. Because four people were only available on weekends and the other five preferred to study together on workdays, two groups formed naturally and easily. We gathered in our new group configurations to "feel" them out. Because I had been one who did not want to change study partners, I noticed that, although I was satisfied with the new group configuration and felt that it was workable for me, there was still inside of me a little attachment to the old group and a resistance to change. Someone in my new group recognized that I needed to express my grief for the dissolution of the old group. With that I was able to let go and become fully involved in starting over with my new study partners.

After psychological reorientation to the newness of the configuration, everyone expressed satisfaction and hope that these groups would work out. Enthusiasm was felt throughout the class for having accomplished a major cooperative effort with such success. One person commented in her reflection paper, "I felt real excitement in the way we fell into our study group formation." We had completed our task on time. Moreover, we had started our 2nd year with an incredibly collaborative group experience.

11

Synergic Inquiry in Action: The Expansion of Racial Consciousness

Carole Barlas, Angela Cherry-Smith,
Penny Rosenwasser, and Colette Winlock

W e are four female doctoral students, two Black—Angela Cherry-Smith and Colette Winlock—and two White—Carole Barlas and Penny Rosenwasser. We were part of a cohort of 19 doctoral students in the School of Transformative Learning, California Institute of Integral Studies, San Francisco. Our field of study is learning and change in human systems, where we work at the individual, group, and community levels to understand how people learn and how systems change. This is a case study of our cohort's participation in an intensive 6-month process of synergic inquiry (SI) about racial consciousness.

As authors, we are both the researchers and the researched; we participate in exploring ourselves as part of the dialectic of self-knowing and other-knowing at the same time as we explore our entire cohort's SI process. In writing this case study, we continued to move through cycles of action and reflection, of self-knowing, other-knowing, difference-holding, and difference-transcending. Our data sources are our collective memories, individual reflection papers, team reflection papers, e-mail communications, and videos documenting the cohort process.

This case study is an example of the application of SI at the group level. It is told through our collaborative lens. Along with describing our SI experiences, we attempt to share our changing racial consciousness as we experienced it during the inquiry process.

Project Context

Cohort 5 is the formal name for our learning group, which consisted of six Black (5 women and 1 man) and 12 Whites (9 women and 3 men), and 1 Israeli woman. Two of the White women and the Israeli woman are Ashkenazi Jews. We ranged in age from 36 years to 58 years and have a variety of spiritual and religious practices and sexual orientations. We originate from all over the United States, except for the one citizen of Israel; currently, one of us lives in Wisconsin, one lives in Montana, and the rest live in the San Francisco Bay area. Almost all of us identify as middle class.

Our racial diversity caused tension and conflict among some of the members in the cohort. One of the White members vividly remembers that first sunny August morning when 24 of us first met with our faculty as an incoming class of doctoral students:

> I remember walking in from the parking lot toward the church in Mill Valley and noticing four African American women getting out of a car, chatting with each other. I felt excited that they would be part of my class. Once inside the room they sat together down the circle from me. I felt my desire to connect with them—as well as my envy of what seemed to be their connection to each other. I also scanned the circle, mentally counting how many of the rest of us I assumed were White and how many were people of color.

Some of us remember comments that first day about issues of race and racism, about the suggestion of diversity training for the cohort. By the end of our 1st week together, small explosions were already beginning to erupt, some in response to diversity exercises but most in response to the formation of our study groups. Although there were two other Blacks in the cohort, a group of four Black women had chosen to study in a group together with one White, Jewish woman. Many other White people in the cohort objected because, as one put it, "there are enough people of color for one each to be in six or seven small groups of White people!"

Thus, study group formation became the first critical incident to reveal our varying levels of racial consciousness—White and Black. Another example of these disparities is how most of the White students in the cohort missed the significance of the Million Man March to the Black community and the Black students in the cohort. Discussion about this upcoming historical event revealed Black students' fears for the safety of the men attending the march and White students' failure to understand this fear. Racial consciousness also came up as we expressed responses to the curriculum, noticed different styles of learning, and expressed differences in epistemologies. The Whites lacked depth in knowing about the values and beliefs underlying the racial consciousness of the Blacks in the cohort; that is, they had little other-knowing.

We continued to wrestle with issues of cultural differences and power imbalances for the next 18 months and eventually decided that we would use the SI framework to focus on exploring more deeply the racial tensions in our cohort. For the previous 18 months, we had experienced 2 weeklong intensives and 16 three-day intensive weekends. As individuals and as a learning community, we had gone through a transformative learning process: We had deeply examined and changed some of our underlying assumptions about ourselves and each other, as Black and as White.

Using SI to engage with racial differences allowed us to learn new awareness and to expand our capacities for consciousness. Our individual lives and our group life have been enriched with new meaning. What have we learned, what awareness and capacities have we developed, and how do we take our learning into the world? The Black and White teams each surfaced deeply held myths and beliefs that shaped our unique consciousnesses.

Design Process and Implementation

Six members of the cohort had previous experience with SI through projects in China and India, and they were recruited by Dr. Tang to form the SI design team. This team was initially made up of three Blacks and three Whites. Throughout our 6-month process, other cohort members also participated as members of the design team. Before each cohort session, the team met with Dr. Tang to discuss the next stage of work and how to facilitate a learning process. This often meant designing strategies and experiential exercises to help us embody the SI process.

The process can be briefly described as follows. We collectively decided to differentiate the whole cohort into two teams—a Black team and a White team. Both teams engaged in an intraracial synergy cycle to come up with a collective self-knowing about their racial consciousness. Then, we had an intense interracial synergy cycle through which we learned about each other's racial consciousnesses. During the interracial synergy cycle we also continued the learning processes at the subteam level so that two levels of synergic learning were occurring at the same time. During the 6-month SI process, the Black and White teams also met for extended periods of time between the monthly intensive weekends. Sometimes our professors, Dr. Yongming Tang and Dr. Elizabeth Kasl, participated in these meetings as well.

Intraracial Synergy Cycle

The initial differentiation process between the Black team and the White team helped surface hidden differences between them. At the beginning of the subteam process, some White team members openly questioned the necessity of separating into two teams, and others said that they missed the Black folks' presence. Black team members felt differently. Colette and Angela made the following comment:

> In contrast, we found that we welcomed the opportunity to share our experience with each other without the presence of the White members of the cohort. As Black people living in a dominant White culture and often feeling constrained by an oppressive society, we found relief in having the opportunity and space to express ourselves authentically with one another. Our richest experiences of expanded consciousness resulted from exploring the differences between ourselves as Black people.

White Team: Self-Knowing and Other-Knowing

We were at 13 different levels of racial consciousness. Our first experience of White team self-knowing qualitatively accelerated our individual awareness about what it meant to be White. To begin the intraracial synergy experience, each of the White team members prepared a story about herself or himself. Other-knowing involved telling each other our individual life stories and sharing different oppressions or pains we had experienced in our lives, including issues of gender, class, sexual orientation, anti-Semitism, and spirituality.

This sharing, accompanied by deep listening, created a rarefied atmosphere, or sacred space, as we came to name it, leading us to deeper connection with each other. It helped us value ourselves through the act of sharing and being heard. We began to learn about each other, thus experiencing other-knowing while doing self-knowing. The flow and relationship between self-knowing and other-knowing began the process of our expanding consciousnesses as individuals and as a White group. Penny observed, "We as a White team have a family history now."

In sharing our stories, we noted the diversity of our experiences as Whites. This was a different experience from anything we had done before in the cohort. By framing our various perspectives in the synergy language of "differences," we began to hold all of these, without judging some as "right" and others as "wrong," to value a "both-and" rather than an "either-or" way of thinking. Holding multiple perspectives was one of the major learning themes of our inquiry.

Penny expressed her experience of this process as feeling "more expansive, less reactive, less of a need to convince others of my point of view as long as they hear me. . . . I rock and roll between new and old perspectives in a creative-tension boogies." She felt herself begin to embody a change in consciousness, of holding new awareness:

> Another part of my shell is cracking. . . . I am learning to live more in color than black and white, moving between fixed and transforming, embracing questions and living into answers: uncomfortable, but wide open and present and very alive.

An example of differences in White and Black consciousnesses was illustrated during this period in a critical incident. Carole and Penny wrote:

> We were meeting in two separate teams, and the White team was intensely engaged in a process of trying to hold differing perspectives between us. Between the tension and the tears, those of us cofacilitating from the design team realized we needed more time and asked the White team for agreement to revamp the schedule. We sent Carole to tell the Black team about our decision to reschedule the remainder of the day.
>
> After lunch, when we reconvened as a cohort, Taj (from the Black team) quietly mentioned noticing that the White group had taken it upon themselves to change the day's schedule without consulting a third of the cohort: the Black team. Many of us on the White team then realized how we had just behaved in a way that showed our embeddedness in dominant (i.e., White middle-class) group thinking, in taking it upon ourselves to make a decision for the whole cohort. We had felt entitled to change the structure—whereas the Black team was striving to work within the structure.
>
> This was a powerful moment of revelation and self-knowing for many of us on the White team, as we acknowledged that as a dominant group we are oblivious to our dominant consciousness. Yet we force those groups that we marginalize or oppress to take on an oppressed, marginalized consciousness.

Black Team: Self-Knowing

Our first meeting as the Black team began with a combination of excitement and fear. Our team consisted of Angela, Bola, Colette, Earthlyn, Lewis, and Taj. Entering the self-knowing phase would bring challenges to our perceptions of each other and possibly point out our major differences, a fear we would learn later to be part of our racial consciousness. As "the" Black students in the program, we already knew we were an identifiable group. The SI process was going to make legitimate our need and desire to be together without the presence and influence of our White classmates.

Comments made by members of the Black team during that first meeting ranged from "Hey, this is all right" to "What a treat, now we can stop explaining ourselves." Someone asked, "Are you sure they can't hear us?" a reference made to the presence of the White team only a few yards away. We even joked about being careful so they would not think we were revolting or conspiring. We were both excited to be together and fearful of what would be projected on us.

This first cycle of intrateam self-knowing gave us a chance to share our unique experiences with each other and was a rare opportunity that we looked forward to. In mixed cultural groupings, particularly in the educational system, Black people getting together by themselves during class time is almost unheard of. SI provided us the space to explore our sameness and our differences. We were all Black and comfortable identifying as Blacks, with common sociopolitical and cultural experiences, but it was also evident there were threads of difference running through the group.

We were different from each other, and it was important to claim this difference in developing a racial consciousness for the team. Our differences were visible in our mannerisms, cultural expressions, and even dress and hairstyles. Historically, for survival, we had been taught to reduce our differences, so we found ourselves wondering if, in examining our differences, our unity would weaken.

To begin the SI process, we had to give permission for each of us to differentiate from the group. We needed assurance that being different would not provoke the stigma of "not being Black enough," and we all wanted to learn how to embrace difference as a strength. To accomplish this, we began listing the ways in which a Black person could be different from another Black person. Our actions did not represent the views of all Black folks, although some things we shared could be generalized to other Black people.

We noted that even in naming our differences we still moved in community; we were doing it together. We came up with 21 differences we believed influenced our individual consciousness as a Black person. Since meeting as a cohort some of our differences had surfaced, so many were already in the forefront and visible realm of our consciousness. The kinds of differences included class orientation, shade of skin color, sexual orientation, gender, upbringing (in Black or White neighborhoods), and attendance at Black or White schools. We also looked at where we grew up—in the South or the North—our religious preferences, whether we had a single-parent or two-parent rearing, our age and level of involvement with the civil rights movement and Black liberation, the number of people in our families and our birth order, the music we listened to, and even our experiences with interracial dating.

One of our team members reflected that she didn't realize how different we all were from each other until then. She remarked, "You know I'm a Southerner and for us, all Black folks are alike." Another shared how she could identify with many things that we had listed, but there were a few that for her made up what she called her primary consciousness and identification as a Black person. With that comment everyone began talking about the primary consciousness that they identified with and that shaped their movement in the world. During this process, we began to move past the visible skin identification that linked us to our consciousness as Black people and to share some aspects of ourselves that were not visible. We started to share our epistemologies and the individual assumptions that represent the logical dimension in Vachon's model of consciousness.

We went deeper into our individual self-knowing through the process of intrateam other-knowing. In the context of SI, we were able to look at each other sometimes as an other and sometimes as the same. Throughout this process, our reflections centered on what was involved in holding these two states of consciousness. The real excitement of SI was the opportunity to hear each other's stories. In the Black community, "who you be" is important for establishing relationships. We all knew something about each other, but we didn't really know our stories.

Telling our stories served multiple purposes. Self-knowing occurred with the storyteller and other-knowing with the listeners, who also cycled into self-knowing as they reflected on their reactions to the content of the story. This means that we learned more about ourselves by noticing our reactions to each other's stories. Storytellers went deeper in self-knowing as they reflected on how they reacted to others' reactions.

Storytelling was a critical process in getting to the racial consciousness of our team. We began our stories in the cramped foyer of the classroom where we met for the cohort weekend intensives. Our environment became a metaphor for how we felt trying to tell our stories. We felt restricted from giving full expression because we feared causing too much commotion or being overheard; the call and response we all were familiar with was tepid. The environment reinforced our feelings of oppression and our constant watch for how our other (White people) might react to our behavior. We were unable to complete all the stories during this weekend, so we agreed to meet at someone's home to finish this portion of the process.

Meeting in a home was a qualitatively different experience: the food, the ambiance, the reflection of our culture while we sat in a circle created the feeling that we were now in sacred space. The fear of having our space invaded had dropped away, and many of us felt a sense of relief that our stories would be told in a safer and more personal environment. We were doing something much more than a school assignment; we were exploring our relationships with each other as Black people. Although this was exciting, it was also scary and brought up many fears about becoming too vulnerable to each other.

One of our team members feared telling her story because she felt afraid of rejection; she believed somehow her story would validate that she was not the right kind of Black person or that her experiences were outside what some call the Black experience. Angela shared her fear very poignantly when she said, "White people can hurt your feelings, but Black people can break your heart." We shared how differentiation was scary and felt dangerous. For survival reasons, Black people have had to stick together; racism created the need to unify. In telling our stories, we were removing the assumption, maybe even the facade, that we were together. We were revealing that in our consciousness we held the fear of rejection. This is how someone's self-knowing could stimulate cycles within cycles of self-knowing by other group members. After discussion, the team member continued with her story. The outcome of that cycle of action and reflection enabled us to listen to each other's stories with even greater compassion and empathy for how difficult a process this was.

Often in telling our stories, it surfaced that someone in the group represented an other to someone else and symbolized the type of Black person who had persecuted them for being different. This created tensions and moments of anxiety within the group, as we watched the two individuals involved in conflict try to work with their feelings and frustrations. In these moments the SI process was invaluable because it gave us a language and way of explaining what was going on. Angela recalled a particular incident that illustrates this dynamic:

> During a Friday night meeting at a team member's home, a critical incident occurred that spurred me on to deeper Self-Knowing and helped the group in holding differences. The atmosphere was to me a typical Friday night for many African Americans, with libations, soul food, and music being offered up by the hostess. The warm environment helped to set a mellow tone for our togetherness. There were personal effects of childhood pictures and other African American art.
>
> However, the atmosphere began to take on a new tone when the issue of classism surfaced. This once mellow and comfortable atmosphere began to turn into a tense setting involving myself and another team member. As we engaged in the dialogue process, I felt my palms grow sweaty and my face glow in a heat of redness when she revealed some of her negative experiences of being rejected by the upper middle-class Blacks in her community growing up. She commented, "It's because of people like you that I am the way that I am!"
>
> As she continued to give example after example, I didn't fully understand her reasoning. I began to feel myself become defensive. I responded to how her

experiences of rejection were not representative of how I interacted with others in my community who were not from the same socioeconomic background as me. I wanted her to know that members in my community, in spite of socioeconomic differences, embraced each other from our need for survival against racism. She said how she was afraid to trust people who represented the upper and middle class.

As she shared her experiences of rejection, I began to feel disconnected from her because of our differences. I was taking her experiences personally, although I was not personally involved. Using the cultural synergy process, I recognized that Taj was sharing her Self-Knowing and that her knowing did not have to be my knowing. Personally, I am not responsible for the negative actions of others in my same social class. I used the process to hold the differences that we had and tried to put myself in Taj's place to understand what she was feeling. We had a container where we could creatively hold the tension we were experiencing caused by our differences.

This narrative gives an example of our Difference-Holding processes and the depths to which we engaged in looking at our racial consciousness. We developed a racial consciousness that reflected all of our beliefs. It had at least four parts that we termed Elements of a Long Note, a phrase from a one-woman play titled *Twilight,* by Anna Deaveare Smith. Ms. Smith portrays Cornel West in a monologue about the suffering of Black people and how we are always holding the long note; we can withstand pain and suffering for a long period of time.

As a subteam, we felt the long note. Our collective consciousness was steeped with pain, fear, intrusion, and a host of suffering. A Black woman wrote about how the elements of a long note represented our collaborative view of Black consciousness as we interpret it from our experiences and personal histories in the United States. We agreed that it wasn't easy being a Black person in this country, and the consciousness we identified through many cycles of Self-Knowing and Other-Knowing reflected this uneasiness. The elements of the long note we surfaced in this differentiation phase of the inquiry process are as follows:

1. Consciousness of Harmony: We belong together

2. Oppositional Consciousness: Living in two worlds; holding opposing thoughts simultaneously

3. Consciousness of Other-Knowing: Priority of other-knowing over self-knowing for our survival

4. Fear-Based Consciousness: Our legacy of rejection and survival

These four elements reflected what we saw as our Black subteam racial consciousness and what we would present to the White team during the integration phase. We looked at this next step with some trepidation because it required us to reveal our thoughts to the White team, a group representative of the enemy, and allow ourselves to become vulnerable to them. Even though SI creates a process where opposing groups can meet in a respectful and safe space, we were still doubtful that this would happen.

Interracial Synergy Cycle

At the end of the intraracial synergy cycle, the Black team wrote a single essay documenting the various levels of their Black consciousness and including the significant points of commonality and differences between them. In contrast, the White team chose to submit 13 individual essays about their consciousnesses. The essays were exchanged between the two teams, which helped each team to have some initial conceptual other-knowing about each other's work on racial consciousness.

The next step in engaging other-knowing at the whole-team level was for both teams to meet to witness presentations of each other's racial consciousness. Penny remembers when the design team was trying to decide whether the Black team or White team should go first:

> I suggested, "Since White people have the institutional power in this society and tend to control the agenda, why doesn't the Black team go first, in an effort to change the power imbalance?" Taj gently responded, "I don't want to use the 'R' word [racism], but don't you see how, by doing that, you're still holding on to the power and control, by you deciding we should go first?" I literally felt my head open up, as I felt the truth of Taj's words. I experienced other-knowing in terms of her reality and also learned more of my own self-knowing.

White Team's Presentation of Self-Knowing to the Black Team

We decided to enact our individual consciousnesses as a White team to demonstrate who we are as a team. We found ourselves shuffling slowly in 13 different directions and yelling out, "I want it my way, my way!" and "You're doing it wrong!" This accelerated to a chaotic bumping into each other, hurling reams of white crepe paper around each other to pull each other in and shove another away and grasping White cardboard body parts with words printed on them like "Conformity," "Individualism," "Loneliness," and "Alienation." We were fighting, hugging, veering off alone.

At the completion of this presentation, we sat in a circle as a White team to reflect about our enactment. Many of us expressed feeling isolated and disconnected as White people. We discovered a deeper level of self-knowing that we desperately wanted connection and despaired that we did not know how to "do it." We saw how we feared being unliked, being judged, and we learned how this fear keeps us from reaching through and creating the strong connections we yearn for. For us, the self-knowing process was one of unraveling and of evolving consciousness. Carole expressed it metaphorically as when one veil is lifted and another veil is revealed: "And in the process, making our consciousness a little less opaque. . . . We are souls searching for wholeness, and it is a messy business."

Black Team's Reflection of the White Team's Presentation

As a Black team, we watched what the White team presented to us in horror and shock. It validated our knowing about how unconscious White people were. The improvisational depiction of White paper scattered all over the room in no particular pattern with many bodies crying for attention or demanding their right to be an individual and to exert their power was frightening to some of us. We watched as their process desecrated the altar we normally set up for our weekend intensives. They had trampled right over it. For us as Black people, this was a metaphor for how we experienced White culture: being trampled on without concern. The discussion from the White team after their presentation didn't help to bring a collective focus on their consciousness as White people. This clearly was a class assignment, yet the feelings we felt in our bodies were very real, alarming and validating at the same time.

Black Team's Presentation of Self-Knowing to the White Team

After a break, it was our turn to share our consciousness. We gathered in the room with our drums and our musical instruments, and we began a journey to reveal our souls; we started by listening to the long note that Lewis played soulfully on his saxophone. We drummed furiously and expressed our pain through an opening poem titled "The Long Note." We shared individually what the Long Note meant to us: We talked about our fears of rejection, our dilemma of being in the Black world and the White world. We exposed our necessary preoccupation with White people, and we finished with the affirmation that "we belong together." When we were through, we wondered if the ancestors would be mad at us because we had told, and now the White folks knew how we really felt.

White Team's Reflection on the Black Team's Presentation

The Black team's presentation was a powerful experience for us. The racial differences that surfaced created the conditions for us to go deep into our own consciousness. After the Black team presented their self-knowing, Penny summarized her own self-knowing and other-knowing experience:

> Watching the Black team's presentation filled me with such pain and such joy. More than ever I understand that they are empowering themselves; they do not need me to empower them. What I can do is to get out of their way and learn to love myself as they are learning to love themselves. To believe that finding my own wholeness is a vital step toward White people in this country reclaiming our wholeness.

In reflection, we believe our team was acting out our isolation, separation, and embeddedness in the rugged individualism mentality that marks the influence of our White U.S. culture. Although we didn't discuss this as a team, during the April weekend many of us spoke informally in small groups, comparing our individual essays with the Black team's unified essay. As the authors of this chapter, we believe this is a critical illustration of the varying consciousnesses of our two teams at that time: the individualism of White consciousness, specifically indicated by our team's 13 separate stories, juxtaposed to the one inclusive paper from the Black team, which cohered around their team consciousness of "we belong together."

Differences-Holding Cycle 1: Interteam Dialogue

In this cycle, both teams came together to coach each other in clarifying our different consciousnesses. We formed a circle, with the Black team on one side and the White team on the other. Two chairs were placed in the center facing each other. A Black team member sat in one and a White team member sat in the other. The idea was that one person would begin by asking the other person questions to deepen our other-knowing of that team's consciousness. As questions and issues were raised, other team members walked over and tapped their teammate's shoulder taking her or his seat to speak. Taj started the process by asking the White team, "I did not hear you speak of your history. Why is that?"

Donna responded, "Because we are part of the dominant group in this country, we don't have to." Carole responded that she felt embarrassed about her working-class Jewish grandparents: "If I start thinking about my roots, I get ashamed. I don't want to be rooted in that . . . my parents and their mannerisms of East European Jews . . . I want to be American." This began an interaction with the Black team that profoundly affected us. We saw ourselves reflected by them in a way that allowed us to observe how deeply embedded we were in our Whiteness. We began to define White consciousness as our unconsciousness concerning privilege that enables us not to have to view the world through the lens of race. We gained the insight that, as White people, our self-knowing is not influenced by a consciousness of race. In our world, White is taken for granted as normal and human.

Applying Robert Vachon's levels of consciousness, we realized that, at the visible level, we were disconnected from our past. At the logical level, part of our White privilege is that we didn't have to notice how we got here. Others of us expressed the belief that finding our ancestral roots wasn't going to cut it and didn't lend itself to helping us find group consciousness. At the mythical level, Carole and Gail made the following observations:

The Black team consciously presented their [mythical] being level. As a White team, we were unconscious of our mythical level as we presented our crepe paper chaos. . . . Our not being conscious was the problem. We realized that the Black team holds the knowledge about us that we don't yet know about ourselves. (Carole)

What privilege is about is going unconscious: ignoring our history, ignoring our future, ignoring our present. White consciousness . . . by its nature, is waking up in the morning without being aware; moving in the world without regard. . . . So looking for White consciousness is like describing how lucid you are when you're sleepwalking. (Gail)

Despite our feelings of confusion and shame, as we cycled through the action-reflection process with the Black team, our self-knowing and other-knowing increased. We slowly began to embody the ability to hold both Black and White perspectives.

Some of the Black team members did not feel met by the White team. It became evident to our team that being White and having an analysis of what that means in relationship to Black people was not something many of the White team members had explored. This frustrated members on the Black team; as one member put it, "It feels like we got stood up at the river."

Because of this dynamic, we felt we spent more than our share of time trying to bring consciousness to their unconsciousness. At this point, the SI process seemed to wane in facilitating an equal relationship between these two groups. Because of the privilege bestowed on White skin, our classmates were not aware of how this privilege played out in their interactions with Black people. We felt the White team was not able to go much further than the visible or logical manifestations of being White. They weren't able to enter the mythical realm that drove their behaviors. We wanted to hear the myths that were motivating their visible and logical behaviors, actions we were already very familiar with.

We were in a quandary. Do we sit and passively try to hold a consciousness that was at best still on the visible level as deemed by the process? Or do we try to create opportunities to go deeper and awaken new levels of consciousness within our other? We felt we had been drawn into another situation of educating the oppressor, and for some of us this was all too familiar. Yet this inquiry process also offered a structure that allowed for compassionate discourse and facilitated an openness that had been missing in some of our previous interactions with White people.

Difference-Holding Cycle 2: Embodying Differences

To enhance difference-holding, the group as a whole identified some major differences between White consciousness and Black consciousness. After this, the teams again separated to create presentations to embody the other team's consciousness; this was to help us hold differences.

Regarding the White team's effort to embody Black consciousness, Carole remembers:

> Someone suggested that we divide ourselves into two groups, a blue-eyed group and a brown-eyed group. One eye color would represent the dominant group and one the marginalized group. We would then act out scenarios to demonstrate oppression of a marginalized group of people. This would be our way of embodying Black consciousness, as a way to increase our other-knowing of the Black perspective.

For some on the White team, this was a powerful exercise. In one of the scenarios acted out during the skit, a blue-eyed person took the role of a police officer frisking a brown-eyed person. The brown-eyed person, Sandra, later related her experience:

> I was thrown up against the wall, frisked, and physically abused for a characteristic that is a factor of birth and not of choice—the color of my eyes. The inhumanity, brutality, and ugliness of being treated this way was overwhelming (for me). . . . The tears I felt arose from a place deep inside that felt shame and horror for having been unconscious of the Black experience.

However, it was only after acting out the blue-eye/brown-eye skit and reflecting on it with the Black team that the White team realized they had once again "gone unconscious" and had left the Black team unmet. By choosing a blue-eye/brown-eye story about discrimination, we had chosen to avoid the experience of trying to really embody Black consciousness. One of us became aware of "the part of me that in no way can bear being Black (even in a brief skit). The fear of the pain is too overwhelming, so I'll go unconscious to keep my head buried in the sand and hold on to my privilege to protect myself."

Once again, we learned how having trouble working through an inquiry phase can actually stimulate our learning. We were learning more about ourselves, our other, and how to hold different perspectives; attempting to hold Black consciousness equally with White consciousness, and not succeeding, propelled us into a deeper understanding of how White consciousness sees itself as center, rather than as just one experience of being human. And that shedding White consciousness is knowing more about the extent of the privilege that we live with every day. One team member made the following realization:

> It's so hard to give up what you think you know so well . . . it's like jumping across the trapeze and it's that space in midair that's so scary . . . it's about awareness and never seeing things the same way again and the fear of how that will change our lives forever.

Within our team, different perspectives continued to emerge and give us many opportunities to develop our capacities to listen openly and deeply. These ranged from "I don't think today that there's anything good about White consciousness; there's a lot of good about me as a human being" to "I have tremendous resistance to seeing the White team have a self-image of despair. . . . I hold out there's some value in our White consciousness." In the weeks that followed, we were increasingly willing to let go of embedded thinking and surrender to a process of transformation. Said one team member, "Much is shifting for me. . . . It is as though a thick, opaque film that has obscured my seeing, feeling, and thinking has reconfigured into a thinner, transparent membrane which breathes."

Particularly moving was Ace's description of his growing awareness:

> There is an emerging cycle of emotions that move me kind of in a spiral fashion . . . toward removing the barrier to wholeness. . . . It starts with pride, arrogance, and them moves to shame and self-deprecation: "How could you have not seen this before?" It then moves to . . . a dying or a feeling of letting go, a surrender to the . . . truth-feelings. And finally, I . . . awaken with a sense of

responsibility to do something different in my life. . . . My path to . . . accepting my privilege and using it appropriately in the world.

It wasn't difficult for the Black team to embody the White team's consciousness. We were able to quickly assign attributes that represented White consciousness to our team members and step into the process of difference-holding. Our oppositional consciousness from having to know both the Black world and the White world quickly facilitated this cycle for us. We held the consciousness of White people being disconnected from each other, keeping privilege by remaining unconscious, possessing concern only for their individualism, and appropriating others' causes. One of our team members stated, "It was easy being unconscious. I didn't have to do anything, and I even received money for remaining unconscious." After our skit, the White team indicated to us that we had indeed held elements of their consciousness. Many expressed to us it was not easy for them to watch our depiction of them.

Conversely, we as a team felt the White team did not hold our differences in the consciousness of who we were. We are Black people with a consciousness emanating from that fact, and their using the blues and browns of eye color did not reflect this consciousness. We did not feel they had stepped into our shoes, nor did we feel their skit represented the elements of our consciousness. We felt frustrated and once again unmet.

We were asked by the White team why we stayed in the process with them. Responses from the Black team ranged from "even if you do not see our humanity, we can see your humanity" to "I want to heal my wounds by confronting them" to "I want to pass my learning onto my students who are young African Americans." In this phase of synergy, we began to ask if the historical imbalances of Black and White culture were setting the Black team up for reinjury. Experiencing the White team's inability to see us was more than frustrating; it was wounding. It propelled many Black team members to the self-knowing that racism is here to stay.

Difference-Transcending

Because of time limitations, we never formally carried out the difference-transcending cycle as a cohort. Yet we were able to see the benefits of participating in the SI process in our work together the following year on our group demonstration of competency. (This is comparable to the oral examination in other doctoral programs.)

As a result of the action and reflection process during our 6 months together, the White team began connecting with each other in a new way. They began to form the community that they longed for. In their team reflection paper, they revealed the following thoughts:

> Our process of self-knowing has increased our capacities to hold the differences between us. We have less fear of being outcast from our group, and we have less fear of our own "ego god: being challenged when someone disagrees with us, or of our hurting someone else's 'ego god.'"

As a team, the Whites began to take some of their new learnings and extended capacities into expanding their consciousness in new areas. Penny's experience in difference-transcending came in a breakthrough regarding understanding the cost of her assimilation as a Jew into Whiteness:

> I understand now how my assimilation as a Jew, the work to forget where I came from, fed by White consciousness, allowed me to also forget White people's enslavement of Blacks, to forget the effects of that trauma on my people as well—allowed me to disassociate and cut off and fragment. Such is the bounty of assimilation.

We felt how others of us had forfeited our Celtic, Swiss, Polish voices. Still others had cut off rural working-class ways of being in the world or had learned to repress feelings of vulnerability, openness, and fear to fit in the box of the White upper middle-class corporate male. Gail helped us notice how assimilation works to keep us looking outside of ourselves for answers, rather than referencing internally where our wisdom is. "Busting White consciousness includes breaking assimilation to explore life as a question with multiple answers . . . the reclaiming of multiple histories and selves."

Significantly, throughout the inquiry process, the White team found that much of their self-knowing and, hence, their expanded consciousness was informed by their relationship with the Black team. The White team believed that the dialogue with the Black team served as the major catalyst for the White team's awakening from White consciousness. This is shown in the reports on other-knowing and difference-holding. As opposed to the section on White team self-knowing, these involved interaction with the Black team and contained the White team's most in-depth learning.

At the end of the formal inquiry process, as the White team applied SI's three dimensions of consciousness, the team members realized their visible level is the chaos of white crepe paper; it is the disconnection and isolation and the valuing of a rugged individualism that promotes othering, fragmentation, and oppressive behavior. However, the White team is learning that they are not alone. They are responsible for doing their part, and they are connected to many others who are also responsible for doing their parts. Together, the White team members know they can do this.

The White team is asking questions about how to bring their learning about racism into the world in such a way that it will effectively reach other White people without imposing prescriptive ideas. As Whites, the team members are committed to unraveling more layers of their unconscious racial assumptions to work together to change and heal themselves, their communities, and their institutions. Ace revealed, "I want to be a bridge, a catalyst in the transition period of the next few years from White male supremacy to White male compassion."

The White team's logical level is their complicity with assimilation, with giving up who they really are to gain the benefits of Whiteness. They realize how they create safe constructs to remove themselves from fear, pain, and denial. However, they are opening to new ideas and different perspectives as their consciousness expands. They have learned that the White perspective is not the only perspective or even a superior perspective. Yet as they are unfolding, they still fear what they do not know, and they hold on to the power and privilege that is familiar and feels safe.

On the mythical level, the White team is desperately clinging to a mono-lithic singular reality with which they try to subjugate and eradicate all other realities and perspectives. By trying to fit into a single White package, the team members have become emotionally and spiritually starved and have tried to fill this soul hunger with external fixes—alcohol, drugs, sex, food, work, relationships, religion, and appropriation of the spirituality and cul-ture of our other. In the final White team paper, the team members wrote, "We are contradicting our construction, our assimilation into Whiteness. We are beginning to reclaim our history and ourselves and our souls. We are finding our way back home."

The White team proposed envisioning an emerging and fluid power-sharing, holistic consciousness as an alternative to the static White conscious-ness from which they are awakening. Where White consciousness clings to one hegemonic answer, holistic consciousness opens to living in many questions, multiple realities, a web with a million vibrant interconnected centers.

The Black team felt they had started something that they didn't get to fin-ish, at least not in the time frame given in the cohort weekend intensive. The Black team started exploring their relationships with each other as Black people, and they began to get into areas that revealed the depths of their diversity. They finished the process with many unanswered questions regard-ing their relationships to each other as Black people in an academic setting. What does this diversity really mean for Blacks' ultimate ability to support each other, particularly when in a predominantly White academic setting. This continues to be the question that members of the Black team ask themselves and are interested in exploring further.

The SI process created a structure in which the Black team unveiled their diversity. But because of the context of synergizing with our other, Whites, the Blacks once again experienced the embeddedness of the power dynamic of privilege. Either the Black team was sidetracked, or conveniently distracted, from working with themselves. Many of the Black team's members expressed regret that this occurred, and they agreed to continue at another time the process they had begun together.

For most of the Black team, relationships with the White team members expanded their understanding. Still, the process left Black team members feeling as if they had not learned anything new about White consciousness. Having gone through the synergy process together, the Blacks were only given a common language to use for describing to Whites what was going on when they faced a racist system. They were not given anything that would change or add to the depths of their understanding of Whites.

Cohort Reflection on the SI Process

As a cohort, we were able to cut through our veneer of politeness to have authentic and honest conversations about our differences. We began to speak the unspeakable to each other, to give voice to those deeply rooted beliefs and myths that define us as individuals and as a cultural group. We found this capacity to be a powerful tool for transformation.

For many of us in the cohort, the synergy dialogue permeated the context of all of our cohort relationships and experiences. We found that we were using the language of SI as we collaborated with each other during other course work. When we interacted about our differences, we spoke about our behavior in terms of our underlying assumptions, values and beliefs, and enhanced self- and other-knowing. We spoke about our attempt to hold our differences and about the possibility of transcending these differences to find a new way of thinking. Some of us reported responding similarly in our lives outside of the cohort.

As the four authors of this case study met collectively to dialogue about these questions, we realized that we were engaging in a synergistic process. The four of us were using the awareness engendered from the self- and other-knowings of each of our teams, holding our differences and creating new meaning out of our experience together as we cycled through action and reflection, creative tension, and ultimately difference-holding. As we collaborated to write this, we consciously used the SI framework to employ synergistic processes and further our learning.

At the end of our time together as a cohort, we presented a group demonstration of competency to show our ability to create a learning community. We used the SI framework in this process. Aided by our SI experiences together, we changed into a higher quality learning community by examining our underlying values, beliefs, and myths and reframing our thinking and actions.

As our process continued, major questions came into bold relief. How do we continue SI as an open, authentic process when there are historical and present-day institutional power differences between the White dominant culture and the dominated Black culture? How can SI address the dynamics of two cultures coming together, when one has a history of dominating the other and they cannot start from a level playing field? Is it possible to create a process where the oppressed group is not put into the position of making conscious the manifestations of privilege and oppression that are unconscious within the dominating group?

We found that in the cohort, the domination dynamic was affected by the SI process. A new sense of group developed within the White team, demonstrated by the shift in the White team's consciousness, to varying extents, around acknowledging White privilege. Through the SI process, they had become more conscious and aware, and, in effect, the team's behavior changed. They became more consciously able to recognize their tendency to operate from a privileged standpoint. The Black team's consciousness shifted around their own connections and differences among themselves. They reported that is was easier to articulate what their differences were, even if they still were not able to get to the implications or meaning of these new awareness. Both teams found that the dynamics of their interactions could be changed from an either-or to a both-and perspective.

A final illustration of the shifting consciousness of the group is described in the descriptive research report "Soul of Cohort 5." This report speaks in the collective voice of the cohort through the voices of the six researchers:

> The cohort nature is increasingly to value multiple perspectives or realities that exist in this world and at the same time confront views that are exclusive. This means that we have come to recognize and believe that an other's reality can coexist with ours, and ours can coexist with another's.
>
> Our shared spiritual context led to expanded capacities for love, compassion, and commitment toward ourselves and each other. We learned that out of our struggle within ourselves and with each other has come more compassion and commitment. In this way, the love that has held us together is evolving and nurtures our ability to be alive to one another.

As a group, we experienced minicycles of differentiation and integration throughout our various intrateam and interteam configurations. When we concluded our inquiry in June, we realized that, although we had sometimes managed to hold each other's perspectives around race, we had not yet reached synergy. However, during the 8 months that followed, in which we prepared and presented our group demonstration of competency, we had a growing insight: Synergy, for us, is a continuing process of consciousness expansion, and it continues to manifest through our action in the world. We found that other issues had been underlying our group dynamics, such as issues of gender, assimilation, anti-Semitism, and classism, and were erupting with new complexities. Our capacities for expanded consciousness enabled us to accelerate our ability to work with these differences. Thus, we continued to embody capacities of differences-transcending.

Throughout our 3 years together, including our 6-month SI process and our demonstration of competency, we developed new capacities for learning. These capacities enabled us to stay connected and open to learning even in times of discomfort. We extended our capacities for deep listening, for holding multiple realities, and for openness and willingness; we developed our skills for using action and reflection; and last, we uncovered our compassionate natures.

12

Gender Synergy: Using Synergic Inquiry to Work With Gender Differences

Yongming Tang, David Goff, Anna Gatmon,
Marriane Murray, Vickie Zhang, and George Kich

This case study describes how synergic inquiry (SI) was used in a 2-day workshop setting to address gender issues. Authors include 4 of the 5 people designated as facilitators and 2 of the 11 women and 7 men who participated in the study. Although there was a formal facilitation team, during the workshop facilitators also participated heavily, and some of the participants also facilitated the process.

Preparations and Workshop Design

The designated facilitators spent as much time preparing for the workshop as they did conducting the workshop. Of the five facilitators, only two had direct previous experience with SI; the other three brought years of experience facilitating men's, women's, couple's, and community-building groups. The initial task facilitators faced was integrating their various skill sets and perspectives into an effective team collaboration. To facilitate understanding of the methodology, the facilitators employed SI to build their team. Thus, they began the first cycle of this inquiry with a stage-by-stage description of the process. Then, starting with self-knowing, male and female facilitators met separately to explore their own gendered consciousnesses. During other-knowing, they rejoined as one group and shared their findings with each other.

As the facilitators followed the process, they observed their emotional reactions, looking for hotspots from both process and content. These observations helped them stay attuned to what was emerging and helped them develop sensitivity to the energetic and emotional dynamics that accompany movement through the stages. This combination of participation and observation enabled them to maintain a level of reflection as they began to touch on areas that were emotionally charged and anxiety provoking.

Along the way, the facilitators discovered that they felt anxious about the prospective dialogue. Afraid the dialogue would get bogged down in stereotypical thinking and behaviors, the facilitators wanted to avoid what they considered to be well-worn and unproductive paths. They noticed that they had anxieties about being heard and were concerned about how others would respond to their feelings of anger, pain, and vulnerability. Paying close attention, the facilitators discovered how different their various experiences were from one another. Thus, they began the process of identifying and holding differences.

Differences-holding turned out to be very important for the facilitators. By maintaining openness to the differences regarding feelings of anxiety, pain, and anger, they were able to include all of these ingredients as they worked on designing the workshop format. Their capacity to surface and hold these differences as a group enabled them to draw deeply on the full range of sensibilities and expertise that they collectively held. This development was a major factor that contributed to the success of the workshop. The atmosphere of inclusiveness, respect, and inquiry that evolved helped them to trust each other enough to bond as a team.

During the last design meeting, differences-transcending happened. Our experiences of self-knowing, other-knowing, and differences-holding taught the group a lot about each other's experiences, and the facilitators felt a wonderful sense of complementarity arising among them. When the facilitators began to focus on the structures and strategies of the workshop, the design seemed to take on a life of its own. At that point, Yongming remarked, "I am feeling very comfortable about any of us doing any part of the design, and, if we let our uniqueness shine, we will have a fantastic time!" It took very little time for the group to agree on how they would work together.

At the end of the final meeting, they were confident that they had prepared well for the workshop and were ready to work together. They were also excited by the quality of the people who had chosen to participate in the workshop. Feeling that they had a good workshop design, they were eager to see where the process would enable them to go. It seemed like the conditions they had created would give them a good chance to discover how much SI could contribute to furthering gender relations.

The design they settled on was an ambitious one; it had two important goals. First, the facilitators wanted to introduce participants to the SI method of inquiry and help them experientially build the understanding and necessary skills to use it productively. The facilitators wanted to explore male and female consciousnesses separately to reach for a synergic awareness that would be capable of incorporating both forms of consciousness. To fulfill these goals, the facilitators decided to employ three synergy cycles. The first used dyads to teach the method and help participants build their skillfulness with it. This would also provide an opportunity to work with gender awareness within a mixed-gender context and, it was hoped, to help prime the pump for what was to follow. The second cycle, to be conducted in single-gender groups, would be devoted to helping each person discover more about his or her own gender consciousness. The third and final cycle would include the group as a whole and focus on deepening the level of inquiry that occurs between the genders publicly. The goal for the third cycle was for participants to use the skills and awareness built throughout the workshop to address problematic differences between the genders (the differences identified by the workshop participants). It was hoped that participants might begin to experience a new, more synergic awareness during this cycle of inquiry.

The Workshop

The workshop opened on Saturday morning with a welcome and a statement that the group was gathered to participate in a ritual social process that would ask something of each member. Facilitators encouraged the participants to view this particular ritual as a vehicle that could bring them to new ways of seeing themselves and new understandings of the possibilities between men and women. To underscore the point that everyone was beginning a journey together, the facilitators read the poem "Diving Into the Wreck," by Adrienne Rich. A line from this poem, "I came to see the damage done and the treasure that prevails," offered an organizing metaphor to help participants focus their inquiry into gender relations.

After facilitators introduced themselves, everyone met in small groups to describe their current feelings, thoughts, and attitudes about gender relations. The facilitators then conducted a short ritual to acknowledge the legacy of the gender struggle everyone brought with them and to include those whom participants considered their ancestors. The workshop began this way to create space and acknowledgment for all that had transpired in participants' lives. By also naming those who had made important contributions to perceptions of gender, the facilitators hoped to somewhat depersonalize the work so that it could be seen as part of a species-wide endeavor.

This section of the workshop concluded with participants stating the expectations they had brought with them, expressing what it was they hoped would and would not happen during the workshop. The facilitators acknowledged these expectations and used them to underscore the tensions inherent in an inquiry into gender relations. Guidelines to help participants during the process included those for transformative learning put forth by Angeles Arrien as the fourfold way—show up, pay attention, tell the truth, and surrender attachment to outcome. After a brief discussion, the facilitators outlined the agenda for the rest of the workshop.

Introductory Synergy Cycle

After Yongming described the four stages of the SI process, participants were asked to do self-knowing by individually identifying and exploring a gender treasure that they possessed and the damage they had experienced because of this gift. Other-knowing involved forming dyads to share these findings, with partners practicing deep listening and attempting to understand the other's experience. Toward the end of this stage, listeners were encouraged to ask clarifying questions as the partners shifted focus to identifying and holding the differences between the dyad's two forms of knowing. Finally, the dyad members coached their partners as they tried to embody their partner's position. The coaches helped their partners fine-tune awareness until they were able to understand and express that perspective accurately and to their coach's standards.

Later, when reflecting as a group on their experiences with this first cycle of inquiry, the participants learned that many dyads experienced an emergence of new understanding and awareness. Vickie Zhang, a female participant from China, made the following comment:

> I had a deepening experience of knowing about self. I remembered the value I discovered within myself when we were pairing up in the exercise of self-knowing and other-knowing about the gifts we bring as woman or man. For me, I realized that the gift I bring [sic] was balance of yin and yang energy. In Chinese culture, yin stands for feminine and yang stands for masculine. Maintaining good balance of the yin and yang energy leads me to the Tao. My White partner became very interested in my explanation. For her, it was learning another way of being.

Anna, one of the facilitators, also commented on this first cycle:

While listening to the participants' reflections at the end of this cycle, I observed a rise in the energy in the room which manifested in participants' anticipation to go deeper into the process and the content of gender relations, as well as a frustration with the short time allotted to this cycle. I believe that the short time allotted to this cycle and the tightness with which it was conducted built up an energetic pressure in which people wanted to go deeper into gender issues, and both the excitement and the frustration provided fuel for the second cycle of synergic inquiry, which followed in same-gender groups.

After returning from lunch, the second synergy cycle of the inquiry began. Because this cycle focused on increased understanding of participants' own gender consciousness, the group convened in separate gender groups.

The Men's Group

To help the men explore what being a man means to them and describe their male consciousness, a series of questions was used to stimulate self-knowing and help the men reflect on the way they behaved together:

What is it like to be a man?

When do you feel most/least like a man?

What constitutes being male?

How does what we are doing reflect male consciousness?

Each man had also brought in an object or poem that reflected his own gender experience.

The first thing the men did after occupying their separate space was set up an altar and start a round of drumming. The drumming continued until all were all settled and ready to begin. Initiating the process of sharing these items, William described the two items he brought for the altar. These were a Shiva lingam that had four faces, each expressing a facet of the divine masculine, and a large ceramic phallus that was broken into two pieces. He described the meaning these items held for him and what they reflected about male consciousness.

Each man then talked about his experience of being a man as he added to the altar. Other items—a rough stone, a drum, a poem, a wallet—emerged. Metaphors emerged as well: the beast of burden, the brute, the cutoff body, and the experience of being power objects. These items and metaphors expressed differing facets of male wisdom, strength, desire, grief, and longing around such fundamental male issues as work, responsibility, duty, isolation, relationships, sex, privilege, and spirituality.

As the afternoon progressed, the men were drawn closer to one another. There was, however, an acute awareness that the women were meeting on the other side of the wall. Knowing that they were going to be facing them again, the men felt added anxiety in their sharing. In fact, the men's differences didn't begin to manifest until they began to consider what, if anything, they would want to share with the women. As they looked deeper into their feelings, they found that some men felt trepidation about sharing anything with the women. Others felt the need to let their sensibilities, wisdom, and vulnerabilities be known. Much to the dismay and wonder of the facilitators, when it came time to stop on Saturday, there was no agreement among the men that anything would be shared with the women.

On Sunday morning, the men were asked to take positions along an imaginary continuum. One end represented a desire for self-disclosure and the other, a desire to stay silent. After the men made their positions explicit, they were encouraged to move around and explore other positions. What then transpired was a dynamic exploration of their ambivalence about sharing with women. As this procedure progressed, it began to change: The way the men moved slowed down, and their positions began to circle around each other. Eventually, one participant suggested that they touch each other; taking the hands of the men next to him, each man expressed his desire to feel connected. The men then settled into a circle and sat holding hands.

Configured this way, the men continued exploring their feelings and concerns. What unfolded was an awareness that they had a lot to share with each other and that it was easier to do this when they felt connected. Sitting together, touching, the men discovered the method they would employ to share their masculine consciousness. Instead of making a presentation and focusing on the reactions of the women, the men would let the women observe as they stayed focused on deepening their own inquiry into their own awarenesses.

For another 30 minutes the men explored their anxieties about being seen, acknowledging that they would have to be willing to face themselves if they were to allow others to see them. This led to a discussion about men's isolation, about how men live their lives separated from one another by invisible partitions.

At this point, one of the two Asians in the men's group called attention to the difference between Asian and White American men. He shared painful experiences of growing up in the United States as an Asian man. Yongming then spoke about differences between his relations with men in China, which were intimate connections with men who treated each other like brothers, and the lack of connection he felt with men in this culture.

Following this line of inquiry regarding the hunger for touch and real contact with each other, the men examined the tension between homophobia and the desire to feel physically connected. Some acknowledged how much desire they had for an erotic connection and how cut off they felt from themselves, each other, and the world. The men explored the mixture of vulnerability and anger that attends this hunger and acknowledged how much these feelings distort their sexuality and cause emotional dependence on women.

In the final minutes, as the men faced the prospect of letting themselves be seen by the women, a great feeling of solidarity seemed to emerge that was most poignantly expressed by the two Asian men who both said that it was the first time in their lives they had felt connected to White men. The feelings of pain and joy that these comments aroused brought home how much pain men experience because of their separation from each other. One man, anticipating a comment from the women, asked how this sense of solidarity was different from the "old boys' network," prompting an exploration of male privilege.

Although some men were still waking up to what it meant to be men in this society, they did not hesitate to inquire into privilege. They shared what they knew about the responsibility that comes with this privilege and the price that they pay to maintain it. The men in this circle were all actively engaged in seeking alternative forms of power, new ways of expressing themselves and contributing to their communities. As one put it, instead of the old boys' network, the men "represent the new men's network." When the men later chose a problematic area of difference into which to inquire, they returned to the issues associated with male privilege.

This experience was powerful for everybody, and a unity within the diversity of the men's group emerged as the men touched and held onto each other. Yongming made the following comment:

> I am feeling we are transcending our differences as we differentiate and respect each other. I have never felt so close to men, especially Western men. I never could imagine I could go this far. Now, I am feeling so hopeful that I will have a different experience with Western White men. And this is a most precious gift from all of you.

David recalled:

> As the men adjourned for the break, I had a sense that the workshop was primed to enter terrain that is seldom attained by mixed-gender groups. The solidarity the men felt seemed to bode well for greater honesty and a richer form of self-disclosure than typically occurs when men meet with women. The fact that the men were determined to face themselves suggested that they would not allow themselves to be deterred by their apprehension about the women's reactions. It appeared that these men had tapped into a form of male power that

was not a form of "power over" another but instead was a form of "power with" another.

The Women's Group

The facilitators' assumptions were that, unlike the men's group, most of the women's group had done a great deal of talking about what being a woman means in terms of social, economic, and political consciousness raising. The facilitators wanted to use this cycle for the women to continue their individual self-knowing and to reflect on the mosaic of other women's personal self-knowing in ways that might break free of the familiar ways women think about women-ness. To deepen their inquiry into the overarching metaphor of the workshop—"the damage done and the treasures that prevail"—the women raised questions that moved back and forth between the consciousness within their own self and the discernment of the impact of context on shaping one's consciousness.

The goals, as described to the group, were to deepen each woman's personal experience of being female; to welcome and explore the polarities that emerged in the group, including unresolvable conflicts; to identify fundamental unifying themes and images; and to create a collective altar or collage of the feminine.

The women began by working individually, and in writing, with a question: What are my core learnings about what it means to be a woman—or what being a woman is not? These reflections were then discussed in small groups of three or four women. To focus on damage and treasures, as experienced through the body, the women were led through a guided meditation in which each woman took on a posture or movement that expressed the damage and then switched to embody the opposite of this damage—individual femaleness in its full splendor. This was followed by an attempt to move between these two physical positions in a powerful exercise that allowed the women to silently listen to the memories and wisdom stored in their bodies. After this, each woman explicated her self-knowing as a woman.

Then the women gathered in a circle so that each woman could share her own sense of female consciousness, perhaps through the symbol or poem she brought. The first woman to speak expressed a deep level of pain and longing about not being in relationship with a man. In many ways, this seemed to set a theme that recurred implicitly and explicitly throughout the women's processes. How women connect with men is central to them. Is the relationship one of unconscious compromise, depression, and loss of self, as several of women believed about their mothers? For some, staying away from men seemed to be the only way to stay free of these damaging dynamics. Others identified with struggling to be with men but also struggling with these dynamics. Still others mourned the enormity of the losses in regards to children, social status, and financial collaboration that result from not being with a man.

The women spent a long time sharing different aspects of their experience as women, and there was an initial feeling of joining together. However, one facilitator noticed that the energy in the room was low and commented that she was feeling lethargic. This created a shift in the process, and some of the hidden differences among the women began to emerge:

> When we named the feelings of stuckness and disengagement . . . I immediately began to feel enlivened. It was as if, at last, there was the possibility of bringing more of my true self into the room . . . and there was room for disagreement and conflict. (Marianne)

Encouraged to explore the differences that emerged, the women each found a place in the room that fit her own position within the female experience and spoke of this experience to the other women. One group gathered in the center of the room and identified themselves as mainstream—heterosexual women with a partner and children. Another group, made up of women who identified as not following the mainstream, formed on the perimeter of the room; they spoke of their sexual attraction toward women, life without children and a husband, and financial independence.

Another group that formed consisted of women who did not have partners but wanted to be part of the center group of women. Still others stood outside all of these groups. One woman said she felt lonely outside, without a group, yet she didn't want to have to buy into all the implicit values and norms of any of the groups; she wanted the freedom to move from group to group. The women expressed what it felt like to be standing in the positions they had chosen. Those who had chosen the not-mainstream path expressed feeling disrespected by the mainstream group for having chosen independent lives without spouses or children but also shared their pride in themselves. Those in the center group expressed feelings of not only valuing the experiences and status that are part of the mainstream identity but also suffering because membership in this group seemed to isolate them from women in other positions.

The women in each group asked other groups questions about the experience of being a woman in the other group, and they shared their assumptions about the experience of the other positions. The facilitators did not choose to work with one difference at a time; instead, keeping the process organic, they asked each woman to stand in any of the positions they had explored, as long as it was different from where she had originally stood.

New positions that had not yet been expressed were also encouraged to emerge. Those who had originally been in a specific position coached those who had taken it as a new position. This was a way to help each woman embody her own position in a fuller way. Although it wasn't possible for each woman to work with all of the differences that emerged, the women got to experience standing in different positions and consciousnesses of the female experience.

A breakthrough came when one woman from the group seen as more mainstream and privileged expressed a desire to listen to the outsider position. One of the outsiders said, "If I lived in another time or culture, I would be valued; I would be a shaman. But now, because I have made different choices about relationship and career, I feel invisible, like a second-class citizen." This remark opened a bridge between the differing positions. There was a palpable shift for many in the room, and a different kind of dialogue emerged. There was only a brief time left before the conclusion of the day, but the women affirmed the value of what they had experienced before they left and resolved to continue the process the next day when they moved into mixed-gender groups. Marriane commented on her experience in this segment:

> I could literally feel in my body the discomfort that came with the possibility of being labeled in a specific way, or of losing myself in a group identity. And I could very clearly feel the depth of longing, in myself and others, to be seen fully and recognized for who we are as women, not judged or compared with somebody else's worldview of what it means to be feminine. It was very powerful to witness that recognition and acceptance—and the emotional responses that came with it.

After the break, the men joined the women in the larger meeting room. For the third synergy cycle, the two gender groups were again together. Because each gender group had separately done collective self-knowing, this cycle started with other-knowing. The facilitators informed participants that this stage entailed self-disclosure by one group, while the other practiced deep listening, and that each group would be allowed about 20 minutes for self-disclosure. The self-disclosures would be followed by a few minutes for clarifying questions. When everyone understood, the facilitators proceeded to spin a bottle to determine who would present first. Serendipity chose the men.

The Men's Presentation to the Women

The men settled themselves in a circle and joined hands. Their fear and apprehension were apparent. They were determined to support each other through what was going to be a difficult process. After a few moments of silence, they proceeded as they had when they were alone. First they reviewed what they had discovered together, sharing their isolation, their anguish about being objectified as power objects, their fatigue about being beasts of burden who worked constantly for others' benefit, their awareness of how cut off they felt from their feelings and their bodies, and their desire for greater erotic connection. They included their awareness that being cut off in these ways created a distorted focus on women's bodies and sexuality.

The men's demeanor while sharing revealed how difficult it was for them to face these truths about themselves and how much they needed each other's support to do it. Clarifying questions from the women had to do with male isolation, sexuality, and privilege. One woman asked a question that seemed to capture the essence of the confusion for both genders. Did men have any reason for wanting to relate to women? Later, when the men listened to the women, a variation of this same question arose.

The Women's Reactions to the Men's Presentation

Many women were touched by the men's revelations, by their willingness to be present, by their obvious sincerity, and by their connections with each other. They commented on how rare, and how valuable, it was to witness this and on their difficulties listening to the men because of the damages inflicted on them by men:

> My feeling when gathering together with the men was one of excitement mixed with apprehension. This was the moment I had worked toward in creating this workshop. Memories of failed explorations of gender issues in a mixed-gender context kept flooding me as I was trying to stay open and trusting the wisdom of the SI process and of all the participants.
>
> During the men's demonstration of their consciousness, I learned a great deal about the ways in which my mind wants to listen selectively, to screen out what feels difficult or painful to engage with. For example, one of the men talked about not really needing to be with a woman except to have sex, and immediately my anger pulled my attention away and I was off in a tumble of thoughts and responses. I had to keep coming back to what he said to reach below the words to discover the pain that created that sense of separation in him. (Anna)

The Women's Presentation to the Men

The women chose to show men the conflict that had emerged during their process and to see if they could go to the next step themselves during this presentation. They felt that it would be extremely revealing to allow men the intimacy of knowing something that women rarely acknowledge even to themselves. This would also be a way for the women to optimize their own learning. Resuming the process started the day before, the women showed the dynamics between them and how their polarities evolved. Then, the women in the outside position were invited in and encouraged to try the center position, as experienced by those who occupy it.

What came forth was a poignant discovery by one woman who had strongly identified herself as not mainstream. Standing in the center position, she said, "What's here for me is that I really would love to have a child and have the precious opportunity to influence another person to have the values that I stand for." The heartfelt level of this exchange contributed to a deepening of dialogue among the women. This process disclosed how much tension exists in female consciousness around issues of self-sufficiency, independence, relatedness, and identity. The women showed the men their in-the-moment process of coming to terms with the diversity of their experiences of female consciousness. They revealed how many differences exist between contemporary women and how valuable it can be when women are able to hold all these differences as part of what it means to be a woman.

The primary question raised by the men was whether there were any reasons—beyond financial security and the privilege marriage conveyed—for women to want to relate to men. This question, like the one asked by the women, conveyed some of the suspicion that both genders held about being objectified and used. It also conveyed something of the underlying desire of both to be known and wanted for their own sake.

Differences-Holding

After lunch, the participants engaged in an exercise to identify significant and problematic differences between the two forms of gender consciousness initiated during the differences-holding phase of this cycle of inquiry. After listing several differences, participants once more convened as separated gender groups. Each group selected a particular problematic difference for deeper inquiry. In this way, the participants selected the specific issues with which to practice differences-holding and differences-transcending. Toward that end, the men and women were to present the area of problematic difference as it appeared from their own gender perspective and from the perspective of the other gender, as they imagined it. Each group would then have the opportunity to practice holding the differing perspectives on the selected issue. The move toward difference-transcending involved being coached by the other group to embody a more accurate perception of that perspective. When the coaches were satisfied, roles would reverse. Members of the opposite gender group would also try to embody their problematic issue from each perspective.

Once more the spin of a bottle selected the men to present first. The men decided that they wanted to initiate a deeper inquiry into what was perceived to be a difference in the social roles men and women occupy. Of the many differences that had been identified, this one had been most loosely defined. On the mythic level, it was described as the difference between Quan Yin, the goddess of compassion, and Prometheus, the hero who stole fire from the Gods for humanity and in punishment was chained to a rock where his liver was eaten daily by a bird of prey. This difference seemed to portray the elevated status of women's caring when compared with the punishment that men absorb as they act on humanity's behalf. On a more visible level, this difference was portrayed as a conflict between the personal and the systemic forces in American culture. Here the difference was perceived to reflect the systemic, structural privilege men enjoy versus the privilege that women seem to hold in the personal domain.

The men began to portray the problem as they experienced it. Elements of this portrayal included a man carrying a huge weight on his shoulders and being told that he should carry more. The men showed how they were expected to behave to succeed at work and how they were ridiculed and sometimes punished if they revealed any doubts, uncertainties, or weakness.

They showed the personal price they paid, which came in the form of compartmentalized lives, cut off from themselves, other men, and their loved ones. This responsibility and isolation also carried over into their personal lives. At work, men are expected to produce, and at home they were expected to provide. The men revealed how unappreciated and used they felt as they tried to express how difficult it is to open up and show feelings, to know what they wanted, and to be sensitive to others when they had been trained all their lives to ignore these sensitivities for the sake of protecting and providing for their loved ones. They indicated how the pressures they felt from women to be more personally expressive and to shoulder more responsibility for their intimate relationships were experienced as demands for greater performance—for men to work harder.

The men then followed these self-disclosures by portraying the way they imagined women experience this area of problematic difference. This portrayal conveyed the men's sense that women were disappointed in them and that women expected men to be more like women when coming home to their families—more relational, expressive, and emotionally available. One man broke into tears as he shared his perception that women were never satisfied, that they simply wanted him to work harder for them, even at the expense of his health and his sense of self. This man was then told that he was indulging his privilege by collapsing when he was confronted with the needs of those who were less privileged than him. It was made clear that he had no right to collapse.

This moment revealed the sense of bondage that these men experience in their assigned role as primary wage earner. It also made more palpable the sacrifices that men make on behalf of their country, its economy, their families, and their relationships. For a moment, the men were able to show something of the shadowy side of the privileges that they hold: how the quality of their inner lives and relationships is extracted from them as payment for the opportunity to protect and provide for others. From the men's viewpoint, it appeared as though women either didn't understand this aspect of men's sacrifices or didn't care.

Members of one gender coached members of the other as they tried to embody a more accurate understanding of the opposite gender's position. The women acknowledged that it was true that they expected men to be more available emotionally and more willing to share themselves. They coached the men into an awareness that women didn't want men to perform to expectations but instead wanted the men to be more truly themselves. The women were tired of trying to read men's minds and take care of their unexpressed feelings. Many of the women wanted to make it clear that they held no expectations that men would provide for them at all. These women wanted it known that they had opted for self-sufficiency and had no desire to rely on men. The women also helped men understand that the demands men made on women for sex, emotional support, and deference to men's needs were considered oppressive. Thus, the men came to understand that women want men to free themselves from the constraints of their traditional roles so that new behaviors and attitudes can become possible.

The sincere attempts by these men to embody women's consciousnesses proved powerful:

> When the men began to embody our consciousness, I felt humbled by the sincerity and emotional openness that I saw in their faces and actions. The experience of hearing my own words spoken by a man, felt by a man, was stunning. I really felt that, in that moment at least, he absolutely understood that aspect of my being. (Marrianne)

As the women moved to embody the men's consciousness, they indicated their awareness of how burdened men felt by their duties as protectors and providers. The women also showed that they had grasped how cut off men were from their own bodies. What the men felt the women failed to grasp was how little support and understanding was available for men. They coached the women to embody just how confused, hurt, angry, unappreciated, and unloved men felt themselves to be. When several women seemed to grasp this isolation and pain, a man reminded them that they were not allowed to collapse under the weight of these feelings. The silence that followed this comment conveyed the emergence of a more compassionate understanding of what it was like to be a man. This understanding then allowed other men to coach the women to understand men's pleasure in holding privilege and power. This latter point suggested there was a relationship between men's alienation and their interest in protecting the powers associated with their privilege.

At this point, the group turned its attention to the problematic difference that the women had selected—sexuality and eroticism. The women presented their view of this problem by portraying what it was like to make the transition from being a girl to being a woman. They showed how, as their bodies changed, they became the objects of wanted and unwanted attention that focused on their bodies in aggressive and sometimes violent ways. The women revealed how they learned to hide their sense of erotic vitality and their pleasure in their own bodies to protect themselves from male sexual aggression. They expressed their anger, confusion, and hurt about having their feelings of Eros turned against them and showed how women are pigeonholed around their sexuality—being portrayed as frigid if they protect themselves and sluts if they enjoy themselves. They also conveyed how some women withdraw from relationships with men because they can't stand the pain of being invisible as they are objectified. Still others revealed how invisible they felt they had become as they aged. They expressed a mixture of grief and relief that this invisibility brought to them.

The women showed how they experienced men leering at their bodies and how much men appear to them to lie, manipulate, and use violence to control women and make them sexually available. The women also expressed how erotically unsophisticated men are and how contemptuous some women feel about the ongoing pretense that men know more about sex and are more sexually adept than women.

In the half hour that followed, men and women coached each other on their respective viewpoints. Thus, the women understood more about how men's emotional and erotic lives are so severely truncated that all sense of the erotic is channeled through sexuality. They came to see how damaged men's Eros is by male socialization and how men turn to women, and particularly women's bodies, as lifelines to Eros, feelings, and connection.

The men also began to understand how this same process contributes toward a kind of cultural abuse of women's sexuality. Together, these men and women saw how women's bodies and sexuality are widely perceived as beautiful, aesthetic, and desirable, whereas men's bodies are seen as dirty, animalistic, and rapacious instruments of violence. Together they began to understand how polarized male and female bodies and sexuality and desire for erotic connection had become. Together, they also began to see that beneath this polarization was an underlying mutual desire for erotic full-bodied, soulful connection.

The impact of holding these differences was amazing. The level of the group's positive engagement with this difficult schism was impressive to many:

> Throughout this phase I felt we were in an altered state of consciousness. I recall the powerful sense of presence and openness in all of the participants. Different people were moved to speak about different aspects of the female or male experience, at times, while coaching someone from the other gender and other times speaking from their own experience.
>
> Many of the words spoken reflected harsh realities about the behavior and actions of men or women; however, there was a sense of a collective experience where the words spoken seemed to come from the masculine and the feminine, rather than from individual men and women. We had tapped into the collective, and all of us were contributing different aspects of this consciousness. (Anna)

Marriane expressed her experience of holding the men's consciousness:

> Embodying the men's consciousness was difficult in ways that surprised me. There were parts of their consciousness that I could get fairly easily, that resonated with my own consciousness—the frustration at being perceived as a source of income, resources, livelihood; never being enough; being consumed at work and at home; not being seen as feeling; being afraid that opening to feelings would lead to some kind of death; and so on—but it was extremely hard to open up to the more dominant and sexual aspects of male consciousness and the linkage between sex and violence that seems to be such an undercurrent from my perspective as woman. I could feel myself in an inner struggle as I tried to take on that aspect, and I don't think that I ever really brought myself to that place of embodiment. It leads me to more awareness of the schism that I sometimes experience within my own psyche between masculine and feminine.

Differences-Transcending

When this sharing began to wind down, the end of the workshop was near. In its final moments, a sense of mutual understanding and compassion emerged. Participants constructed gender altars side-by-side and then sat in a circle around the altars to share what they had seen of the "damage done and the treasures that prevailed." In these final moments, participants shared expressions of new understanding, a reduction in anger and mistrust, and a newfound sense of hope. One participant, who came into the workshop with little hope of bridging the differences, was very emotional and made the following comment:

> I still cannot believe how powerful this has been. In 2 days, I am totally transformed. Now, I am beginning to be hopeful to have a positive gender dynamic that is healthy and healing. I want to continue this journey into my personal and professional lives.

For Vickie, as a woman from China, the whole experience was tremendously powerful:

> It is a transforming experience for me. As the only woman from a culture other than the White culture, this gender workshop has been an eye-opening experience. It was the first time for me to be in a women's group, especially in a White women's group. I was not sure about the outcome of the workshop in the beginning, and I was anxious and felt insecure. However, it turned out to be a wonderful experience of being heard and deep listening as well. It was a rare opportunity for the female voice from China to be heard in this foreign land. Furthermore, I walked away with the call inside me saying, "What can you do to help the women from your culture being heard in their culture and in different cultures as well?" Efforts will have to be made to undo the harm and damage to women. For me, the SI process did not end in the workshop room; rather, it goes far beyond that. SI has become an evolving process in my personal development.

The workshop concluded with a ritual of acknowledgment. Roses were distributed to all of the participants, and they were invited to give a rose to someone who had helped them to see and understand "the damage done and the treasures that prevail." For 90 minutes the participants exchanged roses, acknowledged the gifts that had been given during the workshop, and embraced each other. Then they said good-bye.

Conclusion

The Gender Synergy Workshop successfully showed that SI can be employed in a workshop setting to stimulate deeper levels of reflection and awareness and to support the emergence of larger, more inclusive forms of consciousness. This inquiry method provided a forum for tapping into the collective realm of female and male consciousnesses by focusing on collective patterns of experience. Although it was the experiences of individuals that created this collective collage, focus on the collective allowed individuals to move freely within these experiences without being boxed into any one of them.

This larger sense of consciousness enabled the members of this workshop to examine and reflect on gender dynamics in new ways, which became particularly apparent on the final afternoon when the process of inquiry became like a shared lucid dream as the various aspects of gender dilemmas surfaced and were explored from multiple perspectives. This collective dreaming seemed to unfold through participants giving voice to their own perspectives and positions, listening deeply to others' viewpoints, and then attempting to embody these other positions. Through movement and embodiment, participants developed a fluidity and depth of consciousness that allowed them to penetrate more deeply into the meanings that were inherent in their various positions. This then allowed women to give expression to something in male consciousness that would increase everyone's understanding of masculine sensibilities or men to grasp something painful about women's experience that had not yet surfaced for the women. In moments like these, the chasm that seems to exist between the genders was bridged, and a palpable atmosphere of healing and community arose within the group.

The Gender Synergy Workshop also succeeded as a social ritual process. The SI process provided a vehicle in which the participants were able to transport themselves to a larger, more inclusive form of consciousness. The primary dynamic processes involved enactment, movement, and embodiment. These elements of the process made positions and assumptions of perspectives explicit, creating a kind of spontaneous social psychodrama in which the contents of the collective unconscious were manifest. Movement between positions, and efforts made to embody others' positions, enabled the participants to integrate these new perspectives into a form of consciousness that was multiperspectival. Thus, the workshop could be described as a collective ritual process that can be employed to evoke more complex orders of consciousness. This new form of consciousness was then employed to address dilemmas created and supported by the less complex orders of consciousness that prevail.

Reflections confirmed the collective nature of this experience:

The workshop enabled me to more fully understand how gender expectations both enriched my life as well as cut me off from claiming all aspects of myself. (Anonymous)

One thing that interests me as I think back on my experience is that I only had one, very brief conversation with a man during that whole time. I said hellos and good-byes but never engaged in talking. There seems to be something important for me in that. It seemed important to keep some distance, not to try and make connections and to know these male beings with whom I'm doing this work. In a way, this anonymity—which I felt toward me, too—seemed to engage a very different part of my psyche than might have been present if this had been a group of friends, or costudents, for example. The thought that comes to mind is that this is work that goes beyond the individual. There was something about working in this way—without the comfortable encapsulation of personal relationship—that seemed very permeable to the collective psyche. (Marianne)

In addition, I believe that one of the significant shifts in the process occurred as the women shifted from being united in our cause "against" men to focusing on our own experience and on the differences among us. Consequently, the men did not have to react to our blaming attacks but, rather, could open their hearts to the experience of being a woman in a male-dominated society. My personal desire was for men to really get a sense of the experience of being a woman, the price paid and the hidden treasures. By letting go of blaming men and instead exploring the rich and complex experience of being woman, we provided an opportunity for the men to witness our experience in a safe and inviting environment. These elements, in addition to an amazing group of participants who were willing to explore the synergic inquiry method as well as the sometimes delicate issues of gender relations, all contributed to a successful workshop and individual expansion of consciousness around gender relations. (Anna)

I'm very aware of the mythic qualities of our experience—the archetypal forces that run through each of us individually and through the collective—and the complexity of the different realms that engage in this dynamic intertwining dance. I keep trying to hold my attention more and more open to see and feel the energies of our interactions. Our process is still very alive to me; I find memories from those 2 days coming into my consciousness quite frequently, and I feel changed by the experience. (Anonymous)

Several questions were raised by the success of this particular workshop. It seemed that the quality of the participants may have been a big factor in its outcome: How much did the outcome of this workshop reflect these participants' capacities for inquiry and reflection? Would a workshop attended by participants with lower capacity achieve an outcome that was similarly stimulating and satisfying to its participants? How big a factor in the outcome was the preparation and dynamism of the facilitation team? Was the facilitators' capacity to move between the roles of facilitator and participant a significant factor in the outcome of the workshop? If so, how great a factor? These questions cannot be answered at this time; only additional workshops of this nature will help define the value each of these elements and their respective contributions to the successful outcome generated by this gender synergy process.

13

Teaching Synergic Inquiry in a High School Setting

Roma Hammel

Last year a 16-year-old Chinese American boy wrote me a note that made my heart sink:

> I've learned to close things off and keep them inside. I don't talk to friends and family about my problems anymore. I had a friend named Joy that I talked to last year, but she decided that we shouldn't be friends anymore, because I depress her when I bother her with my problems. Too many problems. I don't want to bother anybody. I don't ever criticize anybody for who they are, because I've been criticized all my life. I'm becoming such a better person. Seriously!!! I'm becoming everything people have always wanted me to be.

His words signaled a level of isolation that sounded painful. Symptoms of invisibility echoed in his note, as they do in the armored bodies and unheard voices of many other disconnected teens.

I am a high school English teacher—middle aged, White, female, heterosexual, middle class, Western educated, like many of the teachers at our school. Despite good intentions and deliberate efforts to help students succeed, I and other teachers perpetuate a system that separates people from each other and themselves.

My students are diverse: They come from 35 different countries, speak 26 different languages, represent all major world religions, and have varied socioeconomic backgrounds. Many of them strive to do well in my academically competitive school. Indeed, my school report card reflects that the school system excels at its academic goals. However, it does not prepare today's diverse students to address the realities of the current world,

> the complexity of modern society, the seeming intractability of certain social dilemmas, the overwhelming threat of environmental destruction, the global roots and ramifications of many political and economic problems, and the patterns of injustice that tradition has taken for granted. (Hoagland, 1992, p. 80)

Einstein's statement that "no problem can be solved by the same consciousness that created it" challenges us to envision different paradigms. What would the world be like if our schools invited young people to discover paths to wisdom?

Synergic inquiry (SI) shows promise in terms of restructuring education to better address the turmoil of our postmodern world. It fosters a different approach. SI is a radically humanistic process that cultivates communication and capacities for relationship. SI is designed to create an educational world that is democratic and participatory.

As a framework for learning, SI is an ideal process to use in diverse classrooms because it shows how much people can learn from each other. The cycles of action and reflection within this methodology add depth to courses that emphasize social awareness, reflection, and critical thinking. As an English teacher, I have used this method as an integrated approach to the language arts. My students engage in interdisciplinary activities designed to recognize their multiple modes of intelligence, support their different styles of learning, and promote their emotional growth. The nonjudgmental, supportive atmosphere of synergy work in my classes fosters an unusual level of knowledge about self and other; my students subsequently demonstrate greater understanding of significant issues in literature and life.

A few months ago, the high school seniors in my first-period college preparatory English class read Ibsen's play A Doll House. In conjunction with literature discussions, students inquired into the gender differences they observed at home and in our class. A series of self-knowing and other-knowing activities helped them investigate gender roles, communication styles, power dynamics, and relationship issues. The first activity divided students into same-sex groups that shared memories about favorite childhood parties, toys, and movies. Their weekend homework assignment was to observe, take notes, and analyze gender roles and work done by adolescent and adult members of their households. On Monday, students again met in same-sex groups to discuss their observations; then each group reported their insights. On Tuesday, the students analyzed the roles and behavior patterns of men and women in the play and compared their findings to their observations at home. On Wednesday, they reflected on power and communication styles of men and women in the play; spontaneously, students then talked about the power and communication styles evident in our class. Students almost unanimously decided to change the dynamics, once they realized that the majority of the people who spoke out were boys, in contrast to most girls, who typically sat quietly unless called on. Most students then decided they wanted to make sure that everyone participated equally in discussion. They made a collective decision to continue their work through another synergy cycle.

For the next series, students individually generated questions they wanted to discuss. They first wrote personal responses and shared their views in same-sex groups. The following day, I led students in a series of communication exercises designed to strengthen skills in active listening and assertive behavior. The third day, students partnered with members of the opposite sex to talk about their responses. The fourth day, partners worked together again, completing exercises in art and movement that were designed to help them develop more body awareness and skills for self-expression and empathic understanding. The culminating activities included two fishbowl exercises: Both groups had an opportunity to sit in the center of the classroom and talk about their experiences. Everyone shared in the follow-up discussion to seek to understand each other and, through self-observation in these interactions, better know themselves.

After observing how engaged my seniors were in these two cycles of SI, I introduced SI to my two other classes. These students chose to focus on racial and cultural differences. They paired with partners from different backgrounds, and together they researched 10 different topics related to their ancestry, including religion, art, music, clothing, education, and food. After 3 weeks of self-knowing, other-knowing, and difference-holding experiences, these students designed synergistic cultural presentations; their differences served as resources.

Almost every student appeared to be engaged in the research and interviews, eagerly taking notes on the stories their partners shared. They interviewed experts, reviewed library sources, and gathered artifacts relevant to their investigations. The presentations allowed the students to present themselves to their classmates and to reveal thoughts and beliefs about issues critical to their lives. The SI process became a framework to help students understand themselves and each other. It also validated their lives outside the classroom and helped connect that world to the world of school.

Two particular presentations stand out in my mind. In preparation, a Filipino American student and a Mexican American student interviewed each other's families. They each learned to cook a family recipe from the other's mother, and they each shared a family meal at the other's home. They presented their experiences to the class, telling stories they had learned from each other's parents and from their visits to each other's homes. They even served the foods they had learned to prepare, an event their classmates greatly appreciated. The other presentation that stands out for me was organized by three students, a Vietnamese Buddhist, a Salvadoran Catholic, and an African American Baptist. The students researched different religious customs and holy days. In their presentation, they shared this information and created tableaux to show what each believed happens when a person dies. The class was fascinated by the variety of the presentations for this assignment, as was I.

Excited about the possibilities for opening students up to worlds beyond their immediate experiences, I designed a carefully orchestrated series of activities for my advanced placement English literature students as they embarked on Ellison's novel *Invisible Man*. I wanted to help these students—none of whom is Black—to understand how experiences shape worldviews. I also wanted to help them empathize with the book's narrator, a Black man who feels invisible.

I began with talks related to differences in perception, interpretation, and consciousness. Then I presented maps of the world as viewed by ancient Greeks, Isaac Newton, and quantum physicists. Students in advanced physics explained introductory concepts of quantum mechanics, including Schroedinger's cat principle and Heisenberg's uncertainty principle. As a class, we talked about systems theory, chaos theory, and strange attractors. We then reflected on how perceptions of the universe evolve into different worldviews.

After this introduction, I talked about the SI theory of consciousness expansion. After sharing terms and diagrams relating to self-knowing, other-knowing, difference-holding, and difference-transcending, I told the students they would have an opportunity to shift their perceptions and develop a more global worldview. Students selected partners for the next series of exercises, choosing someone they didn't know very well, someone whom they experienced as thinking differently than they did, or someone with whom they had a conflict. Their assignment was to spend an hour outside of class getting to know each other. The class generated a set of questions as prompts, and I suggested that they tell each other stories about their lives. In preparation, we practiced an active listening exercise. I reminded them that the conditions fostering synergy include being open, nonjudgmental, compassionate, authentic, engaging, and supportive, as well as being an effective listener, which involves listening with a learning attitude.

The next day, students seemed connected at a deeper level. In class, I led them through a relaxation and visualization exercise in which they focused on "an experience when they realized what life was really like." They then described that experience in writing. They met again with their dyad partner and talked about what they were learning about themselves and each other through these activities.

The following day, I introduced SI concepts about the three levels of consciousness—body, mind, and spirit. The dimension of body, I told them, includes our body characteristics, bodily sensations, emotions, and feelings. The second dimension—mind—includes our explanations, concepts, theories, and principles. Spirit, the third dimension of consciousness, includes our faith, beliefs and myths, and unthought or unsaid presuppositions that shape our explanations, feelings, and actions. I asked each dyad to identify one key difference at each level, explaining that they would not only hold those differences internally but also embody them through role-playing exercises. The goal was to expand their ability to hold the consciousness of the other person. This activity, however, proved a stumbling block for most of the students for several minutes. But then Dietrich and Tara showed the class how they interpreted the directions. Taking my suggestion to begin coaching each other in gestures and body movements in preparation for the role play, Dietrich taught Tara his idiosyncratic way of opening his day planner. Tara then demonstrated his method to the class:

> Curl the four fingers of your right hand in front of you, just above the fastened strap of the day planner. Then quickly flip these fingers down under the strap and snap it open without using your thumb. Next, with the thumb of your right hand, tap the pen, which is carefully tucked tightly into the penholder. Tap it three times, with sufficient force to pop it out of the holder and into the air, and catch the pen with your same right hand. Then, with a quick backwards twisting of your thumb, push off the cap of the pen at just the right angle so you can catch it between your thumb and fourth and fifth fingers, while holding the pen between your second and third fingers. Deftly insert the cap on the other end of the pen. With one last move, a brisk flip of the plastic divider, the day planner opens to the correct day and date.

Pen in hand, Tara was now ready to write. The students and I dissolved in hysterics as Tara demonstrated and narrated these moves, with Dietrich nodding his approval at each step in the series. Afterward, the room suddenly exploded into activity. Farrah showed James how she flips her hair behind her left ear and tucks it behind her right, and Jake coached Julia how to belly laugh.

Megan invited David outside to teach him how to walk. They came back 5 minutes later, ready to show the class. David, we learned, walks without bending his knees. He takes rapid, long strides, constantly in a hurry to get wherever he's going: "It's the destination that matters, not the journey!"

Megan, on the other hand, bends her knees in a graceful and relaxed manner and strolls down the halls of the school, casually looking around for people to greet. Discussion erupted. Would David be the same person if he started walking with his knees bent and in a more casual way? Could Megan still be Megan if she adopted David's style?

We had been discussing the novel's key incidents in class for several days, both in dyads and in small groups. The students now seemed ready to write a one-page draft about the protagonist's experiences, examining his world and his worldview. The next day, in a 90-minute class, they brought drafts to class and spent 15 minutes silently reading their peers' papers. Afterward, I led them in a brief visualization of the world as experienced by Ellison's narrator. Then, they each made drawings showing symbolically or artistically how they imagined this world to be. After sharing the drawings with their peers, I asked the students to push their desks back against the walls and sit quietly for a few moments. Directing them to again close their eyes, they visualized their drawings, animating their visualizations in their mind to bring the drawings to life. They imagined symbolically how the narrator would move in his world, first by seeing this scene in their minds and then feeling it in their bodies.

Cued by me, they then got out of their desks. With lowered eyes to give each other private space, they moved around the room, representing with their bodies the narrator's experience in his world. One student crouched and slowly maneuvered across the room. Other students moved disjointedly, zigzagging across the room. Several became mimes, demonstrating how they were boxed or closed in. This exercise tested both the students' trust in each other and the depths with which they could embody the consciousness of the narrator. Afterward, the students returned to their desks and wrote what this experience had been like for them. They also described the narrator's experience of his world, synthesizing movement, art, reading, and discussion into their understanding of his worldview. Outside of class, they revised their draft of the narrator's worldview. Several days later, students then shared one-page drafts of their own worldviews. These drafts were prepared for a 2,500-word essay assignment: Examine the experiences and worldviews of narrator and self. What meaning do you make?

In and out of class, students participated in book discussions as well as activities on perception, multiple realities, Western worldviews, oppression, and synergy. The goal was for them to increase their capacities to attend to and witness the experiences of self and other. Understanding the novel *Invisible Man* requires a special relationship between the reader and the narrator, because understanding is dependent on the reader's ability to receive and acknowledge the testimony of this man who feels unseen by others. My intention was to help students understand realities that, on some levels, were very different from their experiences. To help them, I offered another definition of understanding: standing under the same horizon of intelligibility as another.

In their essays, several students examined their core assumptions and questioned their previously taken-for-granted worldviews. Some offered remarkable original theories about groups and how individuals interact with them. Others wrote about how individuals are shaped by society, about multiple realities and multiple selves, about the journey to find and construct an identity, and about what it's like to be torn between different cultures. These students did important work.

Recently, I asked my advanced placement students what they remembered from that unit. Serena, a 17-year-old immigrant from India, reflected:

> There are many ways two individuals may interact with one another. The result is dependent on the depth each individual looks into the other and the level of understanding and overlapping consciousness that occurs between, among, and around them.

Desiree, a 17-year-old who moved to the United States from the Philippines three years prior, wrote:

> The study of synergy and the participation in the dyad exercises ultimately practiced my ability to hold differences in perception or knowing side by side. Seeing the world through another did not only open my mind further but also made me appreciate my own views, set in a bigger picture. I have come to two conclusions. First, by understanding another person's thinking and knowing, an individual obtains an exponential growth in awareness. And secondly, reaching this awareness requires a great amount of energy; embodying another's senses is a difficult process.

The students requested we continue our synergy work "because there is so little opportunity for us to really get to know about people in high school."

Daniel, a 16-year-old Vietnamese American, recently offered his perspectives about the importance of SI, after several gender synergy cycles:

> While we were in our [gender-segregated] groups, I noticed that the girls were more able to share their thoughts and stories. They just seemed to be filled with an unlimited fountain of stories and ideas. They automatically formed a bridge of trust between each other, while we, the boys, had more problems. I really did feel like telling a story. But we just sat there. We still couldn't start. In these 2 days I learned that men have problems in expressing how we feel. We are not able to quickly build a bridge of trust between each other. Girls are better at this than us. Men don't tell each other how we feel because of society. In society men

are expected to be strong and keep their emotions inside and not share them with other men. If you see a man who is able to share his feelings openly, society immediately says that this man is gay or just weird. To solve this, as a society we must teach children, especially young boys, that it is okay to show your feelings and it is not a sign of weakness. Then men and women can come one step closer to understanding each other and hopefully be more equal to each other.

We can be partners on a communal journey for the short time we are together. SI invites people to participate intentionally and with awareness in this world. The hope SI can bring for the future can be represented in the wisdom of students like Eian, a 16-year-old Black boy, who shared these discoveries from his journey: "Even while all the male influences in my life make me loud, strong, and powerful, the female influences keep me calm, sensitive, and caring. I have found a perfect balance."

Reference

Hoagland, S. (1992). *Lesbian ethics: Toward new values.* Palo Alto, CA: Institute of Lesbian Studies.

14

Synergizing Cultural Differences for Improving Organizational Performance: A Case Study of Synergic Inquiry in China

Charles Joiner, Yongming Tang, and Yifu Yin

In July, 1995, a joint synergy project using synergic inquiry (SI) as a methodology was sponsored by the California Institute of Integral Studies (CIIS), located in San Francisco, California, United States, and the Beijing Graduate School of Wuhan University of Technology, located in Beijing, China. These two groups rejected the common view that there is inherent cultural conflict between Eastern and Western perspectives, believing instead that there should be no walls in the realm of economy, nor national boundaries in the realm of business management. They felt that a theory of cultural synergy was needed to replace the existing theory of cultural conflicts. Based on the idea that differences can be transcended into a creative larger whole, this project was developed to study how much could be achieved toward a new global culture that has room and opportunities for all.

The project involved two research teams. One, led by Professor Yifu Yin, consisted of 11 midlevel managers from a state-owned enterprise called Beijing New Building Supplies Company (BNBM), located in Beijing. The other team, led by Dr. Yongming Tang and Charles Joiner, was made up of graduate students from CIIS. This team consisted of 10 people with diverse backgrounds and expertise. Interpreters were used to help with language and cultural translation. For more than 2 weeks, these teams collaborated with each other, using their cultural differences to seek synergistic ideas that could improve the performance of the company. This project had three purposes:

1. To synergize the Chinese cultural perspective with other cultural perspectives for expanding the BNBM managers' consciousness and capacities for problem solving

2. To use the SI process to explore a modern company system with the vitality to improve BNBM's economic performance and employee job satisfaction

3. To provide an experimental model and an example of a learning experience for other state-owned enterprises in China

The joint CIIS–BNBM project team was organized into three bicultural subteams for separate in-depth focus on leadership, human relations, and marketing.

Both the BNBM members and the CIIS members undertook processes of self-knowing and other-knowing to differentiate their two perspectives. The CIIS team interviewed several dozen BNBM employees, observed a number of work settings and situations, and intimately interacted with the BNBM team to seek synergistic outcomes. At the end of the project, the joint team presented its findings to representatives of the senior leadership of BNBM. After returning to the United States, CIIS team members put together subteam reports and a final project report for use by the BNBM management team. One year later, Dr. Tang and a member of the CIIS team returned to BNBM for feedback about the key effects of this project.

History and Context

China is currently undergoing a tremendous cultural transition. The Chinese government is attempting to introduce Western-style business practices, while maintaining traditional Chinese cultural values and the values from which Chinese Communism operates. There is relative freedom of movement within the country, and entrepreneurship is being encouraged and supported by the central government. Many individuals are becoming rich, and those with education, ability, and *guanxi* (the informal relationship or support network of such importance in the Chinese cultural context) are doing very well.

There is also vigorous promotion of joint ventures with foreign companies. At the time of this project, there were about 100,000 joint ventures in operation and 130,000 more were waiting to be initiated. However, state-owned enterprises are generally not performing well in this new competitive economic environment, and many are going bankrupt. Wage gaps are also increasing.

Coupled with these developments is the possibility of unemployment, which, until a few years ago, was thought to be nearly nonexistent in the "Iron Rice Bowl." This potential for unemployment is at odds with both Chinese Communism and basic Chinese cultural values; the former places emphasis on providing for the basic needs of all the country's people, and the latter emphasizes the good of the group over that of the individual.

Because of this dilemma, the Chinese government is attempting to develop what they call a socialist market economy. Capitalistic business practices are being simultaneously encouraged and, to some extent, controlled as the government attempts to manage this critical transition in contemporary Chinese history.

Recognizing that state-owned enterprises are experiencing extreme difficulties in the market system, the government has initiated a nationwide experiment in which 100 state-owned enterprises have been selected and given great freedom to experiment with innovative management systems. It is hoped that these experiments will lead to increased national and global competitiveness for state-owned enterprises. BNBM is among the companies chosen for this experiment.

BNBM is a holding company for more than 40 plants and trading companies and has a research institute on the premises of the company headquarters. It has been cited as one of the 500 most profitable enterprises of China, one of the 100 famous enterprises of China, and one of the 100 largest industrial companies in China.

Founded in 1979, BNBM is a successful state-owned enterprise that manufactures many regionally well-known building material products for China, Southeast Asia, Taiwan, Hong Kong, and other countries. These products include things such as gypsum board, rock wool insulation, and steel studs. Known for its reliable products, present production cannot keep up with demand, especially the demand for gypsum board.

More than a company in the modern Western sense, BNBM has many social responsibilities. In addition to its production facilities, it provides housing for employees, operates a grocery store and a cultural center, supports the schools, and is involved in all aspects of an employee's life. In this sense, BNBM operates as a small village of 2,000 people in which the same person serves as both mayor and chief executive officer (CEO).

The leaders of BNBM were aware of their market position and recognized that they faced stiff competition from joint ventures and privately owned enterprises. They wished to maintain and expand their market share, become more active globally, and continue to provide comprehensive social services to employees; these services include schooling for children, housing near the company, a hospital, grocery markets, a bar, a theater, and a public bath.

Under the advisement of Professor Yifu Yin, a well-known management educator and mentor to many upper level managers (including the CEO), BNBM has been seeking to develop a management system that supports both market competitiveness and social responsibility. It was the combination of interest, guanxi, and governmental support that set the stage for a project of the type described in this case study. This was a large and complex project that was heavily documented. Only a small portion of this documentation is used here to illustrate how SI was applied to issues of international business in China.

Project Design and Process

The CIIS team spent 4 days in San Francisco preparing for this project, and team members conducted two synergy cycles. One used SI to focus on team development. In the self-knowing step of this cycle, team members spent about 10 minutes reflecting on who they are, what attracted them to the project, and the fears and concerns they had about embarking on such a distant journey. During other-knowing, plenty of time was given for them to listen to each other's presentations. In difference-holding and difference-transcending, team members worked together to develop a synergic vision for how they would interact with each other and with the collaborating Chinese team. The resulting team vision included ideas such as trust, common goals, presence, emergent leadership, dialogue, intimacy, mutual respect, support, diversity of awareness, the ability to learn from mistakes, nonjudgmental attitudes, humor, multimember contributions, noncompetitive actions, appreciation of each other, and shared purpose. They also developed the following norms:

1. Maintain cross-cultural awareness

2. Model a learning organization (i.e., learning from each other) and learning processes, including feedback and double-loop learning

3. Accept individual perspectives

4. Engage in action and reflection cycles

5. Make space for everybody and provide monitoring processes to ensure space

6. Recognize an individual's power to stop the process

7. Be mindful about the process

8. Be punctual (express time sensitivity)

9. Keep group agreements

10. Have fun and breathe

After this cycle, participants felt the interconnections needed for good teamwork, and their confidence grew. They learned the SI process by personally experiencing it.

The CIIS team identified a theme question that could provide a central focus for the project: What is the modern company system that will enhance the vitality of BNBM? This question was formulated with the help of Professor Yin and the key BNBM executives before the CIIS team was assembled. To deal with the complexities of a large organization in a different cultural setting, the U.S. team organized into three subteams—a leadership subteam, a human dimension subteam, and a marketing subteam—using an organizational systems perspective (see Figure 14.1). This perspective was chosen because it allowed for a comprehensive look at the organization within its cultural and social context.

After organizing into subteams and preparing for the trip, the CIIS team engaged in the second synergy cycle to develop a CIIS perspective on the nature of a vital company. The full SI process was deployed, and a larger perspective of the makeup of a vital modern company was developed. This synergy cycle helped bring the key assumptions underlying the team's perspective to the surface and helped further build the team.

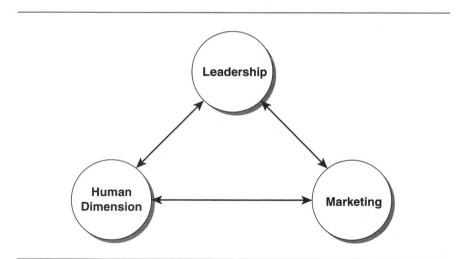

Figure 14.1   The Three-Subteam Strategy

The group also reviewed ethnographic research methods and interviewing techniques to enhance their capacity for entering into and learning about Chinese culture and organizational behavior. Emphasis was placed on the importance of personal journaling for growth at the personal level.

After arriving in Beijing, and before beginning research with BNBM, the CIIS team spent 3 days touring to get a sense of the history and cultural context of modern China. They visited the Forbidden City, the Great Hall of the People, Tiannemen Square, a Confucian Temple, a Tibetan Buddhist lamasery, the Ming Tombs, and the Great Wall. They also wandered around central Beijing, shopping and poking about the streets and alleyways of this old city. The team enjoyed several meals in traditional Chinese restaurants and had the honor of being the first foreign guests at a rustic farm restaurant. After these few days, having gained a sense of Chinese culture based on personal experience, they began their work with BNBM.

The initial 2 days at the company were set aside for formal introductions, tours, presentations, and speeches that were intended for the entire CIIS team. They were provided with structural and financial overviews of BNBM and how it, as a state-owned enterprise, fits into the Chinese system. They were also given overviews on current Chinese cultural and economic realities from the Chinese perspective. They were also able to share many meals with their Chinese colleagues as these helped develop relationships that went beyond those of the actual "work."

Joint Project Organization and Process

In opening the project, the CEO, Mr. Song, said, "I hope you can help improve management here at BNBM. The Chinese have a spirit like those who built the Great Wall." Professor Yin introduced the project and its importance saying:

> This is a day of great significance. . . . The meaning of this project is to expand consciousness and capacities, so [you] can work with any cultural situation. It will help develop the management system with vitality to improve BNBM for greater job satisfaction and provide an experience that can be used to help other state-owned enterprises.

Dr. Tang introduced the synergy process, and the members of both teams introduced themselves. The CIIS strategy for dividing into more focused subteams was adopted by the Chinese, and 12 BNBM managers formed corresponding leadership, human dimension, and marketing subteams to work with the CIIS subteams.

The CIIS team members found that they had to be more flexible than they were at home because it was difficult to do much preplanning. The Chinese business environment is not as highly structured as it is in the United States; it operates on a day-to-day basis. Because the Chinese team did not have the benefit of the same preparation as the CIIS team, it was also necessary for the CIIS subteams to take the initiative. They did this by first developing their own plans and then reviewing these plans with their counterparts on the Chinese teams before proceeding with the inquiry. Among themselves, the CIIS group shared and discussed findings and ideas informally at lunches or dinners and more formally at planned meetings.

The CIIS subteams worked with their Chinese counterparts as often as they could, but the latter's participation was limited due to demands from their schedules and responsibilities at work. The members of the Chinese team were all managers and workers, some of whom were also studying for a master's in business administration under Professor Yin. In the beginning, the CIIS team met formally every evening after dinner to further discuss their data, share patterns and themes that were emerging, and plan future action. As the project progressed and its scope grew larger, these meetings became less frequent.

Self-Knowing

The CIIS team members began their self-knowing (SK) during the initial preparation in San Francisco, where their list of principles for a vital modern company were developed. This SK process continued at BNBM as the subteams conducted other-knowing (OK) through interviews during the first 2 weeks of the project. Participants used the context of the Chinese company situation to help them crystallize their own perspectives.

To develop the CIIS perspective, the teams used the "what," "how," and "why" questions as a framework. The example in Figure 14.2 shows only the motivation portion of a much larger report for SK. This way of organizing perspectives proved to be very useful because it required descriptions of a vision, clear statements about how things work, deeper inquiry into the meaning of observations, and discovery of underlying beliefs by using the "why" question.

Inspired by the ways their CIIS counterparts worked, the BNBM team developed its own perspective on a vital modern company, using a process facilitated by Yongming Tang and Professor Yin. They too used the "what," "how," and "why" framework to develop their SK. See Figure 14.3 for the Chinese perspective on motivation.

WHAT

A vital progressive company is an evolving, living system that is based on uncovering human potential, has ecological perspective, and seeks global sustainability. There are three bottom lines: economic success, social responsibility, and environmental consciousness.

HOW

- Opportunity for individual choice
- Choice of career
- Choice of further education and training
- Equal opportunity to apply for another job
- Rewards and recognition based on achievement
- Financial rewards based on achievement
- Salary based on skills, knowledge, and responsibility
- Promotion to higher salary level based on personal achievement (not seniority or relationship)
- Employees who participate in a way that uses all human capabilities:
  o Work that provides a space for exercising creativity
  o Work that is organized into collaborative teams
  o Employees who can make decisions on how work is done
  o Delegation of decision-making authority so workers can exercise creativity in their work

- Lots of encouragement:
  o Sincere positive reinforcement by supervisors
  o Help accomplishing individual goals
  o Less emphasis on criticism

- Shared understanding of business purpose
- Continual two-way communication of company's activities and goals

WHY

- Each person has a unique identity.
- A person can be creative if able to make individual choices.
- All people have potential that can be developed if given equal opportunity.
- It is important that people be encouraged to bring out their full potential.
- Achievement reinforces and brings forth human energy to better society.
- Quantum physics holds that the universe has a participatory nature; hence, evolution requires full human involvement.
- A human being is also a social being and needs the support of others to develop.
- Shared understanding enhances collective commitment.
- The world is changing fast, and there is a need to act locally and delegate decision making to the lowest levels.
- The chain of command is inefficient in the face of rapid change.
- Mistakes can lead to learning with encouragement and support.
- Punishment and criticism contracts the spirit, creates self-doubt and fear; these effects limit learning and growth.
- Education should be based on the interests of the individual so his or her potential can be developed. This is more efficient.

Figure 14.2   The CIIS Perspective on Motivation

WHAT

New corporate culture exists to move from socialism into a market economy. This is a directive from the central state committee, and we must follow it. We must create a new enterprise with a new concept.

HOW

- Controlling desires
- Regulating behavior by defining punishment and rewards
- Giving positions of responsibility
- Fulfilling material needs
- Increasing income
- Using a salary system (skill, seniority, subsidies, bonus)
- Using an economic responsibility contract
- Providing a technical bonus
- Providing better housing
- Fulfilling spiritual needs
- Providing education and training
- Recognizing achievement
- Providing entertainment
- Creating and promoting a company image
- Educating children
- Encouraging others (i.e., heart-to-heart talks)
- Making horizontal comparisons (competition and face)

WHY

- People have desires; common people are uneducated.
- Bad desires have to be punished.
- Good desires must be rewarded.
- Better income leads to a better life.
- People are social beings, so they need to belong to the community and need the encouragement of others to perform well.

Figure 14.3   The Chinese Perspective on Motivation

Other-Knowing

For OK, the CIIS team presented their SK to the Chinese team. This was followed by the Chinese team's presentation of their own SK about BNBM. To ensure a solid OK process, the CIIS group worked to complete an initial version of this perspective based on a combination of this presentation and their experiences to date at BNBM. They made a presentation of this OK to the BNBM team and received feedback from the Chinese team for accuracy. In a similar way, the BNBM team presented their OK of the CIIS perspective to the CIIS team by comparing it according to their own BNBM perspective. The CIIS team was impressed by how well their perspective had been perceived, and they in turn coached the BNBM team for accuracy. These exchanges worked well to clarify the two perspectives.

To deepen OK, each CIIS subteam organized its own OK activities independently. The OK activities lasted for 2 weeks, with a 3rd week reserved for integration and synergy activities. All of these activities required interaction and discussion with the people in and around BNBM. To facilitate these actvities, each subteam had a Chinese interpreter assigned to it, and, except for those few managers who spoke some English, all discussions were held through interpreters. Chinese members of each subteam took care of necessary logistics and arrangements, such as providing interpreters, making appointments, and providing transportation. There was much informal sharing throughout the process when the teams met in the large conference room that the company provided for the project and as they shared meals in the company canteen.

OK deepened for the BNBM team through their interactions with the CIIS subteams. The functioning of the CIIS team was observed, and endless questions were asked about how CIIS teammates would do things differently and why. It is important to point out that this process helped the BNBM team members understand the CIIS perspective better. One of the managers made the following comment:

> The whole experience with them is very helpful. At the initial joint project organization, some of our team judged their chaotic way of working together and did not feel comfortable. Now, after seeing how they have been working together, I can see the value of democratic participation in which everyone can make a contribution to whatever they do together. It fosters trust and team synergy. It is something I think can be used for improving our company.

Differences-Holding

For the final steps of this project, culturally mixed subteams engaged in the processes of differences-holding (DH) and differences-transcending (DT). The subteams spent a full day and a half interacting as integrated subteams, discussing their differing perspectives without judgment, and clarifying differences when needed.

During this process, all were holding their differences in tension to see if new perspectives could emerge to help the Chinese managers develop new possible strategies to improve their company's performance. For example, the joint subteam for motivation attempted to list concrete examples for both extrinsic and intrinsic motivation. The results of the team's effort are shown in Figure 14.4.

	BNBM	CIIS
Extrinsic	Salary system Technical bonus Better housing Opportunity for training Recognition of model workers Paid vacations Entertainment Company image Horizontal competition Ideology work Rewards and punishment	Skill-based income Performance appraisal Work ethic Mission statement Servant leadership Peer support Delegation of authority
Intrinsic	Better life environment Collegial relationships Sense of belonging Recognition of achievement Reliance on factory	Job enrichment Empowerment Self-directive teams Participation in decision making Job variation Individual choice Self-actualization Allowance for creativity Encouragement to take initiative

Figure 14.4   A Comparison of BNBM Perspective and CIIS Perspective on Motivation

As can be seen from this comparison, U.S. motivation is rich in intrinsic rewards, whereas the Chinese counterpart is richer in extrinsic factors.

It had not been easy to define what belonged to the extrinsic and what to the other; this took much dialogue between the two subteams, and many of the items raised seemed to go into both categories. The probability that all of the items listed go somewhere toward the middle of an extrinsic–intrinsic continuum was acknowledged. Even taking all of this into consideration, participants concluded that the U.S. perspective had a motivation system characterized as intrinsic-high, whereas the Chinese had an extrinsic-high motivation system. Through excited discussions, the group developed the diagram shown in Figure 14.5.

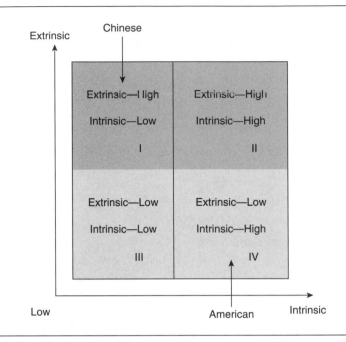

Figure 14.5   Comparison of the BNBM Perspective and CIIS Perspectives on Motivation

Differences-Transcending

These discussions on DH led to a breakthrough in the thinking of the Chinese team. Using their experiences with the U.S. team, the Chinese managers developed new insights about motivation that they could now integrate with their collective viewpoint. Figure 14.6 shows the results of using the "what," "how," and "why" framework during their integrative discussions.

The most important part of this synergy process was that both teams noticed the need to find a balancing point between intrinsic and extrinsic motivation to develop a modern company system. The "dragon of dragons" metaphor gave them a good idea of what this balance looks like and how it should function. The dragon is a symbol for rising power and is also one of the brand names for BNBM products. In China, this image effectively says that BNBM itself has the rising power of a dragon and that it is able to motivate its employees extrinsically. It also says that this power will be maximized only when employees sees themselves as dragons and understand that they too can motivate themselves intrinsically. The shared assumption in this metaphor is that the sum of the parts is bigger than the whole.

WHAT

- A culturally synergistic motivation system that allows BNBM to become a "dragon of dragons"

HOW

- Everybody becomes a dragon.
- A balance exists between intrinsic and extrinsic motivation.

WHY

- Collective synergy: $1 + 1 > 2$

Figure 14.6   A Synergic Vision of Motivation for BNBM

The project ended with two significant final events. A joint presentation of the collaborative findings and recommendations was made to the senior management in a morning session. Key leaders came to listen to the team reports, and the leaders publicly acknowledged and appreciated the work that had been done by both teams. At the end of this presentation, the CIIS and the BNBM teams again worked together. All of the BNBM team members shared how much they had learned through this intense period and how valuable the learnings were for their personal and professional development.

The other closing event was a dinner party hosted by CEO Song, during which he congratulated everyone on the hard work they had done. Company gifts with BNBM symbols were offered to each of the CIIS team members, and all of the participants sang and danced together. Late in the night, as the bus was taking CIIS participants back to their hotel, Chinese team members in unison burst into English to say "I love you!" and CIIS team members responded in Chinese: "Wo Ai Ni [I love you, too]!"

Results and Discussion

Eight months later, BNBM management reported on how this project affected BNBM's growth and development in terms of both economic performance and employee satisfaction. Because the participants from BNBM were plant and department managers who influence production and employee behavior directly, the insights they obtained directly influenced the way BNBM operated.

Through the synergy process, the BNBM management team gained a deeper understanding of their own organization as a whole, as well as the major cultural and managerial assumptions underlying their management approach. Further, through synergic interaction with the CIIS team, the BNBM team expanded the consciousness of the organization in ways that then influenced the positive development of the company as a whole. For example, the synergy project made the BNBM team deeply aware of how their culture emphasizes collectivism and loyal contribution from employees, whereas the CIIS perspective advocates individual motivation, creativity, and team synergy. As a result, the BNBM team was able to create a synergic awareness that enhanced the strengths of both collectivism and individualism. In other words, they developed a new mentality in which both the collective and the individual were equally important. These managers now protect, motivate, and empower individual development and creativity, while at the same time they pay attention to the needs of the larger collective.

Using this synergistic way of thinking led BNBM to experience growth of both income and profitability. Although it is difficult to quantitatively determine exactly what proportion of this growth can be attributed to the participation of the BNBM management team in the synergy project and what is simply a reflection of larger economic realities, the objective gains are as real as the subjective gains.

The cross-cultural dynamics of this project were informative on many levels, and at times dealing with cultural differences was a definite challenge for both sides. For example, when the floor was open to ideas about organizing the project, CIIS team members were very active, rapidly putting out many differing ideas in an attempt to better explore a range of possibilities. The Chinese team saw these efforts as "chaotic"; they could not understand why the CIIS team behaved as it did. CIIS teammates did their best to bring all possibilities to the surface, while the Chinese team as a whole was silent. Gradually, they showed their frustration by calling for more directive leadership from Dr. Tang, Charlie Joiner, and Professor Yin—many of them speaking out at the same time. This in turn struck the CIIS team as chaotic, whereas their own behavior did not. To help all participants recognize that each team had cultural assumptions about team behavior, the facilitators pointed out that each team's judgment of the other's behavior was an interpretation. This experience was an opportunity for both teams to deepen learning about self and other, and afterward the two sides began to avoid judgmental behaviors.

Another revealing cultural dynamic surfaced during the development of the BNBM team's SK. The SI process assumes that every perspective is unique and has a contribution to make to the whole; thus, the process was designed to give every member an opportunity to express and contribute.

However, accustomed to having those with status and power speak for the whole group, the Chinese team had difficulty with the process: It took real effort for them to coparticipate in the process. For example, when Professor Yin was present, those in the group who were his students tended to be silent in spite of encouragement from both Dr. Tang and Professor Yin to have equal say. This encouragement was not enough to get them to behave in ways that their culture would consider disrespectful. Fortunately, Professor Yin was not present at all of the meetings, and these participants had other opportunities for dynamic engagement with each other and the SI process.

In hindsight, it was audaciously ambitious to believe that a nonexpert foreign group, made up of people who had never worked together before, could travel halfway around the globe, immerse themselves in a widely different culture, and in a few weeks grasp the intricacies of a large complex business that was embedded in a radically different political system—and to do this with sufficient insight and depth to accomplish anything. Again in hindsight, it is surprising that the SI process was powerful enough to expose so many hidden assumptions about their organizational system, of which none of the BNBM management had previously been aware. With these assumptions exposed, managers gained greater latitude to propose and implement innovative changes. The key to this unexpected outcome was the SI methodology and the way it enabled these people to view their world from two very different perspectives in ways that would allow them to systematically document, explore, and understand the beliefs that govern their collective choices.

In the process, superficial judgments about each cultural orientation were overcome, and differences between and within the cultures were used to enhance the development of creative alternatives to complex organizational issues. More important, this process did not end up in recommendations made by foreign experts to be implemented later by people who didn't really understand them. The results of this project were fundamental changes in the ways participants thought about their situations. In other words, this project gave all participants new ways of thinking, and those new ways of thinking continue to be applied to the issue of developing a healthy and viable modern company system for China after the conclusion of the project.

15

Synergic Inquiry and Organizational Transformation: A Case Study of Synergic Inquiry Application in a U.S. Organization Working in Mexico

Charles Joiner, Susan Cannon, and Karen O'Neil

World SHARE (Self Help and Resource Exchange), a social business that originated in the United States and has affiliates in Guatemala and Mexico, faced difficult issues that grew out of a need for U.S. internal renewal and a loss of funding sources for their Mexico program. These issues combined with economic chaos in unexpected ways. A group of six members of a doctoral program at California Institute of Integral Studies (CIIS) were exploring synergic inquiry (SI) as a methodology for collaborative action research and accepted World SHARE's invitation to facilitate their organizational transformation. The case study presented here is a summary of their work.

Three members of World SHARE (hereafter SHARE) joined these students as members of a collaborative SI team, and six other SHARE members took part in the project but did not collect data or participate in the ongoing synergizing processes that took place in the field. As a second level of research, a core group of four students also examined how the SI process affects personal transformations for both facilitators and participants.

SHARE is an example of a social business, one of the alternative structures emerging within our economic system that seeks to integrate social values within a capitalist market economy. It originated in the United States and has affiliates in Mexico and Guatemala. In the United States, SHARE is a private 501(c)(3) nonprofit organization that works through a national network of 27 independently incorporated and locally sponsored SHARE affiliates. These affiliate organizations are supported by a corporate staff located in San Diego.

SHARE supports local organizations by helping people obtain affordable, nutritious food and improve their communities. Rather than raising funds through donations, the organization participates in the competitive market economy, creating a service that fills a basic human need. SHARE generates a "profit," or fund balance, which is managed with a business mindset toward efficiency and productivity. All "profits," however, are reinvested in projects to accomplish SHARE's social mission. As a nonprofit, the organization bears many of the social mission qualities of a charity and has a stake in the well-being of the community. The concepts of self-help, empowerment, and community development through voluntary individual participation are key to the SHARE mission.

To serve this mission in the United States, food is purchased in high volumes by the corporate staff and distributed once a month to the local affiliates for redistribution through volunteer host organizations. The host organizations (churches, senior citizens centers, and other organizations) develop volunteer teams that come to the affiliate warehouse each month to pick up and transport the food to their own sites. There the food is packaged by volunteer participants for individual distribution. The participants pay $14 for their food packages and commit to helping others 2 hours a month in exchange for access to food that is discounted from its retail price by approximately 40%. The food packages include 6–10 lb. of meat (e.g., chicken, fish, hamburger patties), several kinds of fresh vegetables and fruits, and three to five grocery or staple items, such as beans, rice, or pasta. Vegetarian packages are available for those who prefer them.

SHARE also receives grants from the U.S. government to distribute food aid in Guatemala and Mexico. This aid was administrated through existing local charitable organizations in Mexico. Eventually, these affiliates gained representation on the SHARE board and sought a greater focus on "U.S. matters." In addition, in 1994, the U.S. government began a "trade, not aid" agenda with Mexico and stopped funding SHARE's food-aid project in Mexico.

Before this funding ended, the 17 affiliated Mexican charity organizations were approached about starting up self-help programs that were based on the SHARE model in the United States. Some of the government grant money was left in reserve to be loaned to the new Mexican startups as seed money. Six of the 17 existing affiliates submitted business plans, received training, and started business. Most of these, as Rotary-sponsored organizations, were more business-like and philosophically aligned with the self-help concept than some of the other charities that had been affiliated with SHARE.

Although SHARE started in Mexico by administrating a U.S. Department of Agriculture (USDA) food relief program through charity organizations, its main experience was not in overseas charity administration but in setting up self-sufficient, semiautonomous affiliates to provide low-cost food to U.S. participants in return for payment plus volunteer work in the distribution cycle. To continue its activity in Mexico, SHARE decided to implement a self-help program based directly on the model of their successful U.S. affiliate program. Due to this lack of cultural adaptation and the prior "charity" perspective of Mexican affiliate staff, this program was immediately beset with problems.

At the time these changes were taking place with the Mexican affiliates, Mexico suffered a sudden, drastic currency devaluation. As a result of the change in the money supply, the self-help concept did not go over very well with participants. They were faced with too many shocks at one time: the reality shock of having their currency suddenly devalued when they were already in great need, the psychological shock of now having to pay for the food that they had previously been receiving as a donation, and the cultural shock of food packages based on U.S. tastes, not on Mexican tastes or needs. The SHARE de Mexico affiliates struggled hard to both follow the U.S. model and satisfy participants who felt angry and betrayed. Loaning seed money to the startups in Mexico from the remaining USDA funds was a controversial move. When the program did not generate the level of initial participation expected, the SHARE de Mexico affiliates requested extended credit.

In the background at World SHARE corporate, a serious interorganizational conflict emerged over the interpretation of the term *self-help* within their mission. Some corporate managers interpreted self-help narrowly to mean "full levels of self-funding and profit creation." Others interpreted it as "providing support such that disadvantaged people could become empowered to help themselves." Further tensions erupted as the U.S. affiliates, feeling that they were already paying too much for SHARE's corporate expenses with their sales fees, resented money going toward "foreign assistance." However, this was a challenge to SHARE's mission statement, which said it was an international network.

The crisis Mexico was facing at that time was not easy for people from the United States to understand. The kind and magnitude of that economic crisis has not been known in U.S. history: Mexican money had been devalued by 50% overnight. Inflation had increased 50% in 15 days. Wages had held firm while buying power had dropped an estimated 70% in less than 1 year. At the same time, interest rates had risen from 20% to as high as

90%, and banks were refusing to allow people to repay loans. Unemployment was pushing 20%, and many of those who were working had been changed from regular employees to contract employees so that their employers would not have to pay benefits. Others found their work hours reduced to only 3 days per week. All of this had come on the heels of the NAFTA agreement, which was promoted by the previous president of Mexico as the final step toward parity with the people of the United States.

The Mexican people felt a deep sense of betrayal and were facing serious hardships. Nonetheless, they maintained a spirit of hope, a determination to go forward, to "reinvent Mexico" and achieve greater democracy and economic parity with the dominant powers of the globe.

Advance Preparations

The project team initially met online, with each person posting an introductory piece that gave an indication of his or her background and interest in the project and included some personal history. Everyone was interested in transformative learning and personal transformation. Other motivators included interest in cultural synergy, participative inquiry, nonprofit organizations, empowerment, grassroots organizing, organizational consulting, and Mexico.

Mental preparation for cultural immersion included reading *Labyrinth of Solitude,* by Octavio Paz, and *Habits of the Heart,* by Robert Bellah, to begin differentiating the two cultures. Before starting active research, a face-to-face meeting for community building and planning was held in San Francisco, but only one SHARE participant was able to attend. Participants in this meeting developed a statement of purpose and two overarching questions to shape the inquiry, helping to give it a clear focus.

The strategy was for this synergy team to facilitate differentiation of the two cultural perspectives within the organization: a U.S. perspective and a Mexican perspective. These two perspectives would need to be checked for accuracy and brought to those who would be participating in a final event called synergy day, where it was expected that new ideas to transcend both perspectives would emerge and provide new insights about the difficulties and new approaches to resolution.

Subteams were identified for focus work, the various levels of synergy and the needs at each level were delineated, and time was built into the schedule for adequate reflection, dialogue, work on the different cultural perspectives, and daily transcription of field notes. Questions and guidelines for a flexible questionnaire were developed, and key actors were identified for interviews that had to be scheduled in advance. One member designed field notebooks with standardized interview recording formats, schedules, and background information.

Facilitation methods were discussed, and the need for balance between content and process was acknowledged. A balance between informational and perspectival processes was determined so that the information collected could be continually updated, integrated, and refined. The form of the final synergy process at the full organizational level was left to emerge. A day was scheduled at the end of the fieldwork in Mexico for the research team to reflect on all of the findings and develop a fitting process for synergy day. It was clear that a research team made up of student members from CIIS and corporate members from SHARE, all participating in the synergy process as both coresearchers and coparticipants on a single team, would be a unique experience.

In the Field—The SHARE Corporate Perspective

Fieldwork began with team members from CIIS convening at SHARE corporate offices in San Diego, where 2 business days were dedicated to interviews and discussions with the staff, with an additional day scheduled for experiencing the activities at SHARE distribution centers. The 1st day in San Diego was spent around a conference table in formal dialogue between members of the synergy team; the two vice presidents with direct responsibility for the Mexico program were included in these discussions. Personal histories, values, and interests in this project were used for introductions and team building. These contributions showed a common thread of interest in startups, a desire to be independent of society's normal institutions, and interest in change as well as efforts toward the greater good.

In an attempt to form a clear picture of the factors leading to the current problems, time was spent discussing SHARE's history, including information about the personalities and vision that shaped the organization, and SHARE's operations from its founding through its numerous reorganizations. The corporate participants gained a number of insights during this process. They remarked that it was the first time that they had a chance to reflect on their past together. Conflicting memories and information that came via informal routes between sessions and at meals revealed power struggles and undercurrents of dissension.

One weekend day was scheduled for taking part in SHARE's monthly food distribution process at their San Diego affiliate warehouse; CIIS team members who weren't yet in San Diego participated by visiting a distribution at a different location. This gave the CIIS team an opportunity to observe and interact with both warehouse staff and participant volunteers. There was also a lengthy group interview and dialogue with the monsignor in the San Diego Catholic diocese, who was a founder and former board chairman of SHARE.

The CIIS team attended the corporate weekly staff meeting on Monday morning and spent the rest of that morning in formal interviews and dialogue with the president and the development director. SHARE's corporate leaders identified a set of primary questions for the focus of this inquiry:

1. Understanding the deep-seated mistrust the Mexican people generally have of others, what actions can World SHARE take to develop better trust and confidence with its affiliate boards and staff and to assist its affiliates in developing better trust and confidence with its host organizations and participants?

2. To what extent is World SHARE able to rely on the development of a host organization network through which to operate SHARE in Mexico (i.e., the registration of participants and bagging, transportation, and distribution of packages)?

3. What actions, strategies or changes need to be made to the SHARE program model to increase participation by the Mexican people?

The existence and focus of these questions were included as part of the SHARE corporate perspective.

The CIIS team then spent a day trying to distill their information into the key elements of SHARE's corporate perspective. As they struggled to develop a clear image from corporate SHARE's combination of detailed data, partial memories, and conflicting stories, three pieces were developed:

1. A linear history of SHARE, which provided the basis for an overall shared picture of the organization

2. A nonlinear, dynamic depiction of World SHARE coming into manifestation from a "spiritual calling," including the general culture of the United States, its business and entrepreneurial culture, the Catholic Church, and numerous strong personalities in its depiction of the forces and influences that had shaped SHARE's mission, perspective, actions, and structure

3. A first attempt to differentiate a SHARE U.S. perspective that identified specific elements in the corporate voice

These pieces were mirrored to the senior manager responsible for the Mexico program, who expressed surprise at the depth, accuracy, and speed with which they had been developed. The perspective piece was also mirrored privately to the president, and he accepted it with virtually no changes.

CIIS team members spent another day in reflection to make sense of the data in such a way that it could be mirrored back to the SHARE members of their team. This was to ensure the validity of the SHARE U.S. perspective early in the inquiry. It was inevitable that personal insights and transformations would arise during reflection on the SI process. With what was going on within the organization, similar elements could be recognized within the lives of the researchers.

One of the major themes expressed by the SHARE staff was that most of them were drawn to begin their work by a spiritual calling, or sense of mission. This mission included feeding the hungry of the world in such a way that they would be empowered to both help themselves and join in spirit within their own communities. During the meaning-making exercises that led to the development of the initial SHARE corporate perspective, it was seen that over time as the SHARE organization became more formed and structured, this calling and mission had reified into an ideology. As the essence of its original mission or calling gradually became confused with organizational methodology and procedures, this ideology created a tight structure around SHARE. As a result, staff members felt strongly that they were right and that their procedures were unquestionable because they were following this spiritual calling.

For example, "doing SHARE" or the "essence of SHARE" had come to mean following a very prescribed method for food distribution, community service, and the organization of the community sites known as host organizations. The distribution process depended on a participant receiving a package of food once a month for which he or she had already paid a month in advance. Distribution happened through an organized church or school sponsor that had access to reliable transportation. Participants helped repackage food or worked at the warehouse, and these activities were viewed as part of their community development work, the essential element of sharing through which one partially "paid" for the food they received.

We experienced a large gap between what SHARE was espousing as important and what was really going on. Although SHARE staff believed strongly that they were empowering people, and that this was what separated them from a commercial food co-op, the staff witnessed examples of host organizations distributing food to a Hispanic community in a demeaning manner. In one organization, each person's basket was doled out while participants waited quietly and passively for their share. The organizers of this program mentioned to us in passing that this was because the Mexicans would steal, so they couldn't be trusted to help in distribution.

In most of the questioning of participants, it was revealed that they didn't feel much "spirit" but simply wanted cheap food. Many people in the field, including the founding monsignor, mentioned to us that the "spirit had gone out of SHARE." As the story unfolded even at that early stage of our work, the doctoral students on the team began to question their own sense of life mission—of sacrificing for the greater good. They asked themselves if they too had created their own limiting ideologies by confusing these ideologies with their callings. Were they also trying to foist their ideologies on others, thinking that they were the ones who had it right?

With this, CIIS team members began to explore the issue of a "consultant" mentality, the point of view of those experts who see their own views as superior to those with whom they are working. From this new perspective, those who were reflecting had to firmly reorient their own approaches as they tried to move away from a consultant-client view of their role to a colearner-coresearcher perspective.

In the Field—The SHARE de Mexico Perspective

The fieldwork in Mexico was designed to immerse the SI team in a representative sample of the general culture and community life of both urban and rural Mexico and to acquaint them with the experiences and perspectives of SHARE's Mexican affiliates. Meetings and dialogues with a number of non-SHARE service organizations gave the team a taste of the different methodologies of the low-cost food distribution and community development already present in Mexico. Presentations, dialogues, observations, and personal and group reflections also gave them insight into the sociopolitical situation of Mexico and its current economic crisis.

Meetings took place at breakfast, lunch, and dinner, in restaurants, food distribution centers, and community centers. Wide-ranging viewpoints were represented in these meetings, from those of grassroots community organizers to those of the wealthy and established with a high sense of noblesse oblige. The problems of high unemployment, high inflation, and the recently devalued peso were discussed, and phrases like "the struggle to live with dignity" and the need for the Mexican people to "reinvent themselves from within" exemplified the themes of the meetings.

As close as possible to every other evening, time was set aside for the SI team to convene as a group to work through issues of both the SI process and the content of Mexican culture, which had to be so rapidly assimilated. Accustomed to fulfilling the role of host to people from the United States, rather than that of equal participants in a process of inquiry, team members from SHARE de Mexico did not join in these early reflections.

The inquiry moved into high gear when the team went to Celaya to visit a rural SHARE de Mexico affiliate. With much to see and numerous groups to interview, the inquiry team had to divide up its work and become more disciplined in transcribing interviews. Short memos began to be produced for team members to exchange with one another. As pressures built, the sub-team studying the personal transformations of participants set aside time each morning for journaling to make sure that personal reflections and this aspect of the project would not be lost amid the bustle of the larger inquiry.

As was expected, the actions and decisions of corporate SHARE had been understood quite differently in Mexico. Some of these decisions seemed to the people in Mexico to be based on misinformation and coupled with a lack of follow-through on agreements or, in some cases, even outright deceit. Rather than participate with the discussion at this level, the researchers added this information to their work on developing an understanding of the Mexican perspective. It took almost a full day of group process work in Celaya to make sense of all of the different experiences in a useful way.

To make more sense of the Mexican affiliate perspective, subteams worked out independent structures for displaying findings and syntheses and for bringing these back to the full group for discussion and further synthesis. For meaning making, the CIIS team used drawings and paintings to depict the Mexican perspective, giving visual form to the effects of crisis on the affiliates. The drawings depicted an image of forces and essences swirling out of a red-hot center. The drawings also used a community organizer's words "born of rocks" to describe the perseverance of the Mexican people.

A reflection exercise to embody the group's understanding of the Mexican experience was powerfully felt. It was one thing to think about what it would feel like to wake up one day with their money worth only half its previous day's value; inflation up 50%, which further reduces the value of their money, and bank policies that won't allow them to pay off debts more quickly but increase interest rates from 20% to 90%. Feeling this as an embodied understanding was an entirely different experience.

Continuing development of the corporate perspective revealed confusion between a consultant-style tendency to analyze and judge from an objective standpoint and the actual corporate perspective. In the process of resolving this confusion, the idea emerged that SHARE was in many respects a countercultural force in the United States. This insight ultimately proved pivotal in helping synergy-day participants from corporate SHARE to step outside of their old understandings and make a different kind of sense of their struggles.

Although the issue of personal transformation was organized as a separate inquiry, the subgroup members found it difficult to step fully enough out of the larger situation to formally reflect on how they were transforming. Their first reflection cycle in San Diego had stayed with the questions of the larger group—those of ideology versus spiritual calling—and the mindset of the expert consultant. It wasn't until the long bus ride from Celaya back to Mexico City that these researchers were able to have a formal group reflection that focused on their specific project. The importance of daily journals was evident: The journals allowed the researchers to capture the feelings and personal issues they experienced.

In the swaying bus, surrounded by economic chaos and social upheaval, faced squarely and sometimes painfully with their own cultural biases and assumptions, the subgroup experienced a powerful, dynamic sense of a cycling, spiraling movement accompanied by strong images and emotions. However, at that time, it was not possible to achieve the distance required for a theoretical description of transformation without forgoing the creativity of synergy. Rather than falling back on the old perspectives to do this, the group decided to allow the creativity to carry them further before attempting to shape theory.

Plans for the team's first day back in Mexico City were overpowered by a Labor Day demonstration that took place on the Zocalo—the main square that is surrounded by key government buildings, which was visible through their hotel room windows. All previous Labor Day parades had been organized by PRI, the political party that exercised exclusive control over Mexican politics since independence. In contrast with the past, this demonstration was the action of independent unions, outlawed political parties, and people who could no longer accept the status quo. This was a powerful sign of new political realities being borne out of the economic collapse of the Mexican economy. The demonstration grew to half a million people. Although there were secret police with cellular phones in all areas of the hotel and riot police in the square, the expected violent confrontation did not take place.

Those in power stood secure behind the thick walls of the surrounding buildings and orchestrated a different reality on TV, while the demonstration on the streets took its natural course. By afternoon, the demonstration had turned into a massive party, and the streets were clean 2 hours after the crowds dispersed. No sign of struggle was evident, and all appeared to have returned to the status quo.

The emotional impact of this experience on SI team members cannot be overstated. From the safety of their hotel rooms, they saw people they'd met actively during their research putting their lives on the line for their beliefs. Those familiar with Mexico's past were astounded and relieved that the demonstrators were not met with violent force. Those who were not familiar with Mexico's past were overwhelmed by the power of this demonstration for change and were appalled by the capacity of authoritarian power to erase all visible traces of it.

Observing this groundswell of desire for change brought a major shift in perspective to the inquiry team. First, it provided an image of a fortress mentality of the corporate SHARE office in the face of critical needs. Further, SHARE's belief that the crises had probably doomed their efforts in Mexico no longer seemed so plausible. It looked like the opposite could well be true.

With Mexico grappling once again with the issues of real democracy, what once looked like a problem might actually be an opportunity for SHARE to live out its mission more fully. Some researchers felt that a focus on self-help in Mexico might assist the original essence of SHARE to find room to flower again—if corporate officials could step beyond encrusted ideology to support this change.

Those in charge of SHARE's Mexican affiliates had repeatedly stressed that they deeply believed in its vision, mission, and values and did not want to change the essence of SHARE. Instead, they wanted to be treated as full members of the SHARE team, or family, and to help translate this essence into something that could be successful in the Mexican cultural environment.

SHARE de Mexico's problems, as seen by these leaders, fell into three main areas: development of participation, the relationship with corporate SHARE, and operational elements of the SHARE model. SHARE de Mexico wanted access to U.S. corporate know-how without being ruled by a corporate staff ignorant of Mexican culture, economic, and political realities within which they operated. Core elements that impeded the growth of SHARE de Mexico were identified, and a number of suggestions were made about how to adapt SHARE to the economic and cultural realities in Mexico.

Pivotal to all of this was the level of initial mistrust due to Mexico's history of using food as a manipulative strategy to control and dominate groups of people. Because this manipulative strategy is not present in the United States, corporate SHARE did not understand that they had unwittingly acted with this same manipulative pattern when they lost their U.S. aid. Their insistence on programs with all of the operational attributes used in the United States had set their Mexican affiliates up to be seen as just another set of self-serving manipulators.

Integrating the Perspectives—Synergy Day in Tijuana

The traveling research team entered this phase with personal misgivings about the feasibility of distilling their Mexican experience for corporate SHARE in the brief time allotted. However, the work rhythms and alignments that they developed in the field allowed them to accomplish what was needed. Holding the two SHARE perspectives without judgment proved difficult. The experience on the Zocalo had been too powerful, and the empathy aroused by this event for the common person in Mexico was accompanied by disdain for those insulated behind walls of power. The Mexican members of the research team and those from the United States expressed deep feelings about this. The Mexicans saw their own reality more clearly, and the U.S. members saw how their own system, and potentially the SHARE organization, contained the same elements of oppression as found in the Mexican political system. The team knew that these feeling had to be set aside, and time was taken to express them. Unfortunately, there was not sufficient time to fully process this issue.

A full day had been allotted to developing the process for synergy day. By now the team was a very effective group, and preparations moved forward effectively. The first part of the day was used to clarify the differing perspectives of SHARE in the United States and in Mexico. The group then focused on approaches for the bringing corporate officials into the intense synergy process that would take place on synergy day.

The cultural position of SHARE within the United States was clarified, and assumptions and beliefs tacitly held by corporate staff were identified. The ways in which these cause confusion and prevent integration of actions and goals were described, and a seven-step synergy process was developed for the second half of the day to help generate innovative solutions from within the organization.

The description of tacit assumptions and beliefs proved to be effective enough to allow corporate managers to step out of their habitual ways of seeing issues, and the self-knowing and other-knowing exercises were very successful on synergy day. Tensions escalated, however, during the differences-holding process.

A powerful mask-making and role-playing exercise was used to help the group hold the differences as equal. All participants created individual masks from paper plates using crayons and markers, glue, ribbon, and other items. Then, with the masks held in front of their faces, the participants created two groups, stood facing each other, and took on one of the two perspectives presented and discussed earlier. As a topic was announced, the two groups engaged in short dialogue, first adopting one perspective and then changing places to adopt the other perspective. After this, masks were removed, and participants were given time to engage freely in the verbal exchange from their positions.

These exchanges were often loud and emotional, and the level of creative tension was high. All participants had a chance to feel both of the positions presented, but, because the power perspective was challenged and the rationales offered were not given much respect, some management participants began to feel that they were under personal attack. These discomforts were acknowledged as an integral part of the process, and time was made to process them.

Part of what emerged from this apparent conflict was that corporate staff still wanted fast, prescriptive, consultant-style answers that would change external circumstances without the need for the staff to make any changes. The staff's discomfort was the result of tension between these unspoken expectations and the process in which the staff members participated. Pivotal in the eventual success of this project was the ability of those who facilitated this exercise to hold fast to the essence of synergy and to trust the process in spite of the tensions. When participants eventually began to see both perspectives as valid, the dialogue shifted and became quite creative.

Time was too short to follow through with transcending differences as was planned. Instead, participants used dot stickers to vote on which question from corporate to address. They chose to focus on the question regarding a deepened relationship between corporate SHARE and its Mexican affiliates. The group brainstormed separate lists of ideas from each perspective and then tried to hold all of the views and ideas that had been expressed to help a third list of synergistic ideas emerge. After clustering the ideas by theme, action steps were decided to stay as close as possible to the schedule. Another day would have been useful to address all of the inquiry questions and developing synergistic solutions for them, but time was not scheduled for this.

Because the CIIS team was by then truly able to hold both perspectives as equals, they were given responsibility for the other two questions; these were to be addressed in a written report based on raw data from the inquiry and another interim report, both of which were due within 30 days. A general report on the entire study was to follow within 60 days.

World SHARE in Transformation

In the weeks and months following synergy day, the Mexico Synergy Project appears to have made a significant impact on the SHARE organization and its leadership. In spite of the discomforts experienced on synergy day, a major organizational transformation was initiated at that time. Both formal and informal follow-up discussions indicate that participants attributed this discomfort to situations in which the values they espoused and the values found in action did not agree. They felt that the synergy process helped bring the problem of discordant values to the surface so that the problem could be processed and addressed within the organization.

Several weeks following the completion of the project, the results of the study were presented to the SHARE board of directors. The director of the Latin America organization gave the SHARE corporate perspective, the director of the Mexico self-help program presented the Mexican perspective, and the vice president of operations described the synergic outcomes and next steps. At this point, plans had already been set in motion for these same staff members to reevaluate the entire Mexican program. Because it was clear that merely transferring rigid rules about "how to do SHARE" was not appropriate for the Mexican cultural and economic environment, the board of directors enacted a resolution affirming the priority of staying the course in Mexico and seeking a culturally appropriate form for the program.

At a subsequent meeting of the board's international committee, it was realized that the economic significance of international activity was greater than was previously believed and that the social value of the international activity relative to the domestic program was discounted. At the following board meeting, it was recommended that the fundamental structure of the organization be reevaluated and that the necessary structural changes be made so that World SHARE could indeed become "world."

In addition to organizational change, there has been continued personal impact on the SHARE staff as a result of the SI project. For example, one manager who felt discouraged about the devaluing of her international efforts found a path of greater influence within the organization because of her international perspective. It appears that there is now a place within the organization for differing perspectives and that this is leading to creative alternatives. Part of the synergy team from CIIS was invited by SHARE upper management help SHARE develop its capacity as a learning organization, and the board approved a major collaborative study within the organization from the bottom up.

Discussion and Follow-Up

Although the CIIS team was experienced in holding the delicate balance between living and empathizing with the experience of others while maintaining an open mind to multiple perspectives and interpretations, the team members still felt that they were to some extent walking a tightrope while preparing the reports and recommendations for SHARE. As a group, they were very serious about background preparations and the focus for immersion into the SHARE corporate culture and into the world of the Mexican affiliates. A tremendous amount of personal and collective transformation took place during the inquiry, and layers of this unfolded as the team members collaborated on these reports. Although deep learning had occurred for them, they recognized that true problem solving and organizational intelligence would have to come from within SHARE itself, not from outside consultants.

They felt that one of the weaknesses of this project was that insufficient time and attention were allotted to training nonstudent participants in methods of inquiry and reflection. The team also was not able to make it completely clear upfront that these participants were in fact coresearchers and that they had both the opportunity and the responsibility to participate as equals. During the process, however, these participants did pick up a considerable amount of this knowledge by association. Nonjudgmental empathic listening, critical awareness, deep reflection, and honesty, as well as the importance of balancing group process and feelings with content and tasks, were all learned in the process of doing. By the end of the inquiry, these "untrained" participants were functioning confidently and enthusiastically as coresearchers and equals within the group.

Group maintenance processes, such as morning guided meditations; the sharing of imagery, art, and dreams; and shared breakfasts on a sunny terrace helped the participants meet their student counterparts on the human level. Perceived boundaries between organizational culture and the academic world dissolved as all became engaged in an inquiry of deep interest to each one. They hoped that the understandings and skills learned during the inquiry would be carried into their work world at SHARE.

With the writing of the initial World SHARE report, the main participatory inquiry was brought to a close. A transformation of World SHARE as an organization was set into motion with both personal and institutional ramifications:

> Significant things have happened since the trip. Andy [president] has become a clear spiritual leader and visionary for the SHARE network. He just completed his public relations blitz, which ended in a 20-minute talk at the national mayors' conference. He has developed a powerful message that positions SHARE as a social business and as an alternative to the current welfare or charity approach to social action. He has come alive and delivers the message with passion as if being moved by spirit.

Advancement was also made toward developing a synergistic SHARE perspective that included the Mexican affiliates as well as corporate views.

Personal Learnings and Transformative Outcomes

After the main project was complete, the subteam that focused on the personal experience of transformation needed more time to complete its inquiry. The action and reflection cycles of this second level of inquiry became intertwined with the action and reflection cycles of the larger synergy project. Influenced by all of the reflections that came before, the SI process took on a life of its own and new cycles continued to emerge. When the team members met to address their question about the experience of transformation while participating in a synergic inquiry, it was clear that major transformations for them were just beginning.

Their next action cycle included a round of interviews with both coresearchers and other participants on the SHARE staff. This gave them an opportunity to interact with the content of their transformative experiences and allowed them to engage in dialogue with others who had participated in a similar experience. Four simple, open-ended questions were crafted to elicit these personal experiences and help others reflect on the synergy experience. Whereas collecting and synthesizing reflections from others was readily accomplished, collecting, reflecting on, and synthesizing personal experiences in a truly collaborative fashion proved more messy and complicated.

The team members' first steps were to write reflection papers and to share them briefly. Themes and categories were extracted from these papers, much as was done with the interview data, and these were exchanged online for distillation and synthesis. Although the papers were exceedingly rich, they did not produce categories that resonated collectively, and meaningful patterns did not immediately emerge.

There had been an expectation that once initial, large amplitude learnings were acknowledged and explored, and data were coded for analysis, attention would easily be focused on the more subtle transformations. However, deep and subtle transformations were still taking place, and these required further reflection, individually and collectively, to surface. Truly synergic understanding of these transformations required letting go of the sense that only one more big reflection cycle would be required. As this expectation dissolved, the inquiry team embarked on a process that was to take them 3 full months to complete. Their focus shifted away from framing "knowledge" gathered from the field experience. In those postfield months, the team began to recognize that authentic knowledge about personal transformation within SI could be constructed only by repeated deep reflections and a collaborative process of synthesis.

When the team members next met, a rich reflective process arose almost spontaneously, and they made what felt like huge leaps in their collective understanding of their experiences. This process was so exciting and generative that they had to apply brakes to their momentum and interject some devil's advocacy. The discussion that followed confirmed their concern that the data up to that point had been comparatively lifeless.

It was during these discussions as devil's advocates that the team members' appreciation for the meaning and power of collaboration became evident. Suddenly capable of crystallizing an idea as a group, they found themselves creating between the spaces in ways that weren't possible separately. In this light of new understandings, their original analysis looked like an intellectual summary of key themes rather than a synergistic use of data to inform their own developing perspectives. Although many personal feelings were identified and an individual mosaic of learnings was recorded in the initial reflections, a collectively experienced pattern of transformation did not begin to emerge until this time.

A variety of factors helped prepare fertile ground for this level of reframing and deeper learning to take place. These factors included time together, but other factors were also as important. Preparations by two members for an upcoming course on participatory research with Peter Reason added both scholarly information and "simmering time" as reflections continued to be exchanged online. Also important were the continued experiences of subtle changes in the team members' daily lives.

Collaborative experiences are often like a roller coaster: Participants experience the collective euphoria of creativity and alignment, as well as the lows of crisis and confusion. Subsequent attempts online to construct a final synthesis of transformative experience fell apart. After many false starts and much spinning of wheels, the original reflection papers were revisited in an attempt to once again work with them in a way that was collectively resonant, a way that showed commonalities as well as contrasts. After successfully working with them online, a three-way telephone conference call led to creating between the spaces, and the team members were quickly able to pull together a meaningful framework of their experiences that had not been evident to them separately. An entirely new level of thought emerged with crisp clarity, and a huge mass of information was distilled to its most essential elements to build a bridge between the synergy process and the personal experience of transformation. The team members' collective experience of transformation could be organized into three main manifestations of transformative experience:

- Seeking critical understanding of lifeworld and self
- Going beyond the self
- New ways of being

Seeking Critical Understanding of Lifeworld and Self

The synergy project immediately immersed these researchers in a contrary environment, a culture that was based on different assumptions and priorities and that operated on an unfamiliar set of tacit rules. In addition, they were consciously and intentionally cultivating a critical, nonjudgmental mindset with the specific goal of discerning their own perspectives as well as those of others and holding both as equally valid. In this way, one perspective became a mirror for the other. The immersion provided the leverage and contrast for illuminating hidden complexities and contradictions of their own lifeworlds and supported the differentiation of their own perspectives from those of others. Their deeply held assumptions and values were painfully visible for the first time, pushing these participants through the initial brick walls of their most entrenched beliefs.

Purposefulness, practice, intention, and even skill building were also enhanced as they attempted to stay true to the SI model. Because participants were breaking through patterns that had operated invisibly and tacitly in their day-to-day worlds, they tended to experience feelings of personal dilemma, contradiction, disorientation, and loss. It was a struggle to resolve the tension between perspectives and to either reconcile them or release the distortions. This did not come easily and effortlessly to anyone.

This experience of deeply seeing that truth is relative and that their own perspectives were not necessarily "right" or "true" but merely relative to other equally valid perspectives was extremely powerful. It opened the participants up to a genuinely nonjudgmental attitude, and they found that they were now able to take an actively interested but nonjudgmental stance on issues in which they themselves had a stake.

Having legitimized their perspectives as merely perspectives, not the "way things are," they were able to step aside and view them from the outside more easily. As consultants, this liberated them from old models and formulas used for consulting. They came to recognize that one assists in another's transformation not by giving right answers but by acting as mirrors through which others can see themselves clearly enough to learn from the experience. In other words, real answers arise from within an individual or organization, not from the consultant. Participants made comments to this effect:

> I was surprised at how he was defensive to my questions and began to notice how I was probably giving them an evaluative tone. I then tried to take off this edge, and it seemed to help. Being able to do this seemed like a higher awareness than I had previously.
>
> I also got in touch with my tendency to assume that my ideals are superior to those of others. This became symbolized for me as a "consultant's mentality," the expert who sees his or her views as superior to those they are working with and who is driven to apply them to clients.

> Throughout the process, it became very apparent to me that as we held each perspective beside each other . . . my sense of "answers" or "knowing what to do"

faded bit by bit. My sense of assuming a position of answers from a "knowing" perspective was alarming and disturbing. . . . Feelings of panic, sadness and disbelief welled up inside me.

Critical awareness of disturbing and contradictory elements in one's own lifeworld helped in deeply understanding how culture, social relationships, and conditioning shape beliefs and feelings. This made the participants more aware of the effects of these forces in their own lives and how these now constrained them. Their own unconscious participation in contradictions as "privileged persons" became apparent, and they had to question the very premises of their reference points and their ways of being in the world:

In Mexico, we experienced a major grassroots demonstration. . . . It was an electrifying sight to see the hundreds of thousands of people amassed on the Zócalo with the palace in the background with its closed doors. The people were expressing their frustration to a government with a closed ideology. The hierarchical organizations that I once led came to my mind, and I saw how they too stood behind palace doors barely penetrable by the workers. This remarkable demonstration became a symbol of our current society with its many palaces where most of us are standing on the outside with only a rock to hurl at a massive wall of stone, steel, and cement.

When I did the mask exercise, I became aware of how it felt to have power. It was a good feeling to be the one with money and able to make the rules. On the other side, as the Mexican affiliate and peasant, I felt helpless and begged for help from those in power. I found I could not hold these two views equally. It made me begin to think about how I had a bias toward hierarchy. This is my history, I realized. Now I experienced the other side for the first time. I now had a real way to empathize with the demonstrators. I now could empathize with the affiliates.

In Mexico, I grasped a sense of the honoring of and dedication to an ideal, to symbols, beyond anything that made daily life work better. Spirit seemed to infuse this honoring, a spirit I sometimes find lacking in my own culture. . . . It added something to the quality of life, some sort of humanness that we don't measure or take into account. I wondered about my own compatriots, with lives so organized and dedicated to productivity and efficiency that the very stuff of life was wrung out of their existence. No time for reflection, relationships, or feeling. This leads me to question in more depth the assumptions about work, productivity, and success in my culture.

With this, sacred personal truths withered painfully into a place of increased ambiguity. The personal missions about which participants experienced so much fervor and commitment were exposed as ideologies, and the participants recognized how these too could be oppressive. Their experiences showed them how answering to something that transcends oneself as a "spiritual calling" can become reified over time by personalities and other forces until the original call is mostly lost. The need for critical reflection, for questioning fanatic dedication to a cause, was obvious:

> [The] leadership center I and five others founded was based on an ideology. I felt that I had a mission to change the world based on my own ideology. This thought made me smile. How arrogant. It's no different than SHARE. So this perspective is helping me get in touch with the way I approach my work.

> I could see how the SHARE members struggled to distinguish between what is universally "right," or even their own spiritual mission, and what was merely the following of an ideology. I began to question that in my own life. I've always felt called to do whatever I've done, yet ultimately, I move on, discovering the cage of my own ideology and breaking free. What cage was I in now?

> Even when confusion and the chaos of splintered beliefs reigned, it was clear that there was a constant movement forward in understanding. An alignment with the movements of change seemed to arise spontaneously from the dialectic of receptiveness to be influenced and the ability to influence.

> It felt as if I had left hold of the trapeze on one end and was now in midair, yet without the view of the second trapeze ahead. This was a time for me to live with the open-endedness, ambiguity, and constant changing circumstance that I ask my clients to deal with on an ongoing basis.

Going Beyond the Self

Critical examination of their own perspectives illuminated the patterns of beliefs and of social and cultural conditioning that had shaped the participants. As they contrasted one perspective with another, they clearly understood the power of perspective and its constricting effect on one's ability to perceive and know the world. Two people with widely differing perspectives were effectively seeing two different worlds in the same space, each one often blind to what was glaringly obvious to the other. Knowing this, they felt ready to shed old skins as snakes do and strained to feel the exquisiteness of fresh life on tingly new skin. As the SI process continued to surface deeper layers of their perspectives, the participants began to describe the layers as mental barriers or veils that barred the participants from wider capabilities of knowing.

The first veil, like the psychological ego, sought to preserve itself. Once this had been breached, the participants were still aware of their perspectives, but the veils had acquired a softer, thinner, more flexible edge. It was as if a shower curtain had replaced a brick wall. In this process, the participants felt as if they had stepped outside or let go of their rational, linear, everyday selves and allowed their nonrational capacities and intuition to flow to the forefront. That which had been tacit, or in the realm of presentational knowledge, became more explicit and vital. They also appeared to transcend their self-defended egos and open themselves to different kinds of connections and influences from others. This took their transformative experience from the purely cognitive and psychological to a dimension of experience that is usually called spiritual.

The expanding capacities of their inner selves opened the participants to greater intimacy with others, providing trust and empathy that allowed them to speak from the heart. As they experienced this melting away of old restrictions and inhibitions, they felt more creative, loving, and connected. One participant described this:

Today at our check-in I began to let my heart speak. I spoke of the frustration I feel and the analogy of the marchers in the demonstration and the palace wall that contains the ruling party. I felt the emotion fill my being as I empathized with those without power. . . . This time I did not justify it or seek a way to avoid it. I let it speak to me. I hope I have the courage to do this at the board meeting. It was spirit that was moving me. I was not trying to understand or rationalize. There was a voice within that began to come through.

The participants began to see with new eyes beyond the surface of appearances to the humanity and spiritual essence of others. This was particularly true in the poor communities they visited in Mexico. At first, their habitual perspectives to see visual manifestations of poverty distracted them, but, after processing and reflection, the participants were able to perceive the human dignity and feel the spirit of the places they visited:

We visited people who lived in very poor conditions, people in makeshift houses without water or electricity. I found it uplifting as here you came in touch with what is life. There were no trappings of a material world. All that took place here was life. The people gathered around us telling us their stories of what they needed, and throughout all of this, their dignity and pride were evident—the government could try to take away things from them . . . but throughout all of this, they still kept their dignity and pride. This deep sense of pride and dignity despite the living conditions was deeply etched for myself following this afternoon.

As consciousness unfolded around the heart and spirit that permeated the lifeworld of the Mexicans they met, these team members report sensing a corresponding lack or restriction of heart and spirit in their own culture, particularly in the work environment. They questioned their own circumstances and dug more deeply into buried assumptions. They were now capable of apprehending the suffering of others, something they had been blind to. Instead of feeling guilt over their privileges, they were able to experience deep compassion. Insights acquired vivid edges and crispness, and emotions were often heightened as the participants experienced intense sadness, grief, anger, and disillusionment at the loss of what had been their earlier sacred truths.

> Feelings of panic, sadness and disbelief welled up inside me. . . . I still did not know what was going on at this point. Tears began to trickle down. . . . It felt as if something sacred which I had believed for a long time was found to be untrue . . . a sacred trust of how one is in society, a role, a contribution . . . had all been displayed as inappropriate. A central belief system that had driven my role and contribution in my communities had become null and void . . . in an instant. . . . My sadness was as much for what was and had been as for what was next. The panic was for a need to quickly redefine something else.

Sensing their capacities expanding in these ways gave participants a feeling of shared meaning with others in their immediate group. As these feeling deepened and intuition increased, they began to develop a group intelligence from which cocreative efforts sparked. The desire to push one's own agenda or to protect one's territory gave way to the flow of the group and feelings of connection. There was a strong sense of familiarity, rhythm, and ease with others, a sense of flow in group processes and operations, one of naturally shared leadership, without the need to speak of or demand it. This led to the experience of "creating in the spaces between them":

> Definitely, I experienced some sort of "altered state" when we'd be processing or just simply talking together. Sense of time was suspended, and absorption was complete. . . . I marveled at the rhythm and unspoken understanding we seemed to have around the conference table. I forgot about fulfilling any personal agenda, yet didn't feel lost or without identity in the groupness. It all seemed so natural.

> By the time we got to Celaya, we had developed a level of intimacy and built a group field that was extremely powerful. I felt very creative, felt that there was innovation and deep penetration that was brought to the surface and easily accessible. It was more than "knowledge amplification"; it was the creation of group intelligence. It was as if we all could access a common consciousness that we had made available by creating the group. The ability to link minds and hearts and higher purposes in this way, to bring about something new, has really transformed my perspective about being in the world. . . . My culture has made historic strides in developing individual potential, in allowing the individual to bring forth the most that [he or she] can. I feel now that I've stepped into the next level, the collaborative level.

As time passed, the participants quoted here continued to experience this group mind, this flow, and a creating between the spaces in their interactions, and this experience became more refined in essence and more of a natural state that was so deeply satisfying that the participants hope to maintain both an awareness of and a reflectivity on the experience, so they can consciously develop it.

Having gained an expanded conception of personal transformation and witnessed the societal work, or transformation of others, as interrelated to their own personal transformations, the participants had new respect for and confidence in the human potential for deep change:

> My confidence is unwavering in how we approached the situation both during the day and afterwards. . . . Yet the memory of how powerful an exercise can be for the group directly involved and those who enter at a later date still reverberates.

> I found that one has to work with a delicate hand and complete integrity—otherwise, damage can occur. During every step of the trip, I was reminded that we are unlocking powerful forces that ripple out into many lives and many levels of existence. Even if one is scrupulously careful, the process of transformation is often inherently painful, and a real change agent must be capable of dealing with that. There is incredible vulnerability in this work—the change agent wields real power and must be wary of slipping into an ideological mindset. We must constantly question our perspective and assumptions and maintain a sense of humility and respect for this work.

From time to time, participants had illuminating insights about their roles within the whole. Dependence on rational focus on people, events, institutions, and ideologies gave way to a sensing of the universal archetypes, cycles, forces, and essences around them. The participants became able to recognize processes of self, organizations, and society and to see the patterns of differentiation and integration in them. Cycles of germination, development, maturation, and recycling or rebirth emerged at many levels, and seeing themselves as parts of these larger, more meaningful or more universal patterns allowed feelings of expansiveness and liberation to surface. As the sense of time continues to expand, they feel more connected to the sense of working at the societal level for the selfless service that their previous ideological stances had imitated:

> This Mexican experience was a powerful opportunity for me to see the underlying connections between theories, to experience the theory in the actions of people on small and large scales, and even connect it to the perturbations in my own life. In some ways, I feel a certain liberation. Liberation in seeing the coherence between large, undulating processes and my own life experience.

In the past, it has seemed rather erratic, as if I've lived multiple separate lives, each one radically different. However, I am becoming increasingly capable of seeing that many of the events are tied to common processes, that I have been riding the surface of one long wave instead of many small ones. I do feel a greater sense of internal control and confidence, an ability to see the whole.

What was it then that interceded to break up these encrusted, rigid thought forms that entrapped individuals and entire societies? In Mexico, I became very aware of the essence of revolution and transformation. . . . The essence of revolution was in the air—sharp, fast, electrifying, violent, and unstable, a sudden jolt that separated the present from the future. . . . A sharp jolt could crack the encrusted shell of an old way of being, and the transformation process could get underway, like a runaway chemical reaction.

Before participating in this SI project, the three members of this subteam understood the transformative experience of SI in rather cognitive, Mezirowian terms, or as an organizational intervention. Since taking their research to this level, their experience of SI has expanded dramatically, and it now provides a bridge into what they experience as the sphere of the spiritual, and their continued processing has led to an enhancement and deepening of their respective spiritual practices.

Creation of a New Way of Being

As the participants' learnings deepened through the continuing momentum of synergy cycles, these learnings integrated with the participants' actions. Life purposes became clarified, and values changed, causing participants to expand into new spiritual practices and seek out collaborative ways of doing things. Finding new motivations, they eventually changed their lines of work. As they let go to adopt their new stances in the world, each gained an empowered sense of self and enacted the new perspectives in daily life in ways that felt more authentic and were deeply satisfying:

I have changed the direction of my dissertation work. I now plan to focus on the idea of a social business and how spirit functions in the formation of such organizations. I am no longer looking for a retreat but a way to become more active in an important social movement. It's like the beginning of an outer phase of my life. I am energized by the prospect of this research project and will have the support of SHARE as a primary coresearcher. I also participated in a leadership workshop where I played a key leadership role. My presence was noticed and important to the gathering. I felt as if I had found a better way to live my heart.

My relationship with the material world fundamentally changed, something that had been in the works for at least 5 years. This was mirrored in the chaos and disruption that I felt returning from the trip, as the last vestiges of my former belief in the industrial, consumer-driven world dissolved. Tremendous progress was made in discerning my own U.S. cultural perspective as a member of the dominant culture and coming to grips with the polar extremes that it sometimes frightens me to confront. Lastly, I had a deep shift by understanding and experiencing the creative spiritual power that can be unleashed through authentic collaboration and finally understood one of the primary pillars of this program. These changes flowed together like the confluence of a great river, and in the 2 months since returning, have resulted in a calm, yet powerful sense of purpose and a new direction in my dissertation work. Not only has my topic clarified and changed, but also I have a completely different outlook on how it might be accomplished, and why.

I arrived home to several issues, which I would have given larger priority before my return yet now they appeared to have a very different relevance. In addition, my work with the area of diversity has really taken a dramatically different turn. I have completed all of my current diversity contracts and have refused any new contracts. My current sense of the methodology we are using in the area of diversity needs to be reviewed for other ways to address it—education and awareness may not bring about the degree and scope of required change. I am also critically reviewing my role as a consultant and work with organizations. I was quite comfortable with the coaching role I had adopted of late, yet I think that I need to take this concept further—to what? I am unsure at this point, but the key question remains to find the most effective means to support transformation with both people and systems.

Exposing participants' own ideologies was liberating, driving them to deeper understandings of empowerment, beliefs, and the divine. As the edges of their accustomed roles in life became blurred and apparently solid realities faded into constant changefulness and uncertainty, messiness and discomfort arose. But feelings of guidance helped them through the uncertainty and chaos, and they acquired an added sense of personal competence. The SI experience embedded within them new understandings of the roles of faith, intention, trust, and confidence in seeing a process through. What had seemed strange or experimental before the project now seemed natural.

A participatory worldview infused their ways of viewing their consulting work and their understandings of the realms of authority and relationship. Sensing judgment and viewing a situation from another's perspective becomes a reflex. Collaboration, once an ideal to work toward, became a natural way of working and of being.

Final Words on the Transformation Synthesis

The three manifestations of experience—critical understanding of lifeworld and self, going beyond self, and new ways of being—were not necessarily stages of transformation in the traditional sense of transformative learning. These three were experienced more like different aspects of the specific kind of transformative process initiated in the SI framework. Although transformation around a particular issue may occur in this kind of natural sequence, things do not necessarily happen this way. Sometimes so many different assumptions and elements are challenged and stretched that all three manifestations occur at once.

Critical understanding is a manifestation of the more rational, intellectual reverberations of the crisis that is felt when a major framework or program is exposed as distorted, untrue, unjust, or lacking. Critical understanding initiates the struggle to think of a way to replace, rework, or eliminate this error.

Going beyond self is more a matter of the feeling and sensing of the intuitive and spiritual aspects of the self, and it brings with it an expansion of capacities. Though some of the feelings that rise with this experience are those of pain, loss, and grief, the salient feature is not the eruption of personal crisis but the unfolding capabilities of sensing in ways that bring participants to a higher level than before. As the capacity to "feel" deepens, one is given access to a more subtle realm of experience. This is what brings greater feelings of interconnection, empathy, awe, and compassion. In this way, creating new ways of being is the manifestation of natural and reflexive embodied change and expansion.

These categories of experience form some interesting patterns. In critical understanding, some essence of destruction can be found in the breaking down and differentiating. The essence of going beyond self is primarily one of opening and creating because it allows the new to enter. Instead of "breaking through the brick wall," this experience brings glimpses past the "shower curtain." In new ways of being, changes are integrated or synthesized into the manifest world, and the participant actually becomes more than before. Although all three of these aspects of transformation involve body, mind, and spirit, critical understanding appears to be oriented primarily toward the mental, beyond self toward the spiritual, and new ways of being toward the physical or manifest.

This three-category description has definite limitations. It gives the appearance of being static, like a break through a brick wall that is followed by an outward expansion toward higher realms and is then embodied: one, two, three, finished. The previous quotations, taken primarily from original reflection papers, enhance this snapshot feel. However, cycles of reflection reveal that constantly changing process is experienced. The shower curtain of yesterday becomes the brick wall of today. From the perspectives of new selves and the new way, barriers once seen as subtle later appear to be entrenched, perhaps even ideological, and there is yet another layer to be peeled away in the dance of continuing evolution and change.

16

Reflections and Implications

W e presented synergic inquiry (SI) as a methodology developed to help alleviate acknowledged problematic situations. We also discussed the problems, crises, and challenges that face people at various levels of human systems, from the individual and personal relationships to collectives as groups, organizations, communities, and global cultures. We state that SI does this by expanding human consciousness and capacities at various systems levels. We addressed the effectiveness of this particular approach and acknowledged and explored the mythic underpinning of SI methodology.

The case studies included in this section of the book document some of the experimentation with SI to date. They serve to expand the discussion of SI's usefulness by providing concrete examples. In this chapter, we revisit the case studies and reflect on issues that have arisen for us. We also explore the implications of the case studies for future work at various human systems levels and in various fields of endeavor.

Applicability of SI

Based on our experiences, the practice of SI can be organized into several categories of use. One function of SI is to help resolve conflicts and confrontations. When differences are polarized in a conflict or confrontation, participants suffer difficulty and pain. SI, when used in these cases, is used to change or transform the situations in such a way that this adversity is transformed into harmony and synergy. Examples of this include the case in which a husband and wife decided to use SI to improve their relationship and solve their conflict over cooking (Chapter 7). In another case, SI is used to help a mother and daughter deal with a housecleaning conflict as well as the deeper issues of traveling across country to college and a mother's memories of her own mother's death from cancer when she was away at college (Chapter 8).

A second use of SI is for social problem solving. Facing the challenge of creating a common vision with high spiritual goals, one group used SI as a creative process that enabled them to engage fully in creating and manifesting their vision at a time when confusions might otherwise have split the group (Chapter 9). The case study that followed this in Chapter 10 shows how SI was used to reframe existing conflicts around learning groups in such a way to eliminate the emotional stuckness the participants experienced.

A third use of SI is to provide a focal point to facilitate the development of a system, such as an individual, a group, or an organization. With this function, differences are intentionally polarized so they can be used as creative resources. Joanne Gozawa used SI in this way to both differentiate and integrate different archetypes deep within her mythic self in a way that led to personal development (Chapter 6). Roma Hammel used SI in a similar way as a new pedagogy for teaching her high school students (Chapter 13). In this classroom setting, diversity was purposefully used as a learning resource. In another such example, a group of doctoral students used SI to develop their fragmented group into a synergistic learning team (Chapter 11). A major business in China called BNBM proactively used SI and graduate students from a school in the United States to leverage differences between a Western framework of management and a Chinese framework of management, using the differences as creative resources for new leadership development as well as new ideas for organizational improvement (Chapter 14). World SHARE also used SI to explore how polarizations between U.S. and Mexican cultures could be used as resources for developing new forms of organization to help their floundering startups (Chapter 15).

Finally, SI can be used for social change and transformation of the "-isms"—racism, sexism, and ethnocentrism—which pervade societies around the globe. A group of doctoral students used SI to address conflicts between Black and White students. Despite its imperfections and lack of a fully synergistic completion, SI led to dramatic new learnings for all participating individuals and for the group as a whole (Chapter 11). In an experimental workshop, Yongming Tang worked with a group of facilitators experienced in other disciplines. They used SI to address gender relations in a way that produced new hope and excitement for participants (Chapter 12). SI facilitators Charles Joiner, Susan Cannon, and Karen O'Neil used SI to transform U.S. cultural ethnocentrism into responsiveness and renewal for an organization working in both the United States and Mexico (Chapter 15).

The common thread that runs through all of SI's uses is that whatever the specific purposes of an inquiry, SI enables participants to take an inward journey for learning and growth. When done well, the outcomes are mental development, harmonious relationships, a healthy social environment, and creative solutions.

Outcomes of SI

It is apparent that SI has made a powerful impact on many of the participants who have engaged in its process. These impacts range from raising awareness about oneself and others to gaining new skills for dealing with differences to making a significant transformation of consciousness in which new ways of being and behaviors emerge.

A recent in-depth study of nine people who participated in at least one of the global SI projects used narrative analysis to show that most participants experienced a personal transformation of consciousness (Takano, 1997). Through their experience with SI, these participants also obtained or reinforced the following skills and capacities (Takano, 1997):

a. The capacity to withhold judgment

b. The ability to openly and compassionately listen to and accept different perspectives

c. Greater ease in tolerating ambiguous situations

d. Improved skills in exploring assumptions as cultural conditioning

e. The ability to hold different perspectives simultaneously

f. Enhanced confidence to deal with differences

Some of the case studies in this book also demonstrate how SI has affected individuals. Charlie Joiner, Susan Cannon, and Karen O'Neil address this in great detail with their description of three manifestations of their transformative experiences while participants in an intense synergy process with World SHARE: (1) a new critical understanding of lifeworld and self, (2) more facility going beyond the self, and (3) the creation of new ways of being in the world (Chapter 15). They also clarify that these three are dynamic, interrelating aspects that sometimes occur simultaneously as different assumptions and elements of the self are challenged and stretched. They are not sequential stages as in traditional descriptions of transformation.

The changes in understanding described by this team were due to reverberations from having their intellectual frameworks and internal programs exposed as distorted, untrue, unjust, or even absent, combined with a deep intention to arrive at greater integration and integrity. They understand this process begins as one of destruction—a breaking down—and differentiating; they find that going beyond self is primarily a process of opening, allowing the new to enter, and creating and integrating. The latter is also a matter of feeling and sensing, of expanding these capacities, intuition, and the spiritual aspects of the self, rather than a matter of logic and thought. Although pain, loss, and grief were often involved in going beyond self, the authors' salient point was not a sense of personal crisis but one of the unfolding of ever-greater capabilities to feel and to access subtleties of experience, empathy, interconnections, and awe.

This combination of understanding and expansion manifests as new ways of doing things and as the desire to do and be more than before as a reflexive embodiment of change that naturally emerges as a result of the process. This differs radically from the conventional idea of self-improvement, which usually involves making efforts toward predetermined goals. As creative expressions of capacities not previously seen or known emerged through SI, transformation was naturally integrated and deeply satisfying.

Transformative effects also are also found in other cases. Briefly, gender synergy (Chapter 12) shows how an intensive SI exploration taking only 2 days can be genuinely transformative to at least some of the participants. Roma Hammel, in Chapter 13, demonstrates how thoughtful application of SI in high school classrooms can have transformative effects that excite and benefit teen students. Joanne Gozawa (Chapter 6) describes how she lives synergy by integrating the synergy principle into the nature of her being. This case indicates that some can experience a new way of life by embodying SI.

The difference that SI makes for individuals also has an effect on their relationships. Vennie and Eric (Chapter 7) discussed how they used SI to learn about themselves and add to, renew, and strengthen an already good relationship. Although this was a simple inquiry, it led to a significant improvement in their feelings for each other and their relationship.

Lien Cao (Chapter 8) discussed how an application of SI expanded her awareness of her own issues in relation to her daughter. Through deep self-knowing (SK), she discovered that their issues around housecleaning were only the tip of the iceberg. Through continuing SK, Lien also uncovered deeply hidden layers of guilt about being a good enough mother, of sorrow over the death of her own mother, and issues of significant cultural differences between herself, born and raised in Vietnam, and her daughter, who was born and raised in the United States. The deep, emotional synergy that followed these discoveries produced immense empathy and strengthened the mother–daughter relationship. This study also shows that SI changed the participants as individuals and changed their relationship.

It appears that SI also affects group work or team development. In Chapter 9, Lien Cao presents how SI helped a whole team move through the difficult issue of reforming their learning groups. This application of SI also expanded the group's consciousness to such an extent that an extraordinary new understanding of each other as individuals was achieved, one that transformed difficult interpersonal relations on the part of some members of the group and fostered new ways of being and behaving at the whole-group level.

Carole Barlas, Angela Cherry-Smith, Penny Rosenwasser, and Colette Winlock in Chapter 11 show how multiple cycles of SI helped their group expand its collective consciousness around perpetuating dynamics of domination in a way that transformed the relationships between Whites and Blacks at the group level. Their intense experiences with SI over a period of 6 months led to expansion and learnings at both the individual and the group levels, and they claim that the group became able to embody synergy in their spontaneous behaviors.

SI has also affected organizations. In the case of BNBM (Chapter 14), some of the Chinese managers were able to use both the Chinese value of collectivity and the Western value of individuality in their work settings; this led to perceived improvements in performance and job satisfaction.

In the case of World SHARE (Chapter 15), SI had a dramatic impact on the organization's development. This inquiry clarified the differences in perspective between the corporate leadership and their SHARE de Mexico affiliates; holding both of these perspectives as equals ultimately stimulated transformation and renewal for the entire organization. The direction of SHARE's work in Mexico, as well as the corporate policies and strategies of World SHARE, were profoundly affected by this SI application.

One SI, Many Manifestations

The SI methodology manifests differently in the various case studies presented. In what follows, we discuss the differences in terms of the numbers of SI cycles, the forms of facilitation, the multiple ways of knowing, and the balance between the processes of differentiation and integration.

Number of Synergy Cycles

Among the case studies included here, a few of the applications used only one synergy cycle. To a large extent, this choice depended on the purpose and strategy of the application. In Chapters 7, 8, and 12, only one synergy cycle was used because the purpose was limited. SI was used either to resolve a limited conflict or to solve a single and specific collective problem. Once these were achieved, the inquiry ended.

In other case studies, more synergy cycles were used. For example, in Chapter 11, the group engaged in several synergy cycles over a period of 6 months; through these cycles, the group learned to embody SI and integrate it into the nature of their group being and behavior. In a similar way, Joanne Gozawa presents in Chapter 6 how she integrated SI into her behavior as a life practice. She used SI over time until the explicit steps of SI no longer required conscious attention and became completely integrated into the nature of her being and her behavior. In the Gender Synergy Workshop described in Chapter 12, multiple synergy cycles were used with a powerfully successful result in a brief span of only 2 days.

We note two significant points regarding the number of synergy cycles. First, our experiences show that multiple SI cycles tend to be more powerful than a single SI cycle. However, a single synergy cycle can be transformative as demonstrated in some of the cases here. Multiple SI cycles enhance expansion of consciousness, develop skills and capacities for working with differences effectively, and help incorporate the synergy principle into the nature of being. Second, although the SI cycle is usually designed for a collective, in which a group experiences the various steps, cycles can be designed to help beginners get started and learn the SI process. Some of the participants in groups seem to psychically move through cycles faster than others. This is another demonstration of how synergy is a natural and organic process.

Forms of Facilitation

The various case studies show very different ways to facilitate SI. These differences range from self-facilitation to cofacilitation by participants to heavy facilitation by designated facilitators. An example of self-facilitation is Joanne Gozawa's presentation (Chapter 6) of SI as a life practice. Vennie and Erik (Chapter 7) used written information describing the SI methodology to facilitate their process. We suspect that Vennie's previous experience with SI was also helpful. Lien and her daughter (Chapter 8) used an external facilitator, Lien's classmate Dacy, to take them through the synergy process. However, this study does not make clear the ways in which this external facilitation helped the participants.

In the Blacksburg study about the development of an intentional community (Chapter 9), participants codesigned and cofacilitated their own synergy process, whereas a small group of doctoral students in Chapter 11 codesigned and cofacilitated the SI process over a 6-month period with the help of an external advisor. In the Gender Synergy Workshop (Chapter 12), a lead facilitator was in charge of the first synergy cycle. Members of the facilitation team who designed the workshop later took an active part in facilitating the gender subgroups in the cross-gender synergy process; they both facilitated the process and engaged in this experience as participants. In addition, some of the other participants spontaneously took on the tasks of facilitation.

These forms of facilitation are fascinating to experience. The key lies in artfully deciding how the SI process should be facilitated in a specific situation. In our experience, as a general rule of thumb, facilitators need to enable participants to learn how to self-facilitate as much as possible because this allows them to develop their own skills and capacities. However, different situations call for different facilitation forms, and participants need to feel safe and open enough to engage SI whatever the circumstances. It is always safer to have participants experience an SI process that is facilitated before they try to self-facilitate. We also find that inadequate mastery of SI hinders participants from engaging with each other synergically.

Multiple Ways of Knowing

Among these case studies, it is clear that multiple ways of knowing are employed as an integral part of the SI process. In most of the case studies, the rational/logical way of knowing was dominant, and verbal exchange was the medium for most of the synergy work.

However, in Chapter 6, Joanne goes beyond this logical level to work in the mythic dimension with what she calls mythic selves. She used symbols and mythic archetypes extensively in this process. The mythic level is a dimension of intelligence that has yet to be adequately explored. This use of symbolic representations functioning as components of consciousness demonstrates an alignment with Ramon Panikkar's (1979) and Vachon's (1995) arguments to more fully recognize mythic realities.

Mythic elements also appear in the chapter on community development (Chapter 9). In this study, a spiritual drawing exercise was used to bring the multiple dimensions of participants' consciousnesses into the synergy process. The experience was powerful enough to allow participants to honor and include differences that could otherwise have caused setbacks.

We believe that multiple ways of knowing are critical to the SI process. First, this approach provides an invitation to people with different learning styles to engage with each other synergically. This creates space to acknowledge each other as equals. By addressing each of the three different dimensions of knowing, participants are encouraged to expand their consciousness from one preferred dimension to multiple dimensions. In the SI process, participants should also be asked not to limit themselves to verbal language as the medium for knowledge transactions; they should be reminded that nonverbal behaviors and ways of being are also tremendous resources for communication.

We share the position of Panikkar (1979) and Vachon (1995) who recognize the necessity of creating new myths that better match the complexity of the reality of this era. Thus, it is of critical importance for SI participants to engage with each other at the mythical level by learning to surface their own underlying myths, to try on different mythos, or to create a new myth of being and behaving. Some of the learning strategies are designed to tap into this realm of knowledge, which is so often unconscious. The imaginal ways of learning described by Elias (1997) is one example of the kinds of learning strategies that can be helpful for this.

Process of Differentiation and Process of Integration

The optimal balance between the two subprocesses of SI—that of differentiation and that of integration—seems to differ based on the differing foci of inquiries. Apparently, when SI is applied to a conflict, the process of differentiation is more prominent than that of integration. For example, in the case of husband and wife (Chapter 7), self-knowing plays a major role in helping the participants deepen their awareness of who they are, what their values and assumptions are, and where these came from. Other-knowing also helped them communicate with each other with openness, respect, and empathy. After these phases, the processes of holding differences and of integration appear to have been relatively easy to achieve. Differences-holding was almost treated as another opportunity to know both self and other, and by that point, the polarization that caused the bad feelings between them seems to have already collapsed, bringing the conflict to its natural end. Differences-transcending did not need to be approached rationally and explicitly because it emerged organically out of their compassion and love for each other.

It is interesting to note that a similar emphasis on differentiation occurs in the experiences between mother and daughter (Chapter 8) and in the group conflict resolution process (Chapter 10). In the former case study, the issue of housecleaning was no longer so important once the deeper issues were recognized through self-knowing and other-knowing. However, the inquiry was continued and eventually led to transcendence with a deeper emotional bonding between mother and daughter. In the group conflict resolution study, once the group consciousness expanded to include everyone more fully, the emotional charge around group formation was gone.

Options that had not previously been available to the group automatically became viable, and the logistical issues that most affected each member of the group organically became the deciding factor for group formation.

On the other hand, when SI is used for collective problem solving, the process of integration seems to take on more prominence than differentiation. For example, in the community development study (Chapter 9), after self-knowing and other-knowing the group members began to automatically shift their focus to integration. Through the differences-holding exercise, the group's consciousness was expanded in such a way that it could readily include all members; that is, everyone's needs were recognized and honored. Differences-transcending then produced a creative solution in terms of the form that the community took in the beginning stages. The original stumbling block of the members' location of residency dissolved as a problem, and members became comfortable with the possibility that some would move to join the rest of the group later as their personal circumstances changed.

Similarly, in the case study of organizational performance improvement (Chapter 14), once the differentiation work was complete, the group's focus spontaneously shifted to an integration that would allow participants to reach new, creative solutions to improve BNBM's organizational performance. At that stage, all of the subteams wanted to join the others and work together to produce the synergic outcomes that emerged.

In the case of Mexico's World SHARE (Chapter 15), the integration process was also emphasized. The CIIS synergy team endeavored to achieve integration among themselves during the first parts of the SI process and coparticipated with the leadership of World SHARE for the events of synergy day. The outcomes on synergy day led to a change in both the orientation and the policies of World SHARE and gave a sense of renewal and vitality to corporate leaders.

When SI is applied using differences as the stimuli for learning and development, a level balance between differentiating and integrating appears to be maintained. In Chapter 6, Joanne describes how she both differentiated and integrated her two mythic selves, which enabled them to dance with each other for complementarity and synergy. In a similar way, Roma describes how both the process of differentiation and that of integration were used to enhance learning for her high school students (Chapter 13).

In the Gender Synergy Workshop (Chapter 12), three SI cycles were used to sufficiently deepen learnings about self and others. In the first cycle, participants learned to practice SI through an entire cycle that included both differentiation and integration in balance. Then the two subgroups formed for another full cycle of differentiation and integration in which both the diversity and the unity within each gender group was explored. Finally, a third cycle of differentiation and integration was used to gain deeper learnings about gender dynamics, resulting in a powerful experience for participants.

Upon reflection of these experiences of balancing the process of differentiation with that of integration is that, whatever the circumstances, participants need to do both quality differentiation and quality integration, and it is important to start with differentiation. Without adequate differentiation, there can be no adequate integration. Differentiation allows the differing identities and perspectives to form, and it is through these that participants gain clarity about self and other. We caution potential SI practitioners never to rush to solving problems by integrating because that may actually cause additional problems. As demonstrated in case studies, when identities or perspectives are clearly differentiated and participants have received each other well, integration occurs either naturally or relatively effortlessly. Thus, in situations where identities and perspectives are already well clarified and recognized, greater time and energy ought to be spent on integration. In other situations where there is a lack of clear differentiation of perspectives and this lack is causing problems, starting with the focus on quality differentiation is of the utmost importance.

In addition to these considerations, determining whether a unity fallacy or a separation fallacy is involved in a particular situation can be helpful in terms of deciding where the balance of energy should be spent. In our experience, when individuals suffer from a unity fallacy, the challenge is to differentiate. In these cases, a significant amount of work is needed to provide the necessary support for participants so they can value differences safely. They must also have the skills available to help them overcome this fallacy. Conversely, for those who suffer from a separation fallacy, the energy ought to be spent on integration, and support and skills are also needed to facilitate effective integration.

Implications for the Future

As we conclude the book, we feel that we have completed the first cycle for SI and are now at a new beginning. Writing this book has been most rewarding for us. In the process of framing and reframing the SI methodology, we deepened our understanding of it. It has been a great honor to study and learn from the cases that so many other writers contributed to this book.

We feel like SI was being born as we wrote, and we feel the tremendous potential for application and development that lies ahead for many of you, as well as for us. The full range of ways that SI can be shaped and developed is yet to manifest. This is exciting. As authors, we cannot help but have questions to guide future work in SI.

The first questions relate to the synergy principle: To what extent is the synergy principle found in different domains of the universe—matter, life, mind, and human societies? How does the synergy principle manifest in different cultural wisdoms around the globe? There are questions related to how different cultures explain synergy and what they see expressed. Considering the magnitude of difference between traditional Chinese and traditional Western descriptions of physical reality, we may gain new insights from this kind of respectful cross-cultural exploration.

From a different cross-cultural perspective, questions can be asked about the central constructs of a robust theory of synergy and how these constructs relate to each other. How, for example, does one recognize the process of differentiation in differing social systems, or, for that matter, the process of integration? How do the relationships between differentiation, as one process, and integration manifest in different social settings? What are the major factors that shape the relationship between these two processes? How fully are these seen as processes rather than isolated events? Is a relationship that is highly integrated in practice automatically understood in terms of this relationship? What are the contextual factors that call forth emphasis on either differentiation or integration? How do we discover whether individuals and collectives suffer from one of the fallacies—unity fallacy, separation fallacy, or compromise fallacy—that inhibit the capacity to engage in synergy? If the fallacy involved in a situation is known, how can SI be used to address it effectively?

In addition to exploring these kinds of thematic issues in refining a theory of synergy, such a theory would be enhanced through scholarly explorations. A robust (and synergized) theory would benefit from more thorough explorations of its roots in Eastern and Western thought. One personally intriguing option is exploring the evolutionary approaches in such different cultural philosophies and religions as the I-Ching, Taoism, Buddhism, Islam, Hinduism, and Christianity.

Another approach, especially in the contemporary West, would be to explore SI in relation to a theory of dialectical development, as found in Bahm (1977) and Johnston (1991). A third vein could be to address such theories describing the evolution of consciousness as found in Aurobindo (1993) and Wilber (1995). Yet another could be in the exploration of a new root paradigm for participatory research to build on the work of Heron (1996) and Reason (1994). Still another perspective is found in theories of cognitive development following Piaget, especially that focusing on postformal operations, as in the work of Cook-Greuter (1990); dialectical thinking, as in the work of Basseches (1984); and human evolutionary development, as in the work of Kegan (1994).

A practical theory could benefit from entering into its own SI cycles to differentiate and integrate the insights from the domain of transformative learning, drawing on the explorations of archetypal psychology, as in Boyd and Meyers (1988), and on the domain of rational thought, expressed in Mezirow (1991). There could also be synergic explorations of the presentational, propositional, and practical modes of knowing of Heron (1996) and Reason (1994); the practice of conscientization as described by Freire (1970); the development of transformative learning in collectives, as in Argyris and Schon (1995) and Kasl et al. (1997); and integrative theory, as in the work of Elias (1997).

Benefits would also result from an exploration of the relationship between SI and other participatory methods (from heuristics to cooperative inquiry). In the domains of research, as well as in approaching SI as a transformative intervention on a human system, the practice of SI could benefit enormously from other perspectives for identifying its core skills and capacities and for refining the methods and tools that can be used to teach them. The examples included in this book are only representations of our initial reservoir. We believe SI is as sufficiently broad and encompassing as many other tools, and methods from other methodologies could potentially be directly used or reframed to enhance this kind of inquiry.

Taking a different perspective, SI can be extended or reframed to address many other domains of difference, ones not included here. The intricacy and complexity of the issues found in areas such as gender differences, race differences, cultural differences, personality differences, and learning style differences may well call for a reframing—or an entirely different framing—of SI. As some of the case studies show, SI can manifest quite differently in different domains. It is our collective task within SI to find ways to make use of this approach in any manner that might be helpful for expanding human consciousness and capacities.

This also fits into our deep belief, based on our construction that we call the synergy principle of the universe, that SI ought to be integrated into the very tapestry of our being, and once manifest it will creatively shape itself to fit the unique needs of each presenting situation. We look forward to learning through the application of SI in many domains. Our real work is just beginning.

We also look forward to building on this work by engaging with the rich complexity found in the diverse populations in the public schools, higher education, and businesses of the United States. As we explore facilitating

SI in joint ventures between North American businesses and Chinese enterprises, we look forward to the novel and new applications that can inform both countries in a wide range of directions.

We expect to apply SI to education in ways that help address differences in learning styles, however those differences are derived. In organizational development, we expect to apply SI for enriching processes of visioning, strategic thinking, and leadership development. And we expect to use SI as a core process for the development of leaders for global enterprises.

If, as we believe, the root cause of the problems and crises experienced in human societies and environment throughout the planet is limitations of human consciousness, our most relevant response would be to discover and refine ways to develop human capacities and expand human consciousness.

East and West, North and South, mature traditions of mind and spirit evoke and celebrate a fundamental rhythm of differentiation and integration. We hope this book and our work with SI will make a modest contribution to our shared capacity to access this fundamental process and channel creative efforts toward the development of an increasingly just and ecologically sustainable planetary community.

References

Ackoff, R. (1999). *Ackoff's best: His classic writings on management.* New York: Wiley.

Adler, N. J. (1997). *International dimensions of organizational behavior* (3rd ed.). Cincinnati, OH: Southwestern Publishing.

Ani, M. (1994). *Yurugo: An African-centered critique of European cultural thought and behavior.* Trenton, NJ: Africa World Press.

Argyris, C. (1982). *Reasoning, learning, and action: Individual and organizational.* San Francisco: Jossey-Bass.

Argyris, C. (1993). *Knowledge for action: A guide to overcoming barriers to organizational change.* San Francisco: Jossey-Bass.

Argyris, C., & Schon, D. (1992). *Theory in practice: Increasing professional effectiveness.* San Francisco: Jossey-Bass.

Argyris, C., & Schon, D. (1995). *Organizational learning II: Theory, method, and practice* (2nd ed.). Reading, MA: Addison-Wesley.

Aurobindo, S. (1992). *The synthesis of yoga.* Pondicherry, India: Sri Aurobindo Ashram Press.

Aurobindo, S. (1993). *The integral yoga.* Pondicherry, India: Sri Aurobindo Ashram Press.

Bahm, A. J. (1977). *Polarity, dialectic and organicity.* Albuquerque, NM: World Books.

Baker, R. (1997). In the valley of astonishment: An interview with Basarab Nicolescu by Jean Bies. *Parabola, 22*(4), 65-76.

Basseches, M. (1984). *Dialectical thinking and adult development.* Norwood, NJ: Ablex.

Bateson, G. (1979). *Mind and nature: A necessary unity.* New York: Bantam.

Bohm, D. (1991). *Changing consciousness: Exploring the hidden source of the social, political, and environmental crises facing our world.* San Francisco: Harper.

Bohm, D. (1996). *On dialogue.* London: Routledge.

Boyd, R. D., & Meyers, J. G. (1988). Transformative education. *International Journey of Lifelong Education, 7*(4), 261-284.

Buber, M. (1958). *I and thou* (2nd ed.). New York: Charles Scribner's Sons.

Chaudhuri, H. (1977). *The evolution of integral consciousness.* Wheaton, IL: Theosophical Publishing House.

Churchman, C. W. (1968). *The systems approach.* New York: Dell.

Cook-Greuter, S. (1990). Maps for living: Ego development theory from symbiosis to conscious universal embeddedness. In M. Commons, C. Armon, L. Kohlberg, F. Richards, T. Grotzer, & J. Sinnott (Eds.), *Adult development 2: Models and methods in the study of adolescent and adult though* (pp. 79-104). New York: Praeger.

Cooperrider, D., & Srivastva, S. (1987). Appreciative inquiry in organizational life. In R. W. Woodman & W. A. Pasmore (Eds.), *Research on organizational change and development* (Vol. 1). Greenwich, CT: JAI.

Corning, P. (1995a, July). *Synergy: A unifying concept for the sciences?* Paper presented at the 39th annual meeting of the International Society for the Systems Sciences, Amsterdam.

Corning, P. (1995b). Synergy and self-organization in the evolution of complex systems. *Systems Research, 12*(2), 89-121.

Corning, P. (2003). *Nature's magic: Synergy in evolution and the fate of humankind.* New York: Cambridge University Press.

de Roux, G. I. (1991). Together against the computer. In O. Fal-Borda & M. A. Rahman (Eds.), *Action and knowledge: Breaking the monopoly with participatory action research* (pp. 37-53). New York: Intermediate Technology/Apex.

Eisler, R. (1987). *The chalice and the blade: Our history, our future.* San Francisco: Harper.

Elias, D. (1997). It's time to change our minds: An introduction to transformative learning. *ReVision, 20*(1), 2-6.

Ellison, R. (2002). *Invisible man.* New York: Random House.

Flood, R. L., & Jackson, M. C. (1991). *Creative problem solving: Total systems intervention.* Chichester, UK: Wiley.

Freire, P. (1970). *Pedagogy of the oppressed.* New York: Herder & Herder.

Fuller, R. B. (1981). *Critical path.* New York: St. Martin's.

Griffiths, A. J. F., Miller, J. H., Suzuki, D. T., Lewontin, R. C., & Gelbart, W. M. (1993). *An introduction to genetic analysis* (5th ed.). New York: Freeman.

Guba, E. G., & Lincoln, Y. S. (1994). Competing paradigms in qualitative research. In E. G. Guba & Y. S. Lincoln (Eds.), *Handbook of qualitative research* (pp. 105-117). Thousand Oaks, CA: Sage.

Harman, W. W. (1994, May). *Toward a new economics: System in decline or transformation?* Paper presented for discussion at the World Business Academy Presidents' Council, Boston.

Harman, W. W. (1996). The shortcomings of western science. *Qualitative Inquiry, 2,* 30-38.

Hegel, G. W. F. (1971). *Philosophy of mind* (W. Wallace, Trans.). Oxford, UK: Clarendon.

Hegel, G. W. F. (1977). *Phenomenology of spirit* (A. V. Miller, Trans.). Oxford, UK: Oxford University Press.

Heron, J. (1971). *Experience and method: An inquiry into the concept of experiential research.* Surrey, UK: University of Surrey, Human Potential Research Project.

Heron, J. (1996). *Co-operative inquiry: Research into the human condition.* Thousand Oaks, CA: Sage.

Heron, J., & Reason, P. (1997). A participatory inquiry paradigm. *Qualitative Inquiry, 3,* 274-294.

Johnston, C. M. (1991). *Necessary wisdom.* Seattle, WA: ICD Press.

Jugenheimer, R. W. (1985). *Corn: Improvement, seed production, and uses.* Malabar, FL: Krieger.

Jung, C. G. (1984). *Dream analysis: Notes of the seminar given in 1928–1930.* Princeton, NJ: Princeton University Press.

Kanter, R. M. (1983). *The change masters.* New York: Simon & Schuster.

Kasl, E., Marsick, V. J., & Dechant, K. (1997). Team as learners: A research-based model of team learning. *Journal of Behavioral Science, 33,* 227-246.

Katzenback, J. R., & Smith D. K. (1993). *The wisdom of teams: Creating the high-performance organization.* Boston: Harvard Business School Press.

Kegan, R. (1994). *In over our heads: The mental demands of modern life.* Cambridge, MA: Harvard University Press.

Kincheloe, J. L., & McLaren, P.L. (1994). Rethinking critical theory and qualitative research. In E. G. Guba & Y. S. Lincoln (Eds.), *Handbook of qualitative research* (pp. 138-157). Thousand Oaks, CA: Sage.

Kuhn, T. S. (1970). *The structure of scientific revolutions* (2nd ed.). Chicago: University of Chicago Press.

Laszlo, E. (1987). *Evolution: The grand synthesis.* Boston: Shambhala.

Laszlo, E. (1996). *Evolution: The general theory.* Cresskill, NJ: Hampton Press.

Lauter, E. (1984). *Women as mythmakers—Poetry and visual art by twentieth-century women.* Bloomington: Indiana University Press.

Lawrence, P. R., & Lorsch, J. (1967). *Organization and environment: Managing differentiation and integration.* Boston: Harvard Business School Publications.

Lincoln, Y. S. (1995). Emerging criteria for quality in qualitative and interpretative inquiry. *Qualitative Inquiry, 1,* 275-289.

Lipnack, J., & Stamps, J. (1993). *The teamnet factor: Bringing the power of boundary crossing into the heart of your business.* Essex Junction, VT: Oliver Wight.

Mezirow, J. (1990). How critical reflection triggers transformative learning. In J. Mezirow & Associates (Eds.), *Fostering critical reflection in adulthood: A guide to transformative and emancipatory learning* (pp. 1-20). San Francisco: Jossey-Bass.

Mezirow, J. (1991). *Transformative dimensions of adult learning.* San Francisco: Jossey-Bass.

Montuori, A. (1992). Creativity, chaos, and self-renewal in human systems. *World Futures, 35,* 193-209.

Moustakas, C. (1990). *Heuristic research: Design, methodology, and applications.* Newbury Park, CA: Sage.

Mouton, J. S., & Blake, R. R. (1984). *Synergogy: A new strategy for education, training, and development.* San Francisco: Jossey-Bass.

Ouchi, W. (1984). *M-form society.* Reading, MA: Addison-Wesley.

Panikkar, R. (1979). *Myth, faith and hermeneutics*. New York: Paulist Press.

Polanyi, M. (1974). *Personal knowledge: Towards a post-critical philosophy*. Chicago: University of Chicago Press.

Prabhu, J. (Ed.). (1996). *The intercultural challenge of Raimon Panikkar*. Maryknoll, NY: Orbis Books.

Reason, P. (1988). *Human inquiry in action*. London: Sage Ltd.

Reason, P. (1993). Reflections on sacred experience and sacred science. *Journal of Management Inquiry, 2*, 273-283.

Reason, P. (1994). Inquiry and alienation. In P. Reason (Ed.), *Participation in human inquiry* (pp. 9-15). London: Sage.

Reason, P. (1996). Reflections on the purposes of human inquiry. *Qualitative Inquiry, 2*, 15-28.

Reason, P., & Lincoln, Y. S. (1996). Dialogue with Thomas A. Schwandt's article. *Qualitative Inquiry, 2*, 57.

Reddy, W. B. (Ed.). (1988). *Team building: Blueprints for productivity and satisfaction*. Alexander, VA: NTL Institute.

Savage, C. M. (1996). *Fifth generation management: Co-creating through virtual enterprising, dynamic teaming, and knowledge networking*. Boston: Butterworth-Heinemann.

Schwandt, T. A. (1996). Farewell to criteriology. *Qualitative Inquiry, 2*, 58-72.

Senge, P. M. (1990). *The fifth discipline: The art and practice of the learning organization*. New York: Doubleday.

Smith, H. (1991). *The world's religions*. San Francisco: Harper.

Srivastva, S., & Cooperrider, D. (1999). *Appreciative management and leadership: The power of positive thought and action in organizations* (Rev. ed.). Euclid, OH: Williams Custom Publishing.

Swimme, B., & Berry, T. (1994). *The universe story: From the primordial flaring forth to the ecozoic era—A celebration of the unfolding of the cosmos*. San Francisco: Harper.

Takano, M. (1997). *A narrative assessment of synergic inquiry*. Retrieved January 16, 2006, from http://www.edst.educ.ubc.ca/aerc/1997/97takano.htm

Tandon, R. (1989). Participatory research and social transformation. *Convergence, 21*(2/3), 5-15.

Tang, Y. (1994). Communicating across east-west cultural boundaries. *Teoria Sociologica, 2*(3), 78-93.

Tang, Y. (1995). The cultural synergy model: A knowledge tool for the 21st century. *Proceedings of the Third International Conference on Sustainable Civilization*.

Tarnas, R. (1991). *The passion of the western mind: Understanding the ideas that have shaped our worldview*. New York: Ballantine.

Thompson, W. I. (1985). *Pacific shift*. San Francisco: Sierra Club Books.

Thompson, W. I. (1989). *Imaginary landscape: Making worlds of myth and science*. New York: St. Martin's.

Thompson, W. I. (Ed.). (1991). *Gaia 2 emergence: The new science of becoming.* New York: Lindisfarne Press.

Tobert, W. R. (1991). *The power of balance: Transforming self, society, and scientific inquiry.* Newbury Park, CA: Sage.

Union of Concerned Scientists. (1992). *World scientists' warning to humanity.* Retrieved November 6, 2005, from http://www.ucsusa.org/ucs/about/page.cfm?pageID=1009

Vachon, R. (1995). Guswenta or the intercultural imperative. *Interculture, 28*(2), 8-73.

West, C. (1993). *Race matters.* Boston: Beacon Press.

Wilber, K. (1995). *Sex, ecology, spirituality: The spirit of evolution.* Boston: Shambhala.

Wu, J. S. (1985). *Foundations of Chinese thought.* Minneapolis, MN: River City Press.

Wu, Y. (1989). *The book of Lao Tzu (the Tao Te Ching).* San Francisco: Great Learning.

Index

About the Editors

Yongming Tang, a pioneer of the synergic inquiry (SI) methodology, is the founder of the Global Synergy Network, an organization working toward global transformation. Dr. Tang is also the founder and director of the California Institute of Integral Studies Synergy Project, which conducts synergy action research in a number of countries. Dr. Tang teaches at the Transformative Learning Doctorate program within the California Institute of Integral Studies.

Charles W. Joiner, Jr., has extensive experience in the commercial, organizational world, in which he has served as president and general manager of major divisions of large enterprises. Seeking to move beyond the limits of the current organizational and economic paradigm, he received a PhD in transformational learning at the California Institute of Integral Studies. He has participated in or been a coleader of four cultural synergy projects. He founded a community dedicated to living in harmony with nature and spirit. His current interest is orthodox Christian theology. He has published two books and a number of articles.